OFFICE
ON THE
GO

W9-DFT-172

TOOLS, TIPS
AND TECHNIQUES
FOR EVERY
BUSINESS TRAVELER

KIM BAKER / SUNNY BAKER

PRENTICE HALL
Englewood Cliffs, New Jersey 07632

Prentice-Hall International, Inc., *London*
Prentice-Hall of Australia, Pty. Ltd., *Sydney*
Prentice-Hall of Canada, Inc., *Toronto*
Prentice-Hall Hispanoamericana, S.A., *Mexico*
Prentice-Hall of India Private Ltd., *New Delhi*
Prentice-Hall of Japan, Inc. *Tokyo*
Prentice-Hall of Southeast Asia Pte., Ltd., *Singapore*
Editora Prentice-Hall do Brasil Ltda., *Rio de Janeiro*

© 1993 by

PRENTICE-HALL, INC.
Englewood Cliffs, NJ

10 9 8 7 6 5 4 3 2 1

Library of Congress Cataloging-in-Publication Data

Baker, Kim,
    Office on the go : tools, tips, and techniques for every business
traveler / Kim Baker, Sunny Baker.
      p. cm.
    Includes index.
    ISBN 0-13-630906-2
    1. Office equipment and supplies--Handbooks, manuals, etc. 2. Electronic
office machines--Handbooks, manuals, etc. 3. Portable computers--Handbooks,
manuals, etc. 4. Business travel--Hnadbooks, manuals, etc. 5. Businessmen--
Time management--Handbooks, manuals, etc. I. Baker, Sunny. II. Title.
HF5548.B318   1993
651.3--dc20   93-20255
                                            CIP

ISBN 0-13-630906-2

PRENTICE HALL
Career & Personal Development
Englewood Cliffs, NJ 07632

Simon & Schuster, A Paramount Communications Company

PRINTED IN THE UNITED STATES OF AMERICA

Dedication

This book is dedicated to every traveling businessperson who is expected to be productive even when the airplane is late, the traffic is jammed, the bed is hard, and the food is bad. These businesspeople who maintain their professionalism in spite of the obstacles on the road are key to keeping their companies profitable and competitive.

Contents

INTRODUCTION

The world's first pager vending machine—Instabeep from SIMMS Communications—rents Motorola Bravo numeric pagers for $6 to $9 a day.
—Mobile Office Magazine

You're about to discover how to get more work done while traveling. This is important, because the average executive spends the equivalent of nine weeks away from the office on business trips every year—on short trips and long ones. People in sales and consulting positions spend even more time living out of suitcases to get their jobs done. Companies spend billions of dollars annually to move businesspeople from place to place. The efficiency and effectiveness of traveling workers are vital to a company's productivity and profitability. Even so, businesspeople waste immeasurable hours on planes, miss important phone calls while traveling between cities, and squander money on ineffective technologies and services on the road. These common travel problems drain profits from every company.

To help eliminate misspent dollars and profitless hours, *Office on the Go* is a state-of-the-art guidebook for the millions of salespeople, executives, employees, and owners of small businesses who travel across the country and around the world soliciting business, visiting customers, and attending meetings. Every business traveler needs *Office on the Go* to make life on the road easier, more effective, and less expensive.

Instead of sitting alone in a dull hotel room watching TV or waiting in the lounge for another late flight at the airport, a businessperson can use the techniques presented in *Office on the Go* to become "fully wired" while traveling—equipped with notebook computer, electronic organizer, modem, portable fax machine, cellular phone, and other easy-to-master tools that make productive work possible anywhere and any time. You can now have a complete mobile office in a briefcase and keep in touch with office and clients as if you were sitting at your own desk. In fact, *Office on the Go* discloses ways to make working on the road even more efficient than working from a desk and goes on to provide travelers with resources for the best equipment and services in cities around the world.

As traveling professionals who have spent the last ten years exploring evolving technologies and practical methods for keeping in touch, we wanted to do more than just a "gee-whiz" book showcasing technology or yet another book for computer wizards. *Office on the Go* is the result of our research into the practical needs of the real road warriors in business who need quick, authoritative information on technologies and services.

Office on the Go explains how to match the right technology and services to your work on the road and your level of technical comfort. You'll not only learn how to choose the tools effectively but will learn to manage your time and your money better. You'll explore options for on-the-road research and read about proven techniques to maximize communications and establish presence from your "traveling office."

The book includes guides to cellular phone connections, hotel and airline services, credit card options, technology services, and much more. If time really does equal money for businesspeople, then the right technologies and services are vital components to make the most of traveling time. *Office on the Go* not only shows business travelers, like you, how to maximize their time, but also how to improve the results of their trips by increasing communication with clients and building new business using mobile office tools.

What salesperson is content to sit in traffic when he or she could be making appointments with prospective customers and tracking contacts? How many consultants would rather waste potentially billable time sitting in a cramped plane seat instead of working on a project? And how many managers feel comfortable depending on a phone call to the office every day or two to find out about the messages piling up there?

Office on the Go shows every business traveler better ways to do a better job while away from the office and offers options you probably haven't considered for making life on the road more fruitful. Complete with resource listings and practical tips, *Office on the Go* opens up a whole new world of productivity and profit to workers on the move.

WHO SHOULD READ THIS BOOK?

The people who can benefit for *Office on the Go* are diverse. Anyone who travels either occasionally or frequently on business trips can benefit from the tips, tools, resources, and techniques presented in *Office on the Go*. These people include:

- Salespeople and service people who are on the road most of their working time
- Consultants and contract employees
- Managers and executives

- Any businessperson who attends meetings, trade shows, or conferences outside the office

- Writers and journalists

USING THIS BOOK—A ROAD MAP

There are three sections to *Office on the Go*. The first section, Office-on the-Go Technology, is an introduction to the many products and options available for the mobile office. Written in nontechnical terms, the power and simplicity of modern mobile-office technologies are demystified so any businessperson can take advantage of the power of notebook computers, the new personal digital assistants (PDAs), electronic organizers, and other electronic tools on the road. This section begins by explaining the potential of the mobile office and then shows readers how to evaluate their individual requirements as determined by their working styles and business needs.

Starting with the uses of portable computers and personal organizers, the section explains how mobile computers handle reporting, time management, client tracking and billing, sophisticated product demonstrations, and a host of other useful functions. Since state-of-the-art mobile offices can incorporate many portable tools and technologies, including cellular phones, satellite pagers, high-quality printers, short-wave radios, fax machines, and more, readers are shown how to evaluate their own on-the-road office requirements. If you are already up on all the latest technologies, skip this section or flip through it quickly to see what you may not have considered.

The second section of the book, Putting Mobile Office Technology to Work, covers methods for improving productivity on the road and getting the most from the technologies you choose to employ on the road. This section offers tips that even the most experienced travelers and technical wizards can benefit from. Time management, record keeping, and communications tips are covered that will make your life on the road not only easier, but more productive and more profitable. And we have included a special section on international travel that can reduce the culture shock of bringing your mobile office to foreign destinations.

The third section of the book, Resources On the Go, is a compilation of the most frequently used service required by business travelers—especially those who use mobile office technologies.

Listings for mobile product manufacturers are first. Then we provide general access information for hotels, airlines, and car rental agencies. Guides to office services, telephone connections, and other frequently used services on the road are also included.

The section is a must-have guide for prospering as a business traveler, even if you don't use the technologies and techniques discussed in the rest of the book. Hard to find numbers for gaining credit card information, making reservations, and finding services in remote cities are now all in one place. Because we want to keep *Office on the Go* a valuable information resource, we would appreciate your suggestions for things we may have left out and your feedback on products and programs we have discussed in the book. Send us a letter at:

Sunny Baker and Kim Baker
Office on the Go Update
c/o Prentice-Hall Professional Publishing
Route 9W
Englewood Cliffs, NJ 07632

It's our wish that all your business trips are productive and rewarding. If the book helps in this regard, then we have accomplished our goal.

Sunny Baker and Kim Baker
Scottsdale, Arizona
February 1993

Section One

OFFICE-ON-THE GO
TECHNOLOGY

1

WHY YOU NEED
MOBILE OFFICE
TECHNOLOGY

According to a recent report from The Associated Press, a member of Parliament was quickly rescued after being kidnapped, stuffed in the trunk of a car, and driven away. The victim simply called the police with the cellular phone stored in his briefcase.

Time and time again—Nowhere is this cliché more appropriate than when qualifying the plights of the traveling businessperson faced with tight travel times, noisy hotel rooms that preclude a good night's sleep, and a demanding schedule of appointments or lengthy booth sessions at a trade show. Every minute on the road is precious—but time and time again the minutes are wasted away in airports, hotels, and traffic. While the traditional business traveler still squanders time reading paperback books and dozing off while waiting in airports, the fully wired traveler spends his or her trips getting work done. This, of course, is a major competitive advantage, because more productivity means new business and a better bottom line.

While many people now travel with a notebook computer, most are unaware of the ways to assemble and use the full range of mobile office technologies and options now in place. Few business travelers, even the "computerized" ones, are equipped with the gamut of tools and techniques available to them. This isn't out of ignorance, it's simply because until *Office on the Go*, there has been no single source that explains the mobile office options, technologies, and techniques and no reference that demonstrates how to put the tools to work as an integrated system of management.

Let's look at a real-life example of what's possible for the ordinary business traveler today:

Bob is a sales and marketing executive for a computer software company. He spends about two weeks of every month traveling around the United States and Canada visiting prospective customers, sales offices, and existing accounts. He doesn't consider himself a technical wizard. In fact, he often has problems understanding his company's own products. Still, empowered with easy-to-use office-on-the-go technology, Bob stays completely connected to corporate headquarters, employees, and customers while on the road. Bob's mobile office fits in a briefcase—and he has room left over for paperbacks and printed reports.

In a typical day, Bob uses his new digital cellular phone to set up appointments and to fax and receive memos and reports. He uses his notebook computer in airports and hotels to send and receive electronic mail and to search online databases for information on potential accounts.

Bob uses computerized market mapping technology on his trips to locate prospective customers, track his sales performance, and keep an eye on his competition. Of course, he tracks his appointments and manages customer records with his computer, besides using it to generate reports and proposals. He even makes his own confirmed airline and hotel reservations online—instantaneously. Bob saves money on the road as well, by using special business discounts and corporate service rates that only the most savvy businesspeople know about.

Just last week, from a data-capable pay phone in O'Hare Airport while waiting to change planes, Bob contacted his public relations agency and downloaded a press release on his company's new product into his computer. After making minor changes to the release with his word processing software, Bob sent the announcement electronically to potential customers across the country. Without so much as a phone call to the office, Bob began taking orders the very next day for the product while still on the road. When he does meet with customers face to face, they marvel at the self-running, color product demonstration complete with music and sound that he displays with his notebook computer.

Bob laughs about people who waste their travel time reading airline magazines and sitting idle in the passenger terminals. He considers his time on the road the most productive in his schedule.

Are you like Bob? Is your time on the road the most productive in your schedule? For most businesspeople who must travel to meetings, conferences, client sites, and trade shows, it isn't. People have been working on the road since the beginning of time. Marco Polo was sort of an early office-on-the-go enthusiast, tracking his travels in writings and maps and selling goods and ideas from one culture to another. The need for maintaining productivity on the road has always been important. But, until recently, even the most disciplined traveler had to limit work to writing reports on pads of yellow legal paper and making phone calls at pay phones when these were available.

As you know already, traveling can be both the most important and the least productive activity in business. An important meeting with a major customer in a distant city may last only an hour. Although the meeting may mean millions in new business, long hotel stays, uninteresting waits in airports, and fruitless hours spent in planes or cars can negatively affect other business priorities. In fact, it is estimated that more than 70 percent of time spent on business travel is wasted. But it doesn't have to be that way.

The mobile office provides a set of tools for getting work done even when its sandwiched in between connecting flights out of Dallas/Fort Worth or during an insomnia-inspired work session at 3:00 A.M. in a cramped hotel room. Now, with the miniaturization of computer technology and the maturation of services and facilities that cater to traveling businesspeople, your travel time can be productive business time.

With a host of new communications technologies and computerized productivity tools, the office on the go has come into its own. Almost anything that can be accomplished in an ordinary office can now be handled on the road and on the fly. In some cases, on the road is even better than at the office because traveling businesspeople can meet their market face to face by visiting stores, clients, companies, and job sites where their products are for sale or being put to work.

Keeping Up

In today's fiercely competitive markets, increased productivity is the key to success. Time spent on the road must become productive time. If you are wasting business travel time with your nose stuck in a paperback novel, you can be sure that your competitors—be they other salespeople or entire companies—are putting mobile office technology to work to their advantage. While you fritter away precious time, they are improving sales, identifying new customers, or keeping in touch with the office. In a dog-eat-dog marketplace, the one who works the smartest wins.

With fully wired mobile office technology, time on the road is time well spent. Days in the hotel or hours on the plane become a quiet opportunity to concentrate on reports, develop plans, and send important letters.

Airports offer a chance to catch up with the mail back at the office or plant or send a fax with a quote to a new customer. Rush-hour, with its stop and go traffic, is the perfect opportunity to make appointments by cellular phone and keep in touch with employees and clients.

You don't need a fortune or a degree in computer science to master the technologies that will make a difference to you. Mobile office technology is readily available and very compact and is becoming less inexpensive and easier to use. Carrying computing and communications power on trips is as convenient as traveling with a briefcase.

The problem for employees and managers on the go is deciding which technologies to use and learning how to put them to work effectively. Choose the wrong software, for example, and the system may be difficult to learn, the cellular phone won't be able to access online services, and the format may not be compatible with the computer in the corporate office.

Inappropriate or hard-to-use technologies go from place to place unused. But, when effectively selected and integrated, mobile office tools make staying in touch a breeze and working on the road as constructive as a day at the office—sometimes more so.

WHAT EXACTLY IS A MOBILE OFFICE?

A mobile office is simply a set of tools that can be used while traveling or when "camped out" in a hotel room in a city remote from the regular office. For some people the mobile office may include an automobile or a truck. The phrase mobile office is a metaphor for a system of tools and components that provides the complete capabilities of a traditional office at any location where you may find yourself. A mobile office requires more than a portable (or notebook) computer—a fully wired mobile office requires both computerized tools and manual techniques that make you productive while in a car, on a plane, sitting in a hotel lobby, or sailing the globe.

A MOBILE OFFICE IS A COMBINATION OF
TRADITIONAL TOOLS AND TECHNOLOGY

A mobile office combines traditional tools and new technology devices to duplicate the services normally provided in a business office environment. For example, because you most likely don't want to travel with a bulky twenty-pound conventional fax machine, a tiny fax modem that's weight is measured in ounces replaces the office-bound model. Or, when a desktop telephone is not available, a compact cellular phone is an elegant and effective replacement.

The basic components of a typical mobile office include a small computer (preferably notebook size) and/or an electronic organizer, a cellular telephone, a fax/modem integrated with the computer for electronic communications, a portable printer, and a variety of software for writing, planning, organizing, and analyzing your information on the road. The fully equipped mobile office even includes games for keeping your spirits up. (Business travelers need entertainment to remain productive.) Many mobile professionals also carry a pager, and a tape recorder/dictating machine is a must for recording ideas, interviews, and meetings, as well as listening to music and catching up on the latest audiobooks.

But not all mobile office tools are electronic. For example, for the individual who has kept a calendar of appointments in a small leather-bound book for twenty years, there's often no compelling reason to start using a computer to track appointments. And many mobile professionals prefer to use the traditional paper diary to back up the computerized systems. The best of the manual methods provide instant access without waiting for a computer to "wake up," are easy to use, and do the job as well as an electronic organizer. And the same person who keeps the leather diary can still use a computer for other office-on-the-go requirements—traditional and automation-based technologies are completely compatible and often can be used in harmony.

While we use automation for almost everything while we're traveling, you should use only as much new technology as you are comfortable with—and limit it to what you can carry with ease. Add the technology slowly, say, by buying a cellular phone as a replacement for the airport pay phone and then acquire new tools as you master the existing ones. You need to determine what best fits your working style, travel requirements, and budget. Why? Because there are limits to the capabilities of technology. An expensive handheld cellular phone is a powerful tool while you are within range of a cellular transmitter, but it's useless when you travel to Germany which uses incompatible cellular technology. Instead, it's back to pay phones and it helps if you have a pocketful of deutsche marks handy.

DO YOU HAVE TO USE A COMPUTER AND OTHER ELECTRONIC GADGETS?

If you are already a computer enthusiast or technology addict, skip this section. But if you are one of those people who knows that a computer is probably looming in your life, but are still reluctant to take that first big step into automation, then this section is for you.

We urge you to automate. Start simple, but get started. Mobile technology is cheaper and easier to use than ever before. Computers have become compact objects that really do fit in a briefcase, and these machines are central to setting up a productive mobile control center. Or, if you are a hopeless computer-phobe, new electronic organizers from companies including Sharp, Apple Computer, Casio, and others are easy-to-use substitutes for a full-function notebook computer.

If you would like to take the leap into full-feature computerization, the new generation of easy-to-use notebook computers from Apple (PowerBooks) makes learning how to use a computer almost painless. Another option is the use of pen-based electronic notepads or personal digital assistants (PDAs) like Apple's Newton that can process handwriting and/or take commands simply by pointing at the function you want to use. Sharp's Wizard electronic organizers are actually sophisticated computers, but they ask you the questions and require no special computer skills to operate. All it takes is a little practice with these tiny machines while reading the easy-to-understand instruction manuals. We discuss these options more in Chapter 4. Even the formidable IBM and IBM-compatible systems have become far easier to learn with the evolution of Microsoft Windows—a program that makes these machines work somewhat like an easy-to-use Macintosh. Whether it's a notebook computer, a PDA, or an electronic organizer, it is important that you add some kind of computer automation to your mobile office. They are now easy enough to use and affordable enough that there is no remaining legitimate excuse for not becoming "computerized."

You don't have to quit using your day book and notepads—take them along. Over time you'll see how the new and the old technologies together make you a much more productive businessperson. You'll wonder how you ever did it without the electronic tools. Your colleagues who still work without them will be left in the dust, struggling to keep up with you.

A MOBILE OFFICE INTEGRATES TOOLS TO CREATE POWERFUL SYSTEMS

Integration among many tools and techniques, both electronic and manual, is required to get the most from the power of your mobile office technologies. This can be achieved only by carefully choosing the right tools and learning how to put them to work effectively. If the technology and services are properly selected, a mobile office can become more powerful and productive than a traditional desk-based office.

While many people routinely travel with a cellular phone and compact computer, the heart of making this technology work is to learn how to combine individual elements into systems. A system is a combination of several tools that accomplishes a business purpose. For example, most people use their notebook computers for only writing a few notes and maybe creating a spreadsheet on the road. Not Bob. Bob considers his notebook computer the "brains" of his mobile empire. Beyond writing reports and taking notes, he uses it for everything from locating new prospects and making sales presentations to entertaining himself when the day's work is finished. Bob also carries a tiny Sony Walkman tape recorder and playback unit. But, in Bob's hands this cigarette pack-size tape unit is used to not only listen to music but to benefit from relaxation tapes that help soothe him to sleep on the airplane and for taping sales demo sessions for review back at the office. In Bob's mobile office every tool plays multiple functions, and all the tools work together. It's this integration among tools that makes a mobile office an effective environment for getting work done while on the road instead of just a briefcase full of gadgets, wires, and papers that weigh you down.

THE SIX MAJOR BUSINESS FUNCTIONS HANDLED BY A WELL-EQUIPPED MOBILE OFFICE

There are six major business functions that must be performed in any office—mobile or traditional. As you put your mobile office together, you must consider all six functions to make the office fully functional. The functions include:

- **Communication.** Communication is the central function in business. Almost everything in business depends on communication of some sort. On the road you need to maintain intracompany communication as well as contact with customers and other companies. Mobile office communications are facilitated with modern telephone equipment, online communication services, presentation software, and a variety of computer-based messaging systems.

- **Reporting.** Reports of various kinds are vital to informing company personnel, whether management or your staff, on the status of travel activities. These reports are especially important to keeping your organization informed while you're on the road because when you aren't in the office, people at the office may assume that you aren't really working. Remember the old adage, "Out of sight, out of mind." A properly equipped mobile office provides the tools for preparing complete reports that prove to the people back at the ranch that not only are you hard at work, but you are a stellar performer. Of course, office-on-the-go communication facilities can be used to submit your reports whenever you like.

- **Information Gathering and Research.** Access to current information is critical to strategic business decisions and profitable sales activities. With a mobile office system, you can gather data in the field as you travel by accessing online research services and reviewing disk-based information directories. Information can be analyzed right on the road or sent to your company for further processing as required.

- **Analysis and Forecasting.** Data is only useful if it can be analyzed to develop appropriate business objectives. Now data analysis can be performed from any notebook computer. For example, a district manager for a chain of retail stores might travel to a city to analyze the performance of the stores in that city. Then using sales figures entered into the notebook computer, he or she can present the performance of each store in a regional meeting. Past and present figures can be graphed and then future performance extrapolated to show the relative performance of each store outlet. All this is done while on the fly, without the need for home office intervention.

- **Planning and Scheduling**. Sophisticated planning and calendar functions make tracking a complicated trip relatively easy. Many of these tools can be set up to remind you of upcoming events when you turn on your computer or electronic organizer. Programs are also available that automatically track billable time. Capable of tracking multiple projects and clients, these programs can be used to bill phone time at different hourly rates from those other activities. At the end of the billing period, they print a complete report of your activities on behalf of each client that can then be used to bill the client or draft your trip report. In addition to keeping your calendar and tracking your time, the mobile office can be used to plan and manage small projects while in the field. Advanced project management software can be used to manage projects like opening a branch office or as big as redesigning the space shuttle. Because the complete project can be made available on a notebook computer, the project can be planned and implemented while in the field. Other strategic documents such as marketing plans can be created, scheduled, and tracked as well.

- **Organization and Record Keeping**. The mobile office offers a wide range of options for record keeping. The options range from client data stored in easy-to-use handheld organizers from Sharp and Casio to sophisticated database programs on note-book computers that track all operations within a company. For example, a traveling salesperson can keep a contact file of all customers that shows account status, purchases, and money owed. While visiting clients, the salesperson can deliver mer-chandise and bill the client on the spot, instantaneously updating the account data. The resulting sales information is added to the file which is then sent to the parent company's main-frame system via modem.

With the right equipment in your briefcase, about the only standard office comforts not directly available from a mobile office are a desk, chair, and wastebasket!

THE THREE MAJOR PERSONAL FUNCTIONS HANDLED BY A WELL-EQUIPPED MOBILE OFFICE

Remember what Jack Nicholson typed over and over on at least a ream of paper in *The Shining* when his wife thought he was busy writing a book? "All work and no play makes Jack a dull boy." Since you don't want to meet Jack's fate on the road, it's important to know that your mobile office can help maintain balance in your life by satisfying three categories of personal needs—educa-tion, entertainment, and relaxation.

- **Education.** Interactive, computer-based products exist that can teach you everything from the basics of investment banking to foreign languages to advanced mathematics. Entire courses are stored on disks, PCMCIA cards (which you'll learn about later), or CD-ROMs (the disks that store computer information on CDs similar to the ones you use to play music). Many of these products mix fun with learning. The popular game, *Where in Time Is*

Carmen Sandiego? for example, mixes interactive game action with an education in world history. As you play the game, you use a paperback encyclopedia (supplied in the package) to look up references to famous people, places, and events. Of course this educational program was originally designed for kids, and we would never get caught playing it ourselves. There are now online university programs, like the online degree programs offered by the University of Phoenix and other accredited schools, that allow businesspeople to finish a degree and still meet their travel obligations. Students simply connect to the "electronic classroom" from any place with a telephone through the modem in their notebook computers.

- **Entertainment.** A stint on the road can be lonely when you are out of contact with family and friends. If you are gone long enough, even going back to the office seems like a bright spot on the calendar. To keep your spirits up, the mobile office provides many opportunities for entertainment. Very sophisticated games, complete with sound and music, are available for notebook computers. Audio books can be enjoyed via a portable tape player or in the cassette player of a rental car. Full-length books available on floppy disks, PCMCIA cards, or CD-ROM can be read right on your computer screen. In addition to these sources of entertainment, if you can get to a phone line (or use a cellular modem), the many online services including CompuServe, Prodigy, and America Online can keep you entertained with a broad range of news, information services, and games.

- **Relaxation.** One of the most wearisome aspects of travel is trying to get enough sleep while crossing time zones, suffering from jet lag, and sleeping in hotel rooms where the elevator keeps the walls rumbling through the night. The mobile office can provide several relaxation options to reduce the stress and impact of these inconveniences. There are a variety of relaxation cassettes available and even "mind machines" that use laser-impulses to induce meditative states. Several companies sell small devices that simulate the sound of soothing ocean waves to mask the noises endemic to hotels. Because these are designed for travelers, they are compact and lightweight.

With all these options, you can see that a mobile office can not only make you more productive, but can keep you amused, educated, and relaxed. This makes life on the road almost fun. With your mobile entertainment facilities, the drudgery of traveling is minimized, and you'll have better things to do after the day's work than head for a beer in the hotel's Starlight Lounge.

🚐 Rule of the Road

No component of a mobile office—be it computer, cellular phone, or spiral-bound notebook—should have fragile or loose parts, sharp edges, or awkward or weak latches. It helps also that, when closed, all components should be waterproof enough to resist at least a few drops of rain. Who knows, you might need to pull your organizer out and make an appointment on a Seattle street corner...

EVALUATING MOBILE OFFICE TOOLS AND TECHNOLOGIES

We recommend using very specific criteria to evaluate the tools and technologies to be taken on any business trip. First, mobile office components must provide most (if not all) of the functionality of their counterparts in the traditional office. Second, they must be easy to carry and should run without external AC power for at least several hours. And, while individual tools may be compact on their own, by the time a complete office set-up is assembled, the items combined may be bulky and cumbersome. No business traveler late to the airport for a flight wants to charge through the terminal hefting two fifty-pound briefcases! So, when evaluating office-on-the-go tools and technology, you should also evaluate the following:

- **Size and Weight Versus Functionality.** Every ounce counts in a mobile office, especially since you have to carry your office on your back. This means that a five-pound notebook computer that can be used for a wide range of office-on-the-go needs will be considered a more reasonable choice than will a five-pound device that keeps only a calendar of appointments.

- **Ease of Use.** If the average businessperson can't quickly put a device to work, then it's not very useful—regardless of the potential for the device. Some of the computer software technologies such as the mapping software explained in Chapter 9 are very powerful, but they take practice and persistence to learn. Thus we recommend advanced programs only to those who have a specific requirement for their functionality and time to learn them.

- **Set-up Time.** Remember, this book is about making you productive on the road. Because you may want to dash off a quick memo or fax only minutes before a meeting or catching a plane, fast access to the functionality of your office tools is important. For example, if sending a one-page fax takes five minutes just to get the computer ready, then in our opinion the set-up time is unacceptable.

- Ability to Function Without AC Power. While this book isn't solely concerned with electronic gadgets, many of the most powerful devices for maintaining productivity on the road run on battery power and may need to be used without tapping into AC power for extended periods. What good is setting up for work in your comfy first class airline seat when your notebook computer is stone dead? For this reason, battery longevity and recharging considerations are important criteria for most mobile office technologies.

- Life Span Versus Cost. While tools already exist that allow you to use satellites to chitchat with almost anyone on the planet from almost any place you may find yourself, the cost of such technology is still prohibitively expensive for most mobile travelers. At about $8 to $12 per minute (not including the cost of the equipment), only the richest travelers and/or most time-critical assignments will benefit from using satellite services today. But it's no secret that most technology expands in capability while it rapidly decreases in cost. You should keep this in mind before purchasing an expensive item that may be 20 to 50 percent cheaper within a year. In this book, we look at products in terms of what they can do for you now. (Maybe by the time you read this, satellite calls will have dropped to a quarter a call, who knows? Then the technology will make sense for everyone.) If the payback is less than the price tag, it's time to ask whether you really need the tool.

- Reliability. Product reliability is of paramount importance on the road. There's nothing more frustrating than losing a week's productivity on a business trip because your computer or phone or some other device failed to work as promised. This means that the reputation of the manufacturer and

on-the-road service availability should be important determining factors in making individual
mobile office purchases.

Taken together, these criteria provide a framework
for evaluating mobile office products based on their performance in the real world on the road. There are also
specific criteria for evaluating specific components that
we'll talk about more in subsequent chapters when we
show you how to select the specific tools for your office.

CRITICALLY EVALUATE YOUR NEEDS FOR MOBILE OFFICE TECHNOLOGY

We describe many tools and options for on-the-
road use, but we don't recommend that anyone use all of
them. Before you go on a spending binge, ask yourself
what you really need when you travel. For the "fully
wired" professional traveling with a mobile office, it is
always a compromise between everything you'd like to
take and what you can practically carry. Not everybody
needs a full complement of computers, phones, gadgets,
and audio equipment for every trip. You must critically
evaluate your own work requirements and personal preferences to put together the best mobile office for you.
Once you determine your needs, you can match the right
tools to your style, work habits, and productivity
requirements. Do remember that your needs will vary
from trip to trip. For example, a one-day business trip
requires fewer devices than a four-month around-the-
world sales marathon.

As we've mentioned briefly already, for most traveling professionals, the basic mobile office components
for short trips and long include:

- **Notebook Computer or Digital Organizer.**
  Portables and laptops are now obsolete for most
  business travelers. If you want to be mobile, get

the most powerful, smallest machine that meets your needs. We provide a complete list of options and selection criteria in the next chapter for this premier component in your mobile office.

- **A Cellular Telephone or Electronic Pager.** You need some way to remain in touch with the office at all times.

- **A Small Tape Recorder (preferably with an integrated radio).** A tape recorder, like a recording Sony Walkman or one of the many competitive units on the market, can perform a variety of useful business and entertainment functions on the road—ranging from simply playing back music when you're jogging around the hotel to recording an important presentation by a competitor at a trade show

---

Rule of the Road

Never purchase any piece of technology that intimidates you. While you may learn to use such a device, chances are that it will make you nervous enough that you won't. This goes double for devices that you will need to access on the fly such as electronic organizers and mobile faxing systems.

- **An Organizer, Either Manual or Electronic.** Even though you'll take a computer along for most trips, there are times when you just need to take notes or jot down a phone number—and this often happens when you don't have your computer with you or turned on. Thus an organizer of some sort is for taking brief notes and keeping your schedule up to date. This is the device you take everywhere with you. It can easily fit in a coat pocket or handbag. Ideally, the organizer should be compatible with the notebook computer you use. If you use a manual organizer, for example, your notebook computer should be able to print pages that fit the configuration you use. If you use an electronic organizer, then it should be able to share information with the computer you use with a cable and linking software.

THE EXTRA GADGETS

Beyond the basics—computer, phone or pager, recorder, and organizer—there are literally thousands of handy gadgets for use on the road, including the obvious portable printers and fax machines to special purpose devices like handheld translators, mind machines, electronic books, air purifiers, and even portable burglar alarms. Improved battery technologies and battery recharging systems allow manufacturers to produce everything from portable blenders to miniature vacuum cleaners.

We'll discuss some of the more useful devices (and some of the most interesting) for mobile professionals later in the book. As we've mentioned already, when choosing the extra devices you need to evaluate the usefulness of each device in comparison to its cost, size, and weight.

For example, if you suffer from allergies and must carry a ten-pound battery-powered air cleaner with you to be able to tolerate visits to pollen-heavy areas of the country, then you have no alternative but to purchase and carry such a device. Always evaluate the importance of each gadget before purchase and when packing for a trip.

Take it from us—it's easy to acquire so many gadgets that you'll need a separate suitcase just to ship all the toys when you travel. Too many devices can make travel burdensome instead of productive—which is exactly the opposite of what you are trying to accomplish in assembling a portable office. International travelers must be even more selective about the tools they bring because too many gadgets can cause customs hassles and delays.

The best kinds of items to add to your repertoire are those that fulfill more than one function—that's why a small computer, cellular phone, and tiny recorder are so useful—they individually are capable of performing multiple functions on the road.

HOW WILL YOU USE YOUR MOBILE OFFICE?

To make choosing equipment easier, in this book we've described some of the most common uses of mobile office equipment and provided guidelines to help you identify your needs and preferences. Keep in mind that the products and functions presented in this book are not comprehensive—a mobile office can take a number of forms and be used for an infinite variety of tasks. For example, one adventurer built a mobile office complete with working satellite links into a trailer he pulled from his bicycle as he traveled around the world on two wheels. From the control center on the handlebars, he can download and upload electronic mail, choose music to listen to, and track data and other information. The whole arrangement is partly powered by solar panels mounted to the bike's trailer—now that's an office on the go!

After reading the rest of this book, you'll be able to design a mobile office just as functional, but perhaps not as unique as the one just described, that is specifically tailored for you.

2

THE COMPUTER TOOLS THAT PUT YOU IN THE FAST LANE

In Chapter 1 we introduced the advantages and capabilities of mobile office technologies; in this chapter we will cover the central component of the mobile office—the computer that will become the primary repository of information and programs for your mobile business endeavors.

The heart of your mobile office is the computer you will use to maintain information. Every business traveler has different needs for computing power, and the marketing people in technology companies have responded to these diverse needs with a growing range of mobile computing options. As mentioned in Chapter 1, in addition to full-featured mobile computers, there are a wide variety of electronic personal organizers available that are really computers dressed up in easy-to-use clothing. Notebook computers and subnotebooks are covered in this chapter. Organizers, pen-based electronic note pads, and personal digital assistants are covered in the next chapter.

ALL COMPUTERS GREAT AND SMALL

There are literally hundreds of mobile computers

on the market—these range from tiny "palmtops" with keyboards that bring new meaning to the words "cramped fingers" to clunky "lugables" that are portable in name only because they have a handle. There are six general categories of personal computers, and each has its own pros and cons as a part of the mobile office. These include palmtops, notebooks, subnotebooks, portables, lugables, and dockables. And, of course, there is the desktop computer—which should only be considered mobile in very special circumstances.

PALMTOPS

Palmtops are tiny, full-function computers that (almost) fit in the palm of your hand. In addition to being small, they are also light in weight, making them ideal for carrying to any meeting around the world. Unfortunately, they have serious limitations if you need to do typing-intensive work, such as writing reports or working on detailed spreadsheets. Be aware that the line that divides palmtop computers and electronic organizers is a blurry one. The difference seems to be that palmtop computers will actually do traditional computing functions, where organizers are designed to keep schedules and maintain phone lists. Palmtop computers differ from electronic organizers in that they run a wider range of general computer software and work more like a desktop computer. Palmtops run on batteries or with an AC adapter.

Pros:

    ✔ Palmtop computers are extremely compact and light in weight, making them as easy to carry as a paperback book. Because they take a fairly wide range of applications, they are best for taking along on short trips when you don't want to carry too much around. They are adequate for memos and small spreadsheets, accessing online information on the road, and sending E-mail and faxes through a modem (if available for the machine).

✔ The newest models such as the Zeos' Pocket PC and HP's 95LX run standard software. (For example, Lotus 1-2-3 is built into the HP's memory, and other applications can be added). This makes access to the programs fast and direct.

✔ These are good machines to use as a second computer to take along when the notebook computer is just too large or when you don't need to do much writing or keyboard input.

Cons:

✖ While most palmtops now offer the familiar QWERTY keyboard, the small size of the keys makes serious typing difficult if not impossible. Thus, if you have to do more than enter a few names and addresses on the keyboard, palmtops are awkward at best.

✖ These machines are limited by their size in ways other than keyboarding. For example, lacking a hard disk, there's little room for additional software and large data files. In addition, the displays are not all that easy to read because they are typically small, nonbacklit LCD (liquid crystal display) readouts. Although some of the palmtops now use Personal Computer Memory and International Association (PCMCIA) cards for expanding memory and other functions, in most systems you can only use one card at a time. Depending on your usage requirements, this lack of flexibility may or may not be a problem.

✖ For serious productivity, palmtops depend on communication with larger desktop machines to send and receive files and information. This limits the palmtop to second computer status, making it absolutely necessary for users to have two computers. Notebook computers on the other hand can serve both desktop and mobile computing functions admirably for many people.

When buying a palmtop computer look for:

- **A Usable Machine.** The main weaknesses of palmtop units is their minuscule keyboards—similar to those found on electronic organizers. Few adults can do more than type in a few lines with these tiny keys. In addition, the display screens are small and sometimes hard to read. Many palmtops display only a few lines of information on the screen at one time. This slows throughput because you must spend more time moving through the document than on the screen of a notebook computer that typically shows a full eighty lines of text at one time. A good palmtop should have a variety of programs available, memory expansion capabilities, ports for connecting to larger computers, a clear display, and a usable keyboard.

- **A Machine Adequate for Your Work.** Because typical palmtop machines are too small to accept disk drives, most software and information (data) must be kept in the machine's memory. As mentioned, some of the newer palmtops use PCMCIA cards which can hold programs or data or function as modems or other devices. Since even the largest palmtop memories aren't all that big, you may not be able to load the programs you need, or you may be forced to work on only the shortest of documents. If these limitations cause you to make compromises in your work, then you need to use a notebook computer.

- **A Serious Computer.** There are some palmtops on

the market that can only be considered toys. Avoid these units because most of them are so limited that you would be better off with a manual organizer or even a pad and pencil than wasting several frustrating hours trying to put these machines to work. Recognize the toys by their price (usually low), cheap construction, limited program compatibility, and low-quality output options.

✈ Batteries Not Included

One way to recognize the toys from the tools suited for serious mobile use is to study the construction for clues. Quality units are solidly built with nearly invisible seams and durable hinges. An easy way to judge equipment quality is to look at the battery compartment. The batteries should fit precisely in a carefully manufactured compartment—not one like you'd find at the back of a $29.95 talking doll. Look for tight fitting connectors and a cover that won't fall off while banging around inside your briefcase. Also, some manufacturers use specially manufactured NiCad batteries designed for their machines—for larger computers, this is usually advantageous because the batteries have a long life and are rechargeable while in the unit. (Just plug the adapter provided by the manufacturer into the wall at night and the batteries are recharged and ready to go the next morning.) There should also be some type of battery back-up system and a clear warning when the power of the batteries starts to fade. If in doubt about the batteries, ask about them before you buy the computer.

NOTEBOOK COMPUTERS

Notebook computers are probably the most functional and adaptable office-on-the-go option (although there are some new handheld, personal digital assistants from AT&T, Apple Computer, and other companies that are giving notebooks a run for the money). Notebook computers currently offer the best portability-to-power ratio, and although there are still some limitations to what notebook computers can do, there aren't many.

While there are a countless number of different models, brands, and kinds of notebook computers, for the mobile office, you obviously want the most compact unit available that offers the largest, clearest screen and a full-sized keyboard.

Of course, for superior, compact design and extended battery power, you're going to pay more than for a similarly powered desktop computer. This is simply because the components that are used to build the machine are more expensive than are those used for desktop computers—and the designers need to make some money for all their innovations.

Notebook computers can usually run the same wide range of computer programs (software) that runs on the desktop computer in a traditional office. Notebooks can run on both battery power or plug into a wall with an AC adapter.

Pros:

✔ The right notebook computer provides the functionality of a regular desktop-based computer, but can run independent of AC power for up to ten hours (average models clock in at three to six hours of battery time), and these units fit in an average-sized briefcase, taking up about 60 percent of the space.

✔ Notebook computers run standard off-the-shelf software and can be used as your primary computer if you don't mind minor trade-offs such as a limited number of F-Keys and no access to a 5 1/4" floppy disk drive.

Cons:

✖ Notebook computers cost around two to four times what their desktop counterparts sell for, though these prices are falling rapidly. As notebook computers become more standard and because of increased competition, you can expect some bargains out there—so look for them.

✖ Most machines are limited to displaying black and white or 16 to 64 shades of gray. Color notebooks are increasingly available, but these are much more expensive and some models offer limited battery life.

SUBNOTEBOOK COMPUTERS

This subnotebook from Zeos is a near perfect compromise between a notebook computer and a palmtop. It's priced reasonably as well.

If you can work without an integrated floppy disk drive, consider a new generation of notebook computers, called subnotebooks in the trade press, that weigh in at less than four pounds. They're light and compact and they take up only about half the room of a floppy-equipped notebook computer.

Subnotebooks are a step between palmtops and notebook computers. Where a notebook computer typically weighs between five and seven pounds, a subnotebook is usually two to four pounds. Most subnotebooks do not have a floppy disk drive, though they often have quite large-capacity hard disks (over 100 megabytes). There are thin-slice external floppy drives available for people who must have access to disks for file transfers. PC slots are provided to hold PC cards (also known as PCMCIA cards). Modem cards, memory cards, and program cards are available. These machines are not just cute and tiny. Subnotebooks are remarkably similar in performance to larger notebook computers, though the displays may lack clarity and keyboards are a bit smaller. Still, the best ones have keyboards that are usable, and their light weight and increasing performance and the proliferation of the new PC cards make them a definite consideration for someone who must limit the weight they carry on the road.

Pros:

✔ Subnotebooks are less expensive than the best notebook computers.

✔ They are light in weight and still powerful enough to do real computing on the road.

Cons:

✖ Carrying a lot of PCMCIA cards around and swapping them in and out of the machine can be frustrating, especially if you accidentally leave one of the cards at home.

✖ Some people may find the keyboards too small for typing.

✖ Although some subnotebooks offer comfortably readable screens, most of the subnotebook displays are too small for making presentations, and some people find the small displays awkward when working on spreadsheets or long documents. Some displays still lack brightness and clarity when compared to their full-notebook cousins.

✖ The number of applications available on PCMCIA cards is still limited, though it is growing.

✖ Some find the lack of a floppy disk drive an annoyance. Others find that the lighter weight more than compensates for the small inconveniences caused by the lack of an integrated floppy disk drive.

✈ What's a PCMCIA?

An increasing number of computers, and especially the new sub-notebooks and personal digital assistants (PDAs are discussed in the next chapter), are expandable by plugging PCMCIA cards into special slots. These cards look like a thick credit card. PCMCIA stands for Personal Computer Memory Card International Association, which brought together a group of manufacturers who agreed on the technical standards with which to develop PC cards for modems, mass storage devices, and LAN adapters. An earlier PC card specification was developed by Japan Electronic Industry Development Association (JEIDA)—and JEIDA specs were the basis for the later, expanded PCMCIA standards. The PCMCIA's standards detail the kind of devices, interface, data formats, and socket specifications to be used by the cards. This kind of expandability (and compatibility) is especially important in machines too small for plug-in expansion boards or that lack a disk drive—and of course, for the mobile professional, they are the wave of the future.

LAPTOP COMPUTERS

The first computers to run on battery power were called laptop computers. These machines vary in size and weight, and modern laptops are usually an alternative to the mobile office if you need a full-function computer and can't afford a notebook model.

A laptop computer, once considered small and lightweight, is now considered a medium-sized portable computer, sometimes almost as large as a modern desktop computer without its monitor. Laptops range in weight from about nine pounds to nearly eighteen pounds (better have a strong lap!). Like notebooks, a good laptop will run standard software. Laptop computers run on AC and batteries, although some models are intended more as portable desktop machines and run only on AC.

Pros:

✔ They offer full functionality at a lower price than most notebook machines with similar capabilities.

✔ Keyboards and displays on many models are larger than those on a notebook.

Cons:

✖ These units are large and cumbersome to carry, and most are the size of a briefcase instead of fitting inside one. Buy a notebook computer unless you have special needs that only a laptop can accommodate. For example, one large, clunky laptop made by Epson allows you to add a standard AT-style board to its single slot. This board could be used for a network or for driving a special device such as a CD-ROM unit. For most mobile professionals, however, the compromises of the laptop are not worth the bargain price.

LUGABLE COMPUTERS

The first "portable" computers were the lugables (also laughably called "transportables"). These machines are simply streamlined desktop computers and they do not run on battery. Today, the line between laptop computers and lugables is blurring with "lunchbox" models that don't weigh much more than a laptop where once a lugable was a thirty-pound behemoth that deserved its name.

Lugables are not the machine of choice for the mobile professional unless you don't need to work away from an AC outlet, you don't need to move the thing long distances very often, the lugable is given to you at no charge, and you have absolutely no money to buy another computer.

Pros:

✔ These fully functional units are somewhat more compact and easier to move than a desktop computer.

✔ Lugables are great for on-the-job weight lifting sessions while staying in hotels not equipped with a weight room or exercise facility.

Cons:

✘ Relatively large, cumbersome to carry, most units are the size of an overnight bag and require a dedicated hand to lug them through an airport.

✘ This kind of machine is becoming obsolete, and only a few are still available on the market. Notebook computers are becoming so inexpensive that there's almost no reason to seriously look at these machines.

DOCKABLE COMPUTERS

Because your mobile office computer is chosen based on a mix of power, flexibility, and portability, you may find that a compact notebook computer that serves you well on the road lacks functionality and ergonomics to serve as your office PC. You may, for convenience sake, not want to have to own two computers—one for your desk and one for the road. Fortunately, several companies make computers which are both compact on the road and full-featured back at the office. These systems are called dockable or docking computers. A dockable computer is a full desktop computer, usually equipped with a separate color monitor. The unit can be broken into two parts: The docking section, with its full-sized color monitor and (on some units) expansion slots and a notebook or laptop-size computer, with an integrated display, that can be taken on the road, leaving the larger pieces of the system on the desk. When "docked," these machines run on AC power. The removable computer runs on either AC or battery power.

This arrangement is ideal for moving a mobile office back and forth from a "land-based" office. For users who require both a compact portable unit and a full-sized desktop computer, dockable systems may be the ideal solution.

Pros:

✔ The dockable unit provides both full desktop computer functionality and the portability of a notebook or laptop computer.

Cons:

✖ A well-designed dockable may cost more than an inexpensive desktop computer and a separate notebook computer. The dockable provides only one machine when it's separated, not two.

✖ A standalone notebook computer may be smaller and lighter than the portable section of an "undocked" dockable. Typically, the more compact the portable section is, the more expensive the machine will be overall.

DESKTOP COMPUTERS

In contrast to the mobile computers described already, let's take a quick look at the desktop computer. Desktop computer systems are different from any of the computers mentioned because they consist of several units that plug into each other. These pieces are often purchased separately and may be manufactured by different companies. Typically, a desktop computer consists of a main unit (CPU), a separate keyboard, and a display monitor. Desktop computers are the least portable units because of the individual pieces that must be moved separately. Don't even think of trying to carry and use one on the road unless you plan to set the system up at a trade show booth for demonstrating a computer product.

You have now been introduced to the full range of computer options available for your mobile office, but because this is a book for businesspeople on the go, when we talk about a computer in the rest of the book, we are generally referring to notebook computers (or capable subnotebook or one of the new PDAs) which typically are about the size and weight of two hard-bound books and fit into a roomy briefcase. Other computers are simply too large to put in a briefcase and lug through a busy airport.

The smaller "palmtop" computers are okay as a backup system or as an adjunct to be used at meetings or on short trips, but some of these models are limited in functionality because they lack storage and compatibility with the standard notebook computers. There are also a growing number of electronic notebook computers (discussed in Chapter 4) that can take handwriting as input, but since today none of these systems allows you to do much more than scratch a note to yourself, at this writing, we consider the notebook computer to be the central machine for the mobile office. (We expect handwriting recognition and voice recognition will improve with time—so for those of you who absolutely refuse to learn to use a keyboard, there is still hope.)

THREE COMPUTER PLATFORMS—WHICH ONE IS RIGHT FOR YOU?

In addition to the different sizes of machines just explained, it is important to know that you must select the operating environment of the machine (called a platform in computerese) that you want to use. For small computers there are three primary platform choices, based on the CPU chip and the operating system employed by the machines. The platform choices include the PC-compatible, the Apple Macintosh, and proprietary platforms. Choosing one of the platforms (mostly) locks you into running software written for that machine. Your choice of a platform may materially affect how productive you are, based on your ability to learn and use the software for that platform. The issues surrounding the choice of a platform are explained in the next pages.

The IBM-Compatible Platform

The most widely used personal computer platform is the IBM-compatible machine. These computers, made by IBM and other companies, use microprocessors designed by Intel Corporation (286, 386, 486, and so on) and software (called an operating system) made by Microsoft or IBM to run the system (operating systems are explained in the next section). These are generally the most inexpensive computers, with many models and brands made in countries with low-cost manufacturing techniques.

Pros:

✔ IBM compatibles are the most popular computer in the world with literally millions of the machines in use in the United States alone. Because of their popularity, a large number of software programs are available for these machines.

✔ With the large number of PC manufacturers around the world competing to sell nearly identical machines, prices for a complete computer are very low compared to other kinds of computers.

Cons:

✖ Because the machines have been around since 1981, a large number of nonstandard changes and additions to the systems have been made by various manufacturers. As a result, setting up one of these machines can be problematic and very intimidating to the novice computer user. Fortunately, since this book is mostly concerned with the smallest PCs, fewer options are available on these machines to confuse you during set-up.

✖ Even when running Microsoft Windows (described next), you need to learn more than a fair amount about how computers work to use the machines of this platform.

The Apple Macintosh Platform

Apple Computer makes the Macintosh line of computers that use CPU chips designed by Motorola (called the 68000, 68020, 68030, 68040, and so on) and Apple's own operating environment called the Apple OS, commonly referred to as "The System." Macintoshes tend to be more expensive than IBM-compatible machines, although they are generally regarded as much easier to set up, learn, and use. With recent price reductions, the cost argument against the Macintosh is less compelling than it once was. In fact, in a recent JD Power survey the Apple Macintosh was rated higher for overall user satisfaction than any other personal computer on the market. Another survey showed that Apple now sells more personal computers than IBM.

Pros:

✔ The "Mac" is easier to learn than IBM compatibles because the computer uses an integrated operating system and intuitive graphic interface. The system is set up so all programs use similar operating procedures. Once you learn one application on the Macintosh, you will find that all the programs work in largely the same way. This allows you to learn the machine and put it to work in less than an hour after unpacking it from the box.

✔ Apple (the makers of the Macintosh) has kept full control of the machine and allowed almost no one to make clones. As a result, the incompatibilities common to IBM PCs and compatibles are comparatively rare, and machine set-up is fast and easy.

✔ Where IBM compatibles may require extensive fiddling with tiny switches and counterintuitive software to get the machine fully set up and operational, the Macintosh requires little or no hardware and/or software tweaking.

Cons:

✖ Even with Apple's continuous price cutting, Macs remain more expensive than PC clones. However, the price gap is much less significant than it once was and continues to narrow.

✖ There is not quite as much software available for the Macintosh as for IBM PCs, but unless your needs are very esoteric, you can probably find the kind of programs you need for the Mac, and this computer is much more popular than it once was. Many popular applications such as Lotus 1-2-3, Microsoft Word, WordPerfect, and PageMaker (to name but a few) now have the ability to swap files between the Mac and DOS/Windows versions almost transparently.

Proprietary Platforms

There are mobile computers that use unique computer chips and operating systems (explained next) that do not have wide acceptance as standards in the marketplace. We simply advise you not to buy a notebook or subnotebook computer that is not either fully PC or Macintosh compatible.

THE OPERATING ROOM

Part of your decision in choosing between the IBM and Macintosh platforms has to do with the operating system used by the machines. Every computer has an operating system. It is this operating system that gives the machine its character as you interact with it to tell the computer what you want it to do. An operating system is simply the software link between you and your machine so you can instruct it to do what you need done—like running programs and copying files.

Currently there are four standard operating environments that can be employed by mobile computers. All Macintosh computers use the Apple OS (also referred to as The System or System 7), which is an integrated graphical operating environment developed by Apple. The system employs pull-down menus and easy-to-identify icons to represent files and programs. Macintosh computers can also run a version of UNIX called A/UX. For IBM PCs and compatibles, the standard operating environments include MS-DOS (called PC-DOS by IBM), OS/2, and UNIX. There is also the popular graphical interface, called Windows, that adds functionality and ease of use to MS-DOS. When MS-DOS and Windows are combined, they work in a fashion similar to the Apple OS, though the Windows/MS-DOS system is not as well integrated.

In the next few pages we present some of the differences among these operating environments that may help you make a decision about the computer platform that you want to use on the road.

MS-DOS

MS-DOS, often called DOS by computer users, is short for Microsoft disk operating system. This operating system was originally developed for the first IBM PCs (and called PC-DOS) in the early 1980s. The DOS system uses character-based commands (words) to instruct the computer to perform basic functions. The MS-DOS system requires that you learn more about the mechanics of internal computer operations than do more modern, graphical systems. Choose this option only if you are required to because your corporation has adopted it as a standard or if you have already learned and continue to use MS-DOS on another machine.

Pros:

    ✔ Fast and compact, this system takes up little room on your hard disk.

    ✔ MS-DOS comes free with most IBM-compatible computers. Even if you use Windows, DOS will be there underneath it all. DOS is required for current versions of Windows to run on IBM-compatible machines.

Cons:

    ✖ MS-DOS is limited in what it can do, and it makes

you learn more about computers than many people care to know. For old hands at the keyboard, MS-DOS is easy to use, even though its graphics capabilities are limited.

✖ MS-DOS must be learned. It is not intuitive.

Microsoft Windows

Windows is a graphical interface developed by Microsoft, the same folks who brought you MS-DOS. Windows works on top of MS-DOS. Windows uses icons and pull-down menus and eliminates most of the requirements to use the cryptic MS-DOS commands. The Windows interface and operations are similar to those used by the Apple Macintosh. Windows also adds the ability to run multiple programs at one time and other functional enhancements over MS-DOS. This makes IBM-compatible computers much easier to use, though Windows adds complexities in setting up the system and takes up much more memory and disk space than MS-DOS alone. Although there is a version of Windows that will run on 286 processors, the current version of Windows definitely demands a 386 or higher CPU.

Pros:

✔ This system makes IBM PCs much easier to use than with MS-DOS alone. Windows makes PCs work somewhat like the Macintosh although it's not yet as easy to use as the Apple OS.

✔ Windows is often included free with new IBM PC compatibles.

✔ A pen-based version of Windows is available that runs some Windows applications on pen-based computers.

✔ Graphics-oriented applications are facilitated under Windows.

Cons:

✖ Windows is going through a series of changes to make it more powerful and easy to use. As a result, other software may need regular updates to make it work with the current version of Windows.

✖ There are technical difficulties in configuring Windows for novice users, because MS-DOS is still the operating system underneath it all. For this reason, people who have not learned MS-DOS or are new to computers in general usually find the integrated environment of the Apple OS on the Macintosh PowerBook an easier-to-use and more predictable environment for mobile computing. As Windows evolves and MS-DOS is eliminated from the equation, this Macintosh advantage may disappear.

OS/2

Microsoft and IBM originally developed OS/2 together, although IBM has now taken over the development of OS/2 and Microsoft has taken on the development of Windows. (This is actually a simplification of a very complex relationship between the two companies and the fate of the operating systems—but for the purpose of this book, it should suffice.) As IBM's answer to Windows, OS/2 is (comparatively) easy to learn and use. Because OS/2 can run most MS-DOS and Windows software, albeit with a few glitches, this is a very powerful environment. OS/2 is about as friendly (easy to learn and use) as Windows.

Pros:

✔ OS/2 offers superior multitasking and overall processing power to Windows and MS-DOS.

✔ It is comparatively easy to learn and use.

✔ It runs software designed for MS-DOS and

Windows as well as OS/2 applications, making it compatible with the largest number of software applications.

✔ It eliminates the need for many of the add-on software utilities that have proliferated in the DOS world to extend the power of the operating system.

Cons:

✖ It tends to be slow on anything but the fastest machines.

✖ It takes a lot of memory—both RAM and on your hard disk. 16 megabytes of RAM is a recommended basic configuration. This makes it generally less desirable for mobile computing applications. In fact, the system is too large for most current notebook computers to handle. (We expect that OS/2 will become more efficient at the same time memory capacities will expand for notebooks, making this limitation less of a problem in the future.)

✖ Incompatibilities between OS/2 and Windows applications are common, and little OS/2-specific software is currently available.

✖ The future of OS/2 is still uncertain, so many people are not adopting the platform until it is fully accepted as a standard.

UNIX

UNIX, the oldest operating system of the bunch, developed by Bell Labs for minicomputers almost thirty years ago, has continued to evolve as a standard for engineers and software designers. The system works something like MS-DOS and is very cryptic to learn and use, but unlike MS-DOS, it is a very powerful environment. If you are an experienced computer user who demands high performance from applications such as complex spreadsheets and programming languages, this may be the system for you. There are graphic interfaces for UNIX that hide the operating system's difficult interface from you and make the product easier to use, but these systems may not get along with your other software.

Pros:

    ✔ UNIX offers superior processing power to other operating environments. A version is available for PC compatibles and the Macintosh computers.

Cons:

    ✖ UNIX is difficult to learn, although newer extensions of the software work much like Windows.

    ✖ It is less popular (and more expensive) than other operating systems and therefore less application software is available for mobile computing applications.

    ✖ Like OS/2, UNIX takes a lot of memory and hard disk capacity.

Apple OS for the Macintosh

The Apple operating system comes free with all Macintoshes. It is both easy to learn and easy to use. But, because it is large and contains so much screen drawing information to maintain the Apple environment, it is slow on older machines.

Pros:

    ✔ The Apple OS is the easiest to learn and use (except for some pen-based systems) and offers the most consistency between diverse applications.

    ✔ It's included free with all Macintoshes.

✔ The Apple OS offers the most control of sound, pictures, and video, making it the top contender if you plan to use your computer for presentations while on the road.

✔ It can read MS-DOS files and disks. Most Macintosh applications are available for Windows, making the two systems highly compatible across the platforms.

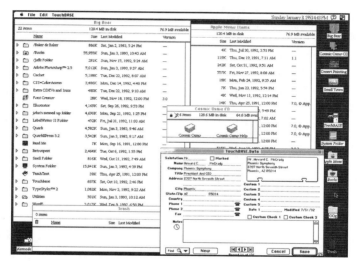

The operating systems of the 1990s employ a graphical user interface (GUI—pronounced gooey). This eliminates complex computer commands by replacing them with a computer desktop that looks something like a regular office environment. Files are kept in (computerized) manila folders, and programs and files that are no longer needed are thrown into the trashcan in the lower right corner of the screen.

Cons:

✖ The system is slow and ponderous on older Macintoshes.

✖ Some people fault the system for not having a command-line interface option (as in MS-DOS) for frequently used commands.

UNIQUE (PROPRIETARY) OPERATING SYSTEMS

Operating systems that are unique to one specific machine are less common than they once were. For example, one of the first notebook computers was Radio Shack's (Tandy) TRS100. This machine offered built-in scheduling software as well as a word processor and spreadsheet. All the software was unique to the machine, so off-the-shelf programs would not run on it.

Pros:

✔ Often machines such as the TRS100 are less expensive than full-featured machines that run standard software.

✔ Typically, because the software offers limited functionality, it is both easy to learn and use.

Cons:

✖ If you want to run other kinds of programs produced for the standard platforms, you're out of luck.

✖ The built-in software may be too limited for all but the most basic mobile applications.

You have now been introduced to the range of full-function computer options available for a mobile office. Confusing isn't it? Well, in the next chapter, we'll explain how you can choose a platform and a computer for your own requirements on the road.

3

HOW TO CHOOSE THE BEST COMPUTER FOR YOUR MOBILE OFFICE

Choosing a mobile computer takes time. First, there are so many machines and brands. Second, it's hard to choose a machine because so many technical issues cloud the purchase decision. And, third, everyone from coworkers to friends to salespeople will give you their opinion on the matter, regardless of how little they know about the topic. Again, we encourage and recommend that you use either a notebook computer (best) or subnotebook computer with reasonable-sized keyboard (good) for the main computing power in your mobile office. Then, add a compatible electronic organizer, electronic notepad, or personal digital assistant (PDA), when a powerful one is finally available, for use when the notebook computer is not feasible because of size or battery limitations.

FIRST CHOOSE THE PLATFORM, THEN CHOOSE THE MACHINE

To choose the computer for your mobile office, we suggest that you first choose the platform for your work. If you're like the majority of mobile professionals, your choice of platform will be between a Windows-based PC compatible or an Apple Macintosh (either a PowerBook or an Outbound).

List the ways you plan to use your computer. That should be easier after you finish reading this book. Then look at the platforms. Look seriously at the IBM-compatible notebooks and Apple Macintosh notebooks before you decide on the platform. Then, after trying both environments, base your final choice of platform on the software you want to use. After all, it's the work you need to get done on the road that is most important and it's mostly the software that determines the work you'll get done.

Not all programs that run on one platform will have an identical version made for the other platform, although many products have a version that runs on both. Select the software and hardware that best fits your needs, and then make the decision. The hardware/software platform choice should be the easiest to use and offer the most flexibility on the road while remaining within your budget. After you make your platform choice, you can use the following guidelines for selecting a specific machine and model within that platform.

SELECTING AN IBM-COMPATIBLE NOTEBOOK COMPUTER

There are literally hundreds of IBM-compatible computer manufacturers, and most of these produce a line of notebook computers suitable for use on the road. The machine that's right for you will combine compact size with adequate performance at a price that makes sense for you. You also want to purchase your computer from a company that makes reliable products and stands behind their equipment with a good warranty program and accessible technical support, preferably providing a toll-free 800 number and one-day turnaround on repairs.

(What good is a mobile computer that's in the shop all the time?)

Start with the Right Microprocessor

Depending on your budget and the kind of programs you plan to run, the choice of your notebook computer's CPU is a critical decision and a confusing one as well. If you decide on a PC platform, the ideal choice is a machine that employs an Intel 486 chip or one with the forthcoming P5 microprocessor. But less expensive machines are available that employ the older 286 and 386 chips. What's the difference? The 386 and 486 microprocessors can do true multitasking with the MS-DOS operating system. This means that more than one DOS or Windows program can run at one time—and this is very useful in mobile computing. (Older versions of the microprocessors, including the 8086 and 80286, can only run one program at a time.) The newer chips are also faster—but that means more expensive as well.

The current Intel 386 and 486 microprocessors are produced in different configurations based on data handling capability and speed. First, there is a 386DX version that is a full implementation of the chip. The 386DX is a full 32-bit chip in all ways—32-bit registers, 32-bit addressing, and 32-bit input/output path—this means that 32 bits of information are being processed at one time—earlier chips were 16-bit microprocessors that only processed half as much information at one time. There is also a 386SX version of the chip that is less expensive but has only a 16-bit data path for processing input and output data. There is also a 386SL version that is primarily for battery-operated models. The 386SX will run the same programs as the 386DX, but will handle input/output more slowly. The microprocessors are produced in various clock speeds as well—ranging from 12 MHz to 66 MHz. The clock speed measures how fast data is processed. The bigger the MHz number, the faster the microprocessor. Faster is more expensive, but faster is more desirable for most applications. (A really fast 386 microprocessor can actually be faster than a 486, even though the 486 has architectural advantages over the 386.)

The 486 family also includes a SX version and a DX version of the chip. Both the 486DX and 486SX are full-blown 32-bit chips. The SX version of the 486 does not contain the built-in math coprocessor that is included with the 486DX. Otherwise, the chips are the same. A 486 chip will have better performance overall than a 386 chip running at the same clock speed, because of the advanced design features of the chip.

The amount of speed and performance you demand is up to you and your budget. If you plan to run Windows most of the time on your machine, you will need to purchase at least a 386-based machine, because the 286 is too slow and cripples some of Window's more advanced capabilities. There are some great bargains around for older 286-based laptops—and if you only use your computer for some simple notetaking, an occasional small spreadsheet, and occasional use of online information services, then you might want to look into one.

But beware—Windows, the powerful graphical interface developed by Microsoft for us on IBM-compatible computers, does not run in its current version on the 286-based computers. This means that the new, easy-to-use, and very powerful Windows applications being developed for PC notebook computers will not run on your system either.

In addition to the 386 or 486 chip that is the brains of your system, you may also need to purchase a special add-on chip called a coprocessor. This chip takes on certain kinds of mathematical functions to free the 386/486 to handle normal chores running your computer. If you plan to crunch a lot of numbers with large and complex spreadsheet programs, a coprocessor will speed your work considerably.

Get Enough Memory

How much memory do you need? The answer to this question rests on the kinds of software you plan to run. If your work is limited to applications that run strictly under MS-DOS, 2 to 4 megabytes (MB) of memory is probably all you'll need, although to make the extra memory work, you'll need to ensure that your machine is configured properly because MS-DOS, the operating system that controls your computer (even if you use Windows) has an underlying 640 kilobyte (KB) limit that must be worked around. Your dealer can help you with setting up DOS properly to take advantage of extended and/or expanded memory. For Windows and Windows applications, more memory is better. A minimum of 4MB is required and your applications may run better and you can have several open at once with 8MB or more of memory installed.

THE HARD DISK MUST HAVE ENOUGH STORAGE

While at one time notebook computers came with only small hard drives—20MB or less—machines today routinely come with 80MB, 120MB, or larger capacity hard drives. The size that's right for you depends on your mobile needs, but it's best to play it safe and buy a notebook with a larger capacity drive than you think necessary. Unlike desktop computers, if you outgrow your hard disk, you may need to purchase a new machine because hard disks are difficult or impossible to replace outside the factory on most notebook computers. (There are shops that will upgrade the hard disk in popular notebook computers although this voids the warranty and this service is available only for very popular models. Look for their ads at the back of the PC magazines.)

You will want a large hard disk for other reasons as well. Most Windows programs tend to be large. Microsoft Word is a case in point—the program, and all of its files take up about 15MB if you install everything and even the "minimum" installation still eats 5.5MB! Another disk space-intensive task is receiving faxes via your modem. An incoming fax is saved as a picture, and these images take up substantial real estate on the hard disk. Should someone send you a ten page fax, you may run out of room on disk before you receive it all on a small, over-crowded system. Other disk-space intensive applications include desktop publishing and multimedia.

Veteran traveler Bob, profiled in Chapter 1, uses his computer to give presentations to customers via mul-timedia software. His current machine has a 120MB hard disk, and even with this much storage he occasionally has to remove less important files and programs to receive a lengthy fax. The bottom line in all this is to get a hard disk with as much storage as possible within your budget.

THE OTHER SELECTION CRITERIA

Buying a PC compatible can be a difficult decision because of the sheer number of machines out there. For a truly confusing introduction to PC hardware options, pick up a copy of Computer Shopper, a tabloid-size publi-cation stuffed with ads from various mail order computer companies and resellers. One way to get to the bottom of the selection process is to look only for machines that meet your criteria for CPU, storage capa-bilities, and hard disk size. Then, there are several other features you can use to further narrow your choices.

The Display

The first question about the display is its size. You must feel comfortable that the screen can display enough information at a time to do useful work. This is more a problem with subnotebooks than standard note-book computers. In our work, the larger the screen the better—but some people jot down only notes and addresses with their notebooks anyway, and occasionally hook up to an online service—and these users don't always need the benefits of a full-sized screen that can display most of a full page at one time.

The next decisions about the screen involves the resolution. Most PC-compatible notebooks offer a screen that displays multiple shades of gray and some manufacturers trumpet that their display can produce sixty-four shades of gray, instead of sixteen or eight, but what's really important to you is how readable the display is in practice. To determine this, you must use the machine hands-on at a dealer, because magazine photos showing machines with crystal clear screens may be misleading or deliberately enhanced. The best machine is one that is clearly readable in any light from total darkness to bright sunlight and that is easy on the eyes. It helps if the screen has normal geometry as well instead of vertical compression to make it fit the machine better. Some early machines, such as Compaq's pioneering LTE notebook, employed a screen that was shorter than a normal computer monitor in relationship to width. That means that a circle displayed on such a screen appears compressed into the shape of an oval.

Is Color Really Necessary?

There are two types of color displays on the market for notebook computers. The first is the passive-matrix LCD display. This type of display is relatively inexpensive and can be powered by batteries, but the color is only mediocre and the brightness and contrast are not great. Comparatively new on the market are notebook computers that use active-matrix LCD displays, which provide a fairly decent color display but eat battery power like crazy.

Although the prices are going down for these higher-quality color displays, they still present compromises in quality for frequent travelers. With these color limitations in mind, in our opinion, there is only a short list of justifiable reasons for buying a notebook computer with a color display:

1. You must make frequent, fancy one-on-one presentations in clients' offices with the notebook computer. This is perhaps the best reason for justifying a color display—but this is not something that most travelers will be doing regularly. Besides, a quality grayscale screen with good resolution and contrast can still present a very impressive presentation if the visuals are professionally designed with one of the presentation packages discussed in the software chapter of the book.

2. You absolutely must play your computer games in color. Games are obviously more fun when played in color than black and white. (Displays that offer 256 colors are more fun than those limited to sixteen colors.)

3. You are a person who must have the latest and most expensive model of everything.

4. You will be designing color documents on the road. This is not recommended, but there may be a few graphic artists out there who actually try to do desktop publishing on a notebook computer.

5. You find Windows difficult to use without the colors you are accustomed to using with your desktop machine in the office. Some people simply find the computer easier to use with color. In this case, buy the active-matrix display, because the other passive-matrix type of display is too murky to be an advantage in graphics-oriented applications.

If you don't meet these criteria, buy a notebook computer with a quality, backlit, grayscale display with clear resolution and good contrast instead. The machine will be less expensive and will run longer on its batteries. In addition, working with ordinary type and data will be less fatiguing than on most color notebook screens.

If you absolutely must spend the money for the prestige and battery limitations of a quality color notebook computer, look for one that offers the best battery life and that doesn't weigh substantially more than a black and white machine. (Because active-matrix color displays are battery hogs, the larger battery required to power them may substantially increase the weight of the computer.)

In a color machine, look also for fast screen redraws because some of the units we tested have been noticeably slow. This makes them awkward for mundane chores such as scrolling through a word processing document. Check also that black and white type displayed in a word processor is still easy to read. Some color displays have great on-screen color but do an unacceptable job of displaying simple black and white text. Such machines are extremely fatiguing to use for writing or data review sessions that last longer than a few minutes.

Pointing Devices

More and more notebook machines are copying Apple Computer's example and building in tiny trackballs that replace an external mouse. If you run Windows or use DOS software that requires a mouse, a built-in trackball may be a useful feature. There are also special pointing devices, like the small trackball made by Microsoft Corporation, that are designed for notebook computers and can be clipped to the side of the keyboard or carrying case. If you want to use one of these, make sure your notebook has a place to plug it in.

Keyboard Functionality

When inspecting prospective notebook computers, pay special attention to the keyboard. Is it a complete

AT-style keyboard or do important functions such as Page Up and Page Down require you to hold down a modifier key along with a cursor key? Make sure that the unit has a full complement of function keys. The keyboard should also have the right "touch" for your typing style. Be wary of keyboards with tiny keys that are jammed together (unless you are shopping for a sub-notebook or palmtop machine).

Floppy Disk Drive

The need for a floppy disk drive is definitely arguable. Still, unless you are shopping for an exceptionally small, lightweight unit, we still prefer a machine with a built-in 3 1/2" floppy disk drive, preferably with one of the new slim-line drives. At the very least, there should be a small, add-on drive available for use with the machine. While you can use an external drive supplied with the machine (often an extra charge) or LapLink to transfer software and data from a desktop PC while you're on the road, you'll be unable to load new software or data without connecting a floppy drive to the machine (if this is possible) or hooking up to someone's desktop computer.

The floppy drive does have a downside—the drive and the slightly larger plastic computer case required to house it add about one and a half pounds to the weight of your machine and add to the size of the machine as well.

Using these criteria together, you should be able to narrow the field of candidate notebook PCs to three or four. The last thing to do before making a decision is to find someone who owns the unit you are interested in and ask his or her opinion about the machine. Take anything less than a glowing tribute to mean that the machine is not as useful or easy to use as the owner expected and move on to your next candidate. If you can't find anyone locally who owns the machine, ask the dealer or manufacturer for several names and call a couple of these people. If you can't find anyone who has one of the little jewels you have your eye on, then think twice about getting one yourself.

HOW ABOUT BUYING A USED MACHINE?

For those on a limited budget, the prospect of saving a few bucks by purchasing a used machine may appear attractive, but unless you're positively broke, we don't recommend it. Here's why:

- Used machines may employ near-obsolete technology. This means they are slower than current models. For example, a survey of the used computer ads in the Los Angeles Times revealed several ads for notebook computers employing 8086 and 286 chips—these can't really run Windows or many large applications. If you want to run Windows, you absolutely must use a 386 CPU or better.

- Older machines invariably have a small hard disk— some as small as 20MB. For today's sophisticated applications, this is simply not enough storage for anyone who will be seriously using the computer on the road.

- A used machine may have hard-to-detect problems. This ranges from a functional but defective hard disk to intermittent memory failures. You may not find out until too late that the machine is dying of old age.

- A machine more than two years old probably needs a new battery pack. Battery packs are expensive and impossible to find for some models.

- The sellers of used hardware may be completely out of touch with the PC price war. They may be selling their machine for more than it costs to purchase a new, more powerful computer. People in this position are often difficult to negotiate down to reality about the machine's actual market value, although you can to try.

If you must take the used route, try to buy at least a newer 286 machine and a computer based on a 386 or 486 chip is that much better. Buy from a store that offers a warranty or take the machine into a service center and have them test it thoroughly. This may cost you $50 or so, but it may save your neck should the machine prove to have fatal technical problems.

✈ Leave It in Memory

If you buy a notebook computer with enough memory, you can leave all your software open on the machine's RAM drive, which uses part of the machine's memory as a hard disk. The only caveat is that should your machine lose power, any unsaved files (to the machine's real hard disk) will be lost. Ask you dealer about this convenient option.

SELECTING A MACINTOSH NOTEBOOK

Once you've decided that an easy-to-use Macintosh is the way to go, the selection of a specific model is relatively easy. As of this writing, there are only two companies (at least that we know about) that make Macintosh notebook computers—Apple Computer, Inc. (which sells its notebook Macs under the name of PowerBook) and Outbound Systems. At this writing, both companies make only a handful of notebook models. This makes the decision less confusing than choosing among the multitudes of PC-compatible notebooks on the market.

Choose a Mac with the Right Microprocessor

The Motorola microprocessors used in Apple and

Apple-compatible notebook computers include the obsolete 68000 as well as the newer 68030 and 68040 chips. Unless you like sluggish performance, pass on any relic that still relies on the 68000 chip. Instead, purchase a 68030- or 68040-based machine, with the 68040 being the superior (and more expensive) chip of choice.

As with PCs, the speed of the microprocessor is important as well. The slowest 68030 runs at 16 MHz—fast enough for most word processors and other business software, but too slow for presentation software and multimedia. For better performance all around, the 25MHz 68040 is the entry-level chip you should consider.

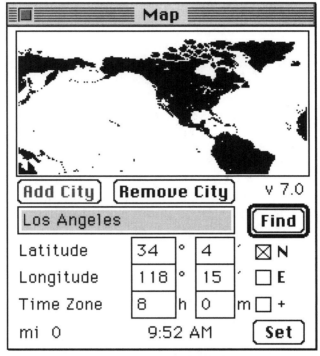

The Macintosh features a control panel for changing your computer's internal clock as you travel. It also instructs you on the time difference between cities of the world and shows their approximate locations.

How Much Memory Do You Need?

Mac notebook computers and dockables typically ship with 4MB of memory as their base RAM configuration. This is (barely) adequate for most software. If you plan to run multimedia presentations on the machine, upgrade to 8MB of memory or (much) more, if possible.

How Much Hard Disk Storage Do You Need?

Buy a Macintosh notebook with at least an 80MB hard disk, and a larger capacity drive is recommended. Apple makes notebook computers with 40MB drives but these are too small unless your activities are confined solely to word processing.

You can purchase a Mac-compatible notebook computer from Outbound Systems of Boulder, Colorado, with drive capacities of 220MB or more. There are third-party drive manufacturers that will upgrade the PowerBooks made by Apple as well.

WHAT OTHER DECISIONS MUST BE MADE?

There are only a few other concerns you must address to decide on the Macintosh notebook that's right for you. Of course, first you must decide whether to buy an Apple PowerBook or Outbound notebook. If you choose the Apple, then you have two basic display options to choose between as well and you need to decide between a dockable unit or a stand alone notebook configuration.

Outbound or Apple PowerBook?

Outbound is a small computer manufacturer that makes quality notebooks that are 100 percent compatible with Macintosh software. While their machines don't offer Apple's unique active matrix display option (described next), their prices are highly competitive with Apple's, and they offer larger hard drives than does

Apple. The Outbound keyboard is a little bit larger than Apple's, and this may make typing easier for some. Outbound also uses a built-in pointing device (called the TrackBar) that works much differently from a trackball. Some Outbound models will not accommodate an internal modem, which makes it necessary to pack an extra device in your briefcase if you need to communicate online from the road. You might make the decision between Apple and Outbound on features versus price and based on the pointing device you find the least awkward.

The Display

In their more expensive machines, Apple uses a pioneering active matrix display technology in which each pixel (dot) on the display is controlled by an individual transistor. This makes for the clearest LCD display in the industry. Unfortunately, the machines with this technology are a little more expensive than Apple's standard LCD or supertwist display technology.

For long hours in front of your machine, you can't beat the active matrix display, and PowerBooks now come with grayscale screens instead of just black and white. As discussed earlier, color notebook computers are becoming commonplace in the DOS/Windows world. A color version of the Mac notebook has already been announced by Apple and there are also third-party companies that offer (expensive) color displays to replace the PowerBook's standard grayscale screen.

Floppy Disk Drive

Apple's obsolete PowerBook 100 and one of its dockable (PowerBook Duo) units lack built-in floppy disk drives. To load data and software, you will need to connect an (optional) floppy drive or hook into a network to get it off another machine. This may prove clumsy for mobile professionals with no easy access to the network back at the office or who need to load data from floppies acquired in the field. For others, the lack of a floppy drive is not as important as the machine's lighter weight and compact size.

Using these criteria, you should be able to narrow the field of candidate Macs to one that meets your needs for power, flexibility, and affordability.

CHOOSING A DOCKABLE

Most of the functional aspects of dockable machines are the same as notebook computers. There are dockable PC-compatibles and Macintoshes. If you need a dockable machine and it makes economic sense, look for one that meets both your needs as a compact notebook computer and as a desktop PC back at the office.

Avoid dockable machines that have a removable portable unit that is the size and weight of a laptop computer or that docks using clumsy latches. Also watch for dockables that tie you directly into the company who made the unit for all of your needs including video display cards and memory—this may lock you into a machine that will date quickly and one that will require you spend extra money to buy proprietary add-ons priced at proprietary prices. (This concern is less relevant with the Macintosh Duo systems, because almost everything is made by Apple Computer.)

It is important that the dockable desk-based unit is compatible with a full range of monitors, keyboards, and add-on cards, similar to those available for stand alone (non-dockable) desktop computers. The desk-based unit should also provide an adequate number of expansion slots for add-on cards.

Last, the "dockability" (there's a new word) of the machine should be taken into account. You should be able to dock, complete with all electrical and mechanical connections, in seconds. A machine that takes much longer than a minute to complete the hook-up will make you less inclined to grab the portable unit for use on quick trips because of the hassle of hooking everything back up when you return. Test connection time—it should take less time than the space shuttle docking an errant satellite!

WHAT TO LOOK FOR IN EVERY MOBILE COMPUTER

After you decide about the size of machine and the platform that best meets your needs, you should consider the features and issues described in the next few pages before you buy any brand or model of computer for your mobile office.

A Solid Machine

For life on the road, you want a solidly built machine that can take the heavy use and jostling that go hand in hand with travel. The durability of the machine is in some ways even more important than its computer abilities because when traveling, a poorly built machine will begin to fall apart in just months, forcing you to replace it once or twice a year if you travel a lot. Since most of the machines are "clamshell" designs with the display section hinging away from the keyboard and CPU, look for a machine with smooth-operating hinges and latches that lock the two parts together firmly when the machine is closed.

Covers over the printer and communications ports should close securely and not be obviously flimsy or located where their hinges may snap. For example, the Compaq LTE, a very expensive notebook computer in its time, had a hinge for connecting the door located near the back corner of the machine. Brushing ours against a table one day broke the flimsy plastic that held the hinge.

To fix this problem, Compaq estimated an outrageous charge of $1,500 for a new plastic case—all because of poor engineering on their part rather than abuse on ours. Lucky for us, the machine was still under warranty at the time and Compaq graciously picked up the tab.

Ease of Use

As mentioned, some machines are easier to learn and use than others. If you are new to computers, consider purchasing a machine such as the Apple Macintosh that doesn't require you to learn much about the computer instead of an MS-DOS/Windows machine that does. For old hands, choose the machine you like best. Other ease-of-use requirements include an easy-to-read screen and comfortable keyboard. Test the keyboard extensively by typing to see if its "touch" is comfortable. Try the screen in a variety of lighting conditions to ensure that it remains readable. (You should be able to adjust the brightness and contrast controls to suit each lighting change.)

Compatibility and Usefulness Back at the Office

If the machine will double as your desktop PC, look for a unit that allows you to connect an external monitor. For use at the office, you may also want to be able to connect a full-sized keyboard to it. At the very least, your mobile computer should be able to exchange data and programs with your office-based computer.

A POWERFUL MACHINE

Software has grown in size and complexity over the last few years, to the point that many popular packages require a fast machine just to run tolerably. Buy a machine with a fast processor. Buy as much power as you can afford—as software evolves you will need more power. If you plan to make presentations with your computer, you will need more power than you can imagine. Otherwise, you will spend a lot of time waiting for the machine before you can continue your work. Waiting for programs is no way to be productive, and long waits may frustrate you to the point that you go back to reading or watching TV while on the road because it's more entertaining than watching the hourglass or watch-shaped cursors that tell you the computer is busy. One caveat, however; the faster a machine you choose, the shorter its battery life, although manufacturers are figuring ways around this problem and battery technology is improving.

✈ Software and a Second Computer

If you use a desktop computer, in most cases you want to use the same kind of operating environment on your portable so that you can easily share files and software. Before you do this, look to see if your software allows you to use copies on more than one machine if you are the sole user. Some products allow this. Others specifically demand that you purchase a second copy.

Communications Capability

For the tiniest computers on the market, the floppy disk drive available for transferring data via disk to another machine is a separate unit (if one exists at all). Should you investigate this option, look for a machine that makes moving information from one machine to another comparatively easy. The small machine should come equipped with a product such as LapLink that allows two computers to send files back and forth. For the smaller machine, such a link is the only way to send software to it. Of course, if the machine has a built-in modem, you can use communications software and the modem to send files back and forth, but the direct approach is more expedient.

By the way, you absolutely cannot take advantage of the information, communications options, or other mobile office functions without a modem. A modem is an integral part of your office on the go. Make sure you buy a modem—either external or internal, with your computer. We have more to say about modems in Chapter 6 when we talk about communications, but we want to mention it here so you don't forget to buy the modem at the same time you buy the computer.

Portability and Battery Life

Notebook computers vary considerably in weight and bulk. One manufacturer makes a "notebook" that weighs in at almost ten pounds—this is really a laptop computer from our point of view. When evaluating portability take into account the weight and bulk of the machine, the backup battery, and the battery charger, because to use the machine in the field, you will need to carry all these items with you.

You may also need to carry diskettes, manuals, and communications cables. When evaluating computers, make a special note to study the power supply. Some otherwise compact machines have surprisingly oversized power supplies which take up more than their share of room in your case. If you don't look at them before purchase, you may be in for a surprise when you try to stuff the system in your briefcase for the first time.

✈ Look for Automatic Voltage Switching If You're Traveling Outside North America

When buying any computer, if you may be traveling to Europe or Asia or other parts of the world, look for a model that switches between 115 AC current at 50 or 60 cycles, the power specification used in most of North America, to 220 AC at 50 or 60 cycles, the power specification used in many other parts of the world.

As already mentioned, battery life is a prime consideration when choosing a notebook computer. There are two kinds of battery technology used in notebook computers today—NiCad batteries and lead-acid batteries. Both systems are rechargeable and can power a notebook from two to ten hours depending on the electricity demands of the machine and how large the battery is. Obviously, larger batteries mean longer life, but they also mean increased bulk and weight because the battery can be the heaviest single component in notebook computer.

The better notebook computers use power management systems and more expensive low-power components to improve battery life rather than larger and heavier batteries. Keep in mind that if you are working with a machine with a backlit screen (and in most cases you should be), the brighter the screen's backlighting, the faster your battery will discharge.

✈ Avoid These Machines

Incompetently designed notebook computers have no way to limit the charge you apply to their batteries. If the instruction manual warns that you must unplug the charger within eight (or fewer) hours to avoid damage to the machine or its batteries, then the machine lacks the sophistication to protect the batteries from overcharging. This probably indicates a machine with other design compromises as well, and you should pass on it.

You should verify the battery life span before purchase in case the manufacturer's claim for battery longevity turns out to be unrealistic in practice. For example, one of our several notebooks is an Apple PowerBook. Apple claims a three-hour battery life, but after two new batteries and a thorough checking out by Apple, two hours is the best we have ever attained with the machine. And once your machine goes dead on an airplane, unless you've got a charged backup battery— you're stuck.

In addition to battery life, you want to evaluate recharge time. While a competent system can fully charge a battery in a couple of hours, some "el cheapo" systems take eight or more hours for a full charge. This makes for a long wait before you can go wireless again.

Power Management Functions

Almost every notebook computer has the ability to go to sleep to save battery power after a predefined interval of time elapses, but some machines are more sophisticated in the way they conserve power than others. The ideal notebook is one with several levels of power conservation. A typical machine with this capability first spins down the hard disk and then slows down the microprocessor and input/output functions to save power after a period of inactivity. It then dims the screen slightly before fully shutting down the system until you press a key or begin typing again.

✈ A Three-Hour Wait for the Airplane Lavatory

An article in The Wall Street Journal *pointed out a new and apparently growing problem—people who camp out in the lavatory cubicles in planes to recharge their dead computer batteries. This results in an inadequate supply of available rest rooms. The use of notebook power supplies with built-in plug ends is breaking the plug fittings that were originally designed for the tiny plugs on electric shavers. More seriously, most of these outlets are deliberately set up to limit the amount of power available so that an electric shaver dropped into the wash basin can't electrocute its owner. This power protection doesn't provide enough electricity for a computer's power supply and may ultimately cook it. The problems are seen most often on international flights because travelers run out of battery power early in the flight and lose the use of their computers. Avoid this problem (and keep your airline trips safe) by carrying extra fully charged batteries on long flights.*

Our favorite notebooks offer a sleep mode that allows you to travel with the machine ready for instant activation whenever and wherever you are. This has distinct advantages over rebooting the machine, which may take anywhere from fifteen seconds to a couple of minutes for the machine to get ready to use. If you are looking for a machine with this capability, check with the manufacturer that the heads for the hard disk park when the machine goes to sleep, because unparked heads can ruin your hard drive should the machine get jostled as you travel.

EXTERNAL POINTING DEVICES FOR USE ON THE ROAD

While on the go, if you are using applications that require a mouse, you will need some kind of pointing device to move around in the windows, choose applications software, and point at words or items on the desktop. While pen-based systems come with a pen and Apple's and some PC-compatible notebooks have a built-in trackball of sorts, other users will need to purchase a pointing device that can be used while on the move. This precludes the use of an ordinary mouse unless all your work sessions will be held at a table. If you will work in the air, the tray table of most airliner seats is too small for a mouse (unless you can afford to sit in first class).

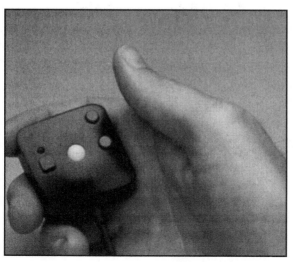

Thumbelina from Appoint is one of the tiny pointing devices that's perfect for the office on the go.

A variety of pointing devices are available for notebooks. Microsoft (and others) makes a trackball that mounts on the side of your computer. Or Thumbelina from Appoint is a tiny three-button trackball that you can use on the smallest work surface. A version is available for both PCs and Apple's PowerBooks. Other options include electronic styli that work vaguely like a pen, and several manufacturers build in special pointing devices on or near their keyboards. For example, NCR offers a device called a FingerMouse and Outbound uses a unique sliding bar pointer.

Choosing the right computer for your mobile office should take some time. Even if you work with computers on a daily basis, with the new models, increasingly compact technology, and changes in the marketplace, you may need to take a week or two just to get a handle on what's out there and how much a good system should cost. Take your time and don't choose a machine until you are absolutely sure that it will fulfill your needs without breaking your budget. If you choose correctly, you can expect some great productivity on the road.

4

ORGANIZERS, ELECTRONIC NOTEBOOKS, AND PERSONAL DIGITAL ASSISTANTS

In the last chapter you learned how to choose the central component of your mobile office—the computer. But not all business trips require a full-function computer—on some short hops around town and in client meetings, an organizer and a notepad are better choices. For some traveling businesspeople, the new personal digital assistants are good alternatives to a full-function computer. This chapter presents the options and trade-offs in current organizer and electronic notebook technology so you can decide if one makes sense as a component in your office on the go.

MANUAL ORGANIZERS

The concept of the organizer dates from the simple appointment books and diaries that began appearing on desks in the nineteenth century. Today's paper-based organizers, like the popular DayRunner systems available from Harper House, have become comprehensive, personalized information systems in a binder. These loose-leaf organizers are available in several sizes and many styles, and a variety of fillers are available for organizing everything from your daily fitness routine to a list of favorite sushi bars.

Many companies make variations of these organizers. Besides the easy-to-find Harper House DayRunner systems, there are the classic DayTimer systems sold through mail order and the Day-at-a-Glance and Week-at-a-Glance organizers available in almost every department, business, and stationery store. While manual organizers can fulfill the functions of an electronic organizer, they are larger and bulkier and contain no electronic "links" to other components of the mobile office. Even so, most traveling businesspeople need a traditional paper-based organizer, because there are still times when it isn't possible to use an electronic device on the road.

We also recommend that you take a compact manual organizer along to act as backup for your schedule and to use when the computer is not feasible. If you carry a portable printer, most organizer software allows you to print appropriately formatted schedule pages from your computer to put in popular paper-based organizer systems. This eliminates the need to duplicate schedule information and notes by hand.

The pros and cons of using a manual organizer are:

Pros:

✔ Inexpensive and flexible.

✔ No learning curve.

✔ No wait for the "system" to start up.

✔ No need for batteries.

✔ No worrying about disk drive or battery failures.

Cons:

✖ No automation to facilitate the search for information that is "lost" in the organizer. Data organization is strictly manual and handled by the user. If you're good at organizing information, great. If not, the information may be lost forever.

✖ No communications capabilities. Of course, you can always fax or copy pages for others to use, but this isn't an ideal way to communicate your schedule to others.

✖ Increased size and weight. To store large amounts of information, manual organizers grow in bulk and weight. A typical full-size organizer that handles 8 1/2" by 11" paper may weigh six to twelve pounds when loaded down with information—more than a notebook computer that can store hundreds of times more information.

✈ Scheduling with a Notebook Computer

While the most sophisticated scheduling software is available for computers rather than organizers, using a computer to set up meetings is not always the way to go. Most notebooks are clumsy when you want to add an appointment after meeting a co-worker in the hallway. You start the machine or bring it out of "sleep" mode, open the scheduling software if it's not already open, page to the date you want, and then use the keyboard to make your entry—all while standing. An organizer that's always ready and always with you is a better option. Then use scheduling software on your notebook that can send and receive data from an organizer to your computer (and back again).

ELECTRONIC ORGANIZERS

Electronic organizers duplicate most of the functions of manual organizers plus use the power of computers to automate the functions and communication with other kinds of computers. You can find these organizers in business supply stores and department stores. The most popular organizers include Sharp's Wizard series and Casio's B.O.S.S. If you create a written schedule in a manual calendar, it's just that—a series of written notes. But, with an organizer, the same schedule can be transferred back and forth to your regular desktop computer or printed out to pass around to other staff members who need to be informed of your whereabouts.

The pros and cons of electronic organizers are as follows:

Pros:

✔ Easy to learn—no understanding of computers is required.

✔ Small and light in weight.

Cons:

✖ Limited in the amount of information they can handle.

✖ Mostly inflexible in the way they work. Some procedures may require non-intuitive or unwieldy steps to carry out.

✖ Limited and expensive expansion possibilities.

✖ Clumsy and unwieldy communications systems that make the use of these systems difficult for anything but the most basic electronic mail applications.

CHOOSING AN ELECTRONIC ORGANIZER

Electronic organizers are the easiest to choose because they are the simplest machines in terms of computer sophistication and features. A review of the machine's instruction manual and a little experimentation with the machine will adequately demonstrate its ease of use and functionality. When choosing an electronic organizer you want to put it through its paces as well as review how expandable it is either with plug-in components or through "cards" that can be added to the actual machine. Keep in mind that there is a range of machines available—from $49.95 "address minders" to very sophisticated systems that blur the border between computer and organizer. Consider the features described next when choosing an organizer that meets your needs.

A Complete Feature Set

An electronic organizer should provide easy to use scheduling of personal appointments, a complete calendar and time feature, an address and phone log that can be instantly accessed, a calculator, and note-taking functions. All of these features should be directly available at the touch of a button, and the address section (which is actually a miniature database) should have a find function that allows you to look for names by the first letter(s). Explore each function to see how it works and make sure that you can instantly switch between functions.

Sharp's Wizard was one of the first electronic organizers. Smaller than a paperback book, this unit is quite powerful and can even send and receive faxes with an optional fax module.

Enough Memory

Organizers store their information in memory—you need a machine with enough memory to save all of the information you require on the road. This memory should be adequate when you buy the machine and upgradable with plug-in memory modules that are not priced ridiculously high (as some are). Read the product's specification sheets to determine how much information the memory can hold.

ELECTRONIC NOTEBOOKS

A wide variety of electronic notebooks on the market masquerade as word processors, electronic tablets, and electronic books. The majority of these units allow you to enter text either by typing or using handwriting. Since these machines offer no computer functionality, they are more akin to a typewriter than either an electronic organizer or personal digital assistant.

The pros and cons of electronic notebooks are as follows:

Pro:

✔ They are very easy to learn.

Cons:

✖ Many of these units are as large or larger than a notebook computer. Because of their extremely limited abilities, their size and weight make them inappropriate for the mobile office because most mobile professionals will need something to keep their schedule and address lists and that can perform other routine chores.

✖ Notebooks can only take notes. This may be adequate for some researchers and writers, but they really aren't a viable option for most businesspeople on the go.

PEN-BASED COMPUTERS AND NOTEPADS

New on the computer scene and not yet fully realized are machines that use hand-printing and pointing
with a pen-like stylus to select functions. These
machines, which use electronic tablets based on digitiz-
er technologies, use special operating systems like GO
Corporation's PenPoint and Microsoft's Windows for Pen
Computing. Some electronic notebooks offer programs
that are compatible with the IBM-PC or Apple Macintosh
platforms. Others are completely proprietary in nature
and support only one kind of function such as inventory
control or data collection in a hospital or building site.

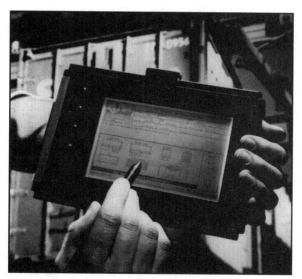

*Pen-based systems, like the GridPAD shown here, are
very easy to use but cost more than other systems and
are still very limited in their overall capabilities.*

Pen-based computers are currently the most
expensive mobile computers available for the office on
the go, although they ultimately may be the easiest to
use for many people.

The pros and cons of pen-based computers are:

Pro:

> ✔ A well-designed pen-based system is the easiest machine to learn and use because eventually the systems will be able to (and can now within limits) recognize your handwriting. This eliminates the need to learn how to type or the need to carry a paper-based organizer for the quick note.

Cons:

> ✘ These machines are not entirely standard (yet), and there is very limited availability of both units and software. The software that does exist is usually for very specific applications, such as inventory control or medical notations.

> ✘ Pen-based systems that use only one brand of software may limit what you can do with the machine and lock you into buying special software at higher than competitive prices.

> ✘ For now, the systems are mostly for software developers to use as they write applications for the machines. There is simply not enough robust software or flexibility to make these machines a central component of a mobile office. When they get more power and software, they'll become a possibility.

> ✘ The handwriting recognition of today is limited to printed letters. The systems cannot yet read true cursive writing and may even have problems with many people's printing. This eliminates one of the major advantages of using an electronic notebook, as it is faster for most people to type than it is for them to print. We expect the next few years to bring major improvements in this area.

> ✘ Fully equipped pen-based machines require a lot of processing power along with special screens and other expensive components. For this and other

reasons, these machines are still more expensive than either PCs or Macintoshes.

What Exactly Can a Pen-Based System Do?

When looking at a pen-based system, check carefully that the machine can do what you need it for. Many of these systems look great when demonstrated at a store, but when you put it to work, you may find that the system is extremely limited in its capabilities. With systems that recognize writing, people with nonstandard handwriting may find that these systems cannot recognize their writing no matter how carefully they print or simplify their character construction. We expect the pen-based systems to improve rapidly—and at the same time become less expensive. We predict that pen-based note tablets will become a standard option for mobile computing in only a few years. In the meantime, they are useful only for very special purposes and limited applications.

PERSONAL DIGITAL ASSISTANTS

While most units on the market such as the Sharp Wizard and Casio's B.O.S.S. system are deemed electronic organizers, a new phrase for more powerful models is emerging. These more powerful devices such as Apple's Newton are called personal digital assistants or PDAs for short. The reason for the name change is that PDAs do much more than a traditional organizer—whether manual or electronic. PDAs are usually pen based and may also offer keyboards. Some incorporate cellular phones, modems, and faxes. The ideal PDAs will eventually do some thinking for you. For example, you may want to find out about when your lunch with Dave is scheduled. By simply writing "Dave" on the PDA's screen, it will come up with the lunch appointment, along with Dave's address and phone number, and remind you that you wrote a memo to Dave that has not yet been transmitted.

As the pen-based computers evolve, they are taking on functions that make them look more like PDAs,

and as organizers evolve, their manufacturers have started calling them PDAs. We expect the division between
electronic organizer, pen-based notebook, and PDAs to
be blurry for some time as the technology for handwriting analysis, voice recognition, database analysis,
heuristic searching, and communications continue to
evolve.

✈ PIA or PDA?

*Personal digital assistant was a phrase used extensively to
describe Apple's Newton, but now it's being called a Personal
Inspiration Assistant or PIA as an attempt by Apple to differenti-
ate the Newton from forthcoming PDA entries. Newton will be
released in 1993 (with less functionality than originally
promised). Other related PDA products designed with mobile
communication and personal organization in mind, including the
Hobbit (the new system that employs technology from the joint
efforts of GO Corp., EO Computer, and AT&T), and similar systems from other companies, are expected to reach the market in
various configurations during 1993. The idealized PDA (or PIA),
which has yet to be developed or announced, is a complete
handheld personal organizer combined with the power of a full-
featured computer and a wide variety of integrated
communications capabilities. Eventually, these devices will facilitate a full range of mobile office functions, including scheduling,
note taking (with handwriting recognition), communications via
modem and cellular phone, paging, contact management, and
other applications. The idealized PDA should be easier to learn
and use than a notebook computer and should be smaller and
lighter as well. The PDA should accommodate the needs of people on the road as well as communication and data access
requirements in the traditional office. Although we don't have
true PDAs to play with yet, they'll likely be here soon.*

The expected pros and cons of PDAs are as follows:

Pros:
  ✔ PDAs are relatively easy to learn, although the
    most powerful PDAs offer so much functionality

that they can be overwhelming to people who are unfamiliar with computers.

✔ They can replace many of the uses of a full-featured computer while still offering compact weight and size.

✔ They offer easy communications with other computers, telephone networks, and online services.

Cons:

✖ They are more expensive and larger than most electronic organizers.

✖ They can't (yet) run ordinary computer software, which limits users to the software built in or available for the machine.

✖ It's sometimes difficult to assess what the most powerful units are fully capable of because much of the machine's "intelligence" remains hidden until you explore it for a month or so.

✖ The PDA technology is evolving so rapidly it is difficult to say what will become standard and what will become quickly obsolete or irrelevant. We recommend waiting until all the bugs are worked out of the early entries before you commit your life savings to one of these devices.

CHOOSING A PERSONAL DIGITAL ASSISTANT

Choosing a PDA-like device is possibly the most difficult of the three automation options. While there are many more functions to evaluate when selecting a personal computer, choosing a PDA is made more difficult because to understand a machine's "intelligence" functions and evaluate their usefulness takes time. The best PDA is one that does everything you need, "thinks" like you do, and makes communications back to the office or elsewhere in an automatic and straightforward manner. To select the right one, look for everything suggested for evaluating electronic organizers, computers, and communications devices, and in addition check out:

How Well You "Identify" with the Machine

While the most inexpensive PDAs work much like an advanced electronic organizer, the better units are intelligent and try to second guess your needs as mentioned previously. Look for a unit that after a week's use seems to be a half step ahead of your needs when trying to look up appointments or automate the process of sending a memo to someone. The machine should automate some of these chores for you by allowing you to scratch out a few words to locate an event tucked away in the future or to make linking to your office easier for sending and receiving electronic mail.

How Well the Machine Identifies with You

A PDA will use hand-printed letters on the machine's "notepad" to take input. That means that instead of typing commands or words into a machine via keyboard, input is hand printed (or in the future written with cursive handwriting) and the machine interprets this input into the kind of text that the computer understands and can process. Commands are replaced by pointing at a picture (icon) of the function you want. You will want to select a machine that can recognize your printing, even when you are in a hurry or one that also offers a keyboard input option.

Because some machines learn from their mistakes interpreting your handwriting, it may take a week or two of use before the machine fully understands your scribble. If even your printing is hopelessly convoluted (as is Kim's), then this feature may be of little use to you and you might be better off with an organizer or computer that accepts straight keyboard input.

✈ Back to the Future (and to the Dealer's)

When purchasing any technology product, never accept a promise that a function you require will be available in a couple of months. Something that may be vital to you may indeed be in the works, but manufacturers are known to drop products, release them months (or years) late, or create stripped-down versions that may not come close to meeting your needs. This problem is so common that the computer industry has a phrase for it. Announced but invisible products are called vaporware. With technology-related products, a bird in the hand is worth ten or twenty in the bush ... or on the drawing board.

Price/Size/Weight

PDAs can be expensive and somewhat larger than an electronic organizer. On the other hand, if the device also incorporates the functions of a cellular phone, modem, and other devices, the size can seem insignificant. As with any component in a mobile office, you need to consider the price and bulk of the unit compared to the productivity you'll gain on the road. When doing this, keep in mind that a PDA may become a companion at your regular office as well as your mobile office.

Communication Capabilities

Central to a PDA is the ability to talk to other computers and access electronic mail and other forms of communications. If you will use your PDA to talk to your desktop computer, tap into electronic mail, read news via satellite, make ordinary telephone calls, or access your company's big computers (mainframes), look for a machine that makes this kind of communication easy. And don't take the salesperson's word for it—try it yourself to make sure it works and doesn't take all day to make the connection. In addition to electronic communication, your PDA should be able to send and receive faxes and print directly to a printer.

The choice of a PDA is highly personal. A machine

that a coworker uses and praises highly may not lend itself to your style of working. Or you may find that by the time you buy an expensive PDA and equip it with all the accessories you need that a full-function computer is cheaper and can handle your work requirements better. If you are close to needing the functionality of a computer anyway, consider its merits against the PDA before making a financial commitment; otherwise, you may ultimately shelve the PDA in favor of a computer. If this happens, the money spent on the PDA is probably wasted (unless you can sell the unit).

HOW ORGANIZERS AND PDAS DIFFER AMONG MODELS AND BRANDS

Organizers and PDAs vary considerably between manufacturers, and like computers, they are becoming more and more powerful at the same time their prices are falling. The differences between models include the following criteria:

Functions Provided

The variety of functions that organizers provide may range from simple tracking of addresses and phone numbers, short note taking, display of time around the world, calculator functions, and of course, scheduling. In some organizers, like Sharp's Wizards, extra functions and programs can be added to via plug-in cards. Because they are just coming to marketing, it's hard to say what PDAs will ultimately offer in terms of functionality, but Apple's Newton and other announced PDAs provide all of the functions of Sharp's Wizards in addition to capabilities to access corporate databases, handwriting recognition (though limited), online communication functions, and the ability to create custom forms right on-screen for such purposes as tracking expenses while on the road. Of course, with more functionality comes higher price.

Storage Capabilities

Like computers, electronic organizers and PDAs are dependent on internal storage to remember names, addresses, notes, and other data elements. Larger amounts of storage allow more information to be kept in the organizer or PDA, but some machines are very limited in the amount of memory they can use. Memory upgrades in some systems require tiny, custom memory components, which may be very expensive.

Battery Life

Look for models and brands that extend battery life through the use of low power electronic components and built-in power management systems.

✈ Batteries

Read the section on batteries in the troubleshooting chapter (Chapter 16) so that you know more about them before purchasing battery-powered equipment that you must rely on while traveling.

Ability to Interface (Talk to) Other Devices and General Communication Facilities

For users that use their organizers primarily as an electronic "Rolodex" or for other basic functions that don't involve sending and receiving information, the ability to talk with other computers may not be important. But, for many people, the ability to talk with another computer over a telephone line, or via cellular phone, or satellite is an important function. Through such a link, it's possible to send and receive electronic mail, send and receive files to another machine, and link up to online services such as CompuServe.

The least expensive organizers may have no communications ability, but most can communicate through a modem, or via a wireless medium such as links to satellites. The best organizers can also share their contents both ways between a standard desktop computer by using a simple cable and software made for that purpose.

PDAs are designed with communications in mind and depending on the model offer sophisticated cellular phone, modem, satellite paging, and other communication facilities. The best PDAs should be able to share data with standard computers as well.

Size and Weight

Just like any other electronic device, organizers and PDAs vary in size and weight between models. Because the very purpose of an organizer is to replace address books and other pocket paraphernalia, these units are much smaller and lighter than a notebook computer. But between models and brands, size and weight vary according to the functionality of the unit. PDAs contain much more computing power and a larger display screen than electronic organizers and are larger and heavier as a result. If you plan on carrying your organizer or PDA in your suit pocket, briefcase, or in a handbag, make sure it will fit with comfort.

Internal and External Expansion Capabilities and Output Capabilities

In addition to plug-in sockets for additional memory, many organizers can take a plug-in card that adds dictionary functions, communications capabilities, games, spreadsheet capabilities, and other options. Choose an organizer with easy expansion capabilities. Sharp's Wizard, for example, has a slot on most models that takes a credit card-size add-on module. Then, check out how many modules are available that may be of use to you. Note: With the limited size and memory capabilities of most organizers, the add-on functions will generally be limited. For example, an add-on dictionary, spelling, and thesaurus module may offer far fewer words than a small paperback college dictionary.

In addition to internal expansion, you may need the ability to connect your organizer or PDA to a printer to produce "hard copy" or to a communications device. Some organizers and all PDAs can communicate directly with full-function computers to exchange information, to a modem to hook into electronic mail or online services, or even to a tiny fax machine for sending and receiving faxes. If you plan to use any of these features, try them out before purchase. Where using an organizer's or PDA's standard features may prove straightforward, communicating with other devices may be less than intuitive or barely work at all.

If you plan to use your device with a printer, test the printer before committing yourself to the organizer. The printer we ultimately purchased for our organizers leaves a lot to be desired in speed and print quality. Sometimes, only one small printer is available to work with a specific brand of organizer, so if you don't like its quality or size, you're stuck unless you send files (with a linking kit and software) to a computer or remote fax machine and print them from there. PDAs should be more flexible in their printing options than organizers and will be able to use many standard and portable printers.

Ease of Use

A large, easily readable screen is preferable even if it means choosing a slightly larger and more expensive model. A light for the screen that can be turned on to read at night would be nice, but at this writing, this feature is not available on most of the organizers we reviewed. If you will be using the machine for even the briefest notes, a QWERTY keyboard is a must, unless you select a PDA with a pen-based notepad feature.

Taken together, this information makes it easy to choose an organizer or PDA. In addition to this purchase advice, you may want to check out how easy each device's batteries are to change, and look for password protection for credit card numbers and other sensitive information that you might want to keep hidden in your organizer or PDA.

Again, the best way to see if an organizer or any computing device is right for you is to buy one with explicit return privileges and then use it for a week. If after a week you like it and use it, keep it. If you find yourself evading the organizer or PDA every time you want to look up a phone number or take a quick note then the machine is the wrong one for you or you need additional training or maybe you really don't need one in the first place.

COMPUTER, ORGANIZER, PDA—WHICH ONE IS BEST FOR YOU?

As the single most important component of a mobile office, the choice of computer, organizer, and/or PDA (or decision not to use one) makes or breaks the usefulness of your office on the go. Choose the right computer (or computer alternative), and you will find your mobile office easy to use, light to carry, and ever ready for the next task at hand. Choose the wrong machine, and it will frustrate you with its weight, frequent breakdowns, or because the batteries always seeming to go dead while you're in the middle of an important project but far from a wall outlet for power.

Again, the way to choose an electronic organizer, PDA, or computer is to work backward from your needs rather than choosing a machine and then trying to make it meet your needs. Trying to make an electronic device adapt to your needs is like driving your car from the back seat—it can be done, but it's not easy and it may lead to disaster.

So which computing option is best for you? It all depends on the work you must complete on the road. Sometimes you will want more than one of the computers or organizers to perform different functions. For example, many people will want both a notebook computer and a personal organizer, even though it means carrying two devices that overlap in their basic capabilities. The notebook is used for work sessions on the road as well as communicating with the office. The personal organizer is used for a quick check on appointments, keeping tabs on client time between meetings, and looking up a phone number in a hurry. If you choose the right combination of organizer (or PDA) and notebook computer, you will be able to share information between the two, so you eliminate copying information from one device to another.

As PDAs evolve, they may take on the role of the notebook computer and the organizer in one package. They will likely perform most of the functions of a full-service computer and all of the functions of good pocket organizers. In addition, they promise to offer communications capabilities and handwritten note taking functions and cellular, fax, and satellite connections that must now be provided with additional devices. At this point, some people will choose to own both a notebook computer for general computing tasks and a compatible PDA for handwritten notes to replace the organizer and other mobile office devices, including pager and phone. Since the PDAs are still in early development, it is difficult to predict how much impact they will make on the notebook computer market or what exactly they will evolve into.

The notebook computer can handle many office on the go functions (except handwritten notes, unless you add a digital notepad), but you have to open the case, wait for the computer to "wake up," and navigate through software to accomplish simple chores. The manual and electronic organizers and PDAs are instantly ready to provide you with the information you need—and thus are better for quick notes and for looking up frequently used information like phone numbers, addresses, and daily schedules. Most organizers can fit conveniently in your pocket to be carried anywhere. Because the personal organizers and PDAs can upload their information to the notebook computers, you can use your organizer to contain temporary information that becomes part of a larger document or database on your notebook computer or to download a series of customer addresses appropriate to the city you are currently visiting.

The two machines—computer and organizer or computer and PDA—can work in harmony in a mother-daughter system that allows you to get the best from each of the two devices. Who wants to juggle a notebook computer to look up a phone number while in a cramped phone booth in Kennedy International Airport or while using the cellular phone during the stop-and-go rush-hour traffic in downtown Los Angeles?

✈ Learn It *Before* You Buy It

In our experience, many of the people who dutifully lug portable computers with them as they travel also carry the operating manuals so that some dark night in a hotel room, they can sit down with the machine and try to learn how to use it—of course few of them ever succeed. Avoid this problem by learning the machine before you buy it, even if it means taking a couple of classes. Otherwise, you may buy a machine that never gets used, and resale on used computer hardware and software is poor once the machine is a year or two old. Computing devices are only worth the investment if you use them.

For many businesspeople (including us), a compact notebook computer is used for heavy-duty work sessions and an electronic organizer supplements the computer with fast access to addresses, phone numbers, and a quick note made in a hurry. And our electronic organizers are small enough to carry in a oversized wallet and a small purse for use anytime and anywhere.

For the rare people who really have no need of a

full-featured computer, a PDA (when they are affordable and available) or a capable organizer is the answer. It provides a wide range of useful functions, it's easy to use, and it's instantly ready to answer any query without the start-up delay of a notebook computer.

CHOOSE EQUIPMENT BASED ON YOUR NEEDS

You've heard us say this before: The first element in choosing an organizer, PDA, or computer is to analyze what you plan to do with the machine. The classic mistake is to buy the equipment first and then try to make it work for your needs later. With some equipment, this is like trying to fit a round peg into a square hole—impossible or at least impractical.

With all mobile technologies, the selection process is as follows:

1. Describe your needs.

2. Identify the products that meet your needs.

3. Test your selections thoroughly before purchase.

4. Purchase the product you (not the reviewers) like the best and use it.

Only by working from your needs and working preferences can you choose the right organizer, PDA, computer, or software. Testing is definitely required before purchase. Many times, the claims made in product literature don't pan out as promised under actual working conditions.

For example, software can turn out to be less capable than claimed or difficult to use because of clumsy design. A PDA's or computer's manufacturer may claim much longer battery life than you will actually experience. Or, you may find that the spreadsheet module for an electronic organizer is as powerful as claimed, but almost impossible to use because you spend more time moving around the tiny screen than getting any useful work done.

If you are new to this kind of technology, you should also carefully evaluate the ease of use of each product under consideration. For example, while you may have no trouble using an electronic organizer, some computer systems are difficult to master because serious computer training is required. That's why you should test each product before purchase by trying it out in a store (or mail order with a sturdy money-back guarantee) with tasks that you will use it for.

For example, if you plan to write long reports on a computer running on battery power, use each prospective machine to write several reports while timing how long it takes for the battery to zonk out—you may find that the battery life is too short or that the word processor you've tentatively chosen is about as intuitive as quantum theory! Also, if you do use both an electronic organizer (or PDA) and a notebook computer, make sure the data can be transferred between the two systems with ease. There are third-party network kits listed in the reference section of the book for doing this and kits available from most of the organizer manufacturers as well. The more compatible the systems, the better you will like using them.

5

ON-THE-GO PRINTING AND OUTPUT OPTIONS

Once you have created a document on the road, be it a one-page memo or a complete annual report, you will want to print it for other people to read. Of course, you could transmit the document in electronic form as a file or a fax, but there are times when that is inappropriate. Unfortunately, the best looking printed output comes from laser printers and similar large and heavy technology, and it is unlikely that you want to travel with such a boat anchor.

Fortunately, there are other on-the-road printing options using either portable printing equipment carried as part of your mobile office or through printing facilities available at rest points on your trip.

ELECTRONIC ORGANIZER AND PALMTOP PRINTER OPTIONS

For the person who uses only an electronic organizer or palmtop computer, there is usually a printer available for the unit from the manufacturer. These tiny units (which are most often small thermal printers that require special paper) print on paper similar to a cash register receipt in width. This makes them essentially useless for printing serious business documents, but we've used these machines for printing expense account information, tracking billable time, and for substantiating in-field consulting hours. Note: The printing on thermal papers will fade in the sun and over time, so make sure to photocopy the thermal output as soon as it is convenient if you want it as a permanent record.

For people who use both an organizer and a notebook computer, a better way to print the organizer data is to use linking software, like IntelliLink or a similar program, and then print the data on a larger printer from your notebook computer.

LETTER-SIZE MOBILE PRINTERS

The first battery-powered printers for the portable computers used thermal paper and low-resolution dot matrix printing. These were okay if you just wanted a record of your work to photocopy for the files, but were not suitable for making presentations to clients. The thermal paper yellowed, and the ink quickly faded.

Now there are portable, battery-operated printers that can produce quality output using dot matrix, ink jet, and thermal transfer technologies. The most expensive are the quality dot matrix printers, which can run more than $1000 for the smallest, lightest, fastest models. Choose one of these only if you need to print multiple-copy forms such as invoices or order forms—as an impact printer (which the dot matrix is) is the only type that can handle preprinted, multipart documents.

For quality output of single pages, look at either an ink jet printer or a thermal transfer printer. Quality portable printers of these types typically cost less than $500 (though some are more) and offer superior print quality. The best of these provide good letter-quality output (not quite as good as a laser printer, but certainly adequate for letters and small reports). These small printers can output a full 8 1/2" by 11" page while remaining compact enough to carry and run on battery power. Of course, they won't win any speed competitions. When you want quality output and portability, the technology still forces us to make compromises.

Commonly used battery-operated printers include Kodak's Diconix, Cannon's BubbleJet, and the Citizen PN48. (By the time you read this there will probably be others to add to the list.) The Diconix saves space by using the printer's paper roller as the battery holder and is about as compact as a printer that takes full-sized paper is likely to get. Some machines suffer from the need for special paper that can either fade or is expensive or both.

Kodak also makes a portable color ink jet printer. The color quality for such a small device isn't bad, but it does not begin to compare to a high quality desktop-based color printer.

If you do purchase a portable printer, follow the manufacturer's recommendations to the letter for choosing NiCad batteries. Our older model Diconix performed poorly with Radio Shack's NiCads. Replacing them with one of the high-current NiCads recommended in the instruction manual substantially raised our page-per-charge ratio.

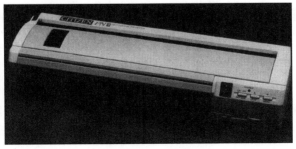

Citizen makes an excellent black and white bubble jet printer that fits in a briefcase and weighs only 2.5 pounds. GCC sells a Macintosh version.

Do You Really Need a Portable Printer?

The answer to this question is again one of job function, but the answer is usually no unless you have priority printing requirements (such as invoices or proposals which must be left with your customers) or are traveling exclusively by car and have trunk space to spare. None of the small printer options we reviewed comes close to printing at the "office" standard of a laser printer. That means that except for letters home, expense reports, and drafts of memos and reports, a portable printer may not prove that useful. As small as these machines are, they are almost the size of the average notebook computer, although the cosmetically identical PC-compatible Citizen and Mac-compatible GCC are unusually compact. They weigh almost as much as well.

✈ Take a Compact But Nonbattery Printer

A number of small nonbattery printers are available, including ones from Epson (ActionPrinter), Apple (the oddly designed StyleWriter), and many others that take up little room when traveling (in a suitcase not a briefcase). These require AC power to run and their output doesn't look quite as good as a laser printer's, but if you want good quality printing at a reasonable price, look for these small AC-powered units and skip the battery option machines. When choosing such a device, look for one with quick set-up and design that makes the unit easy to ship. Avoid units that have parts that fall off, can be easily broken off, or make the unit clumsy to pack.

For people who need laser-quality printing on the road, Hewlett-Packard recently introduced a personal, portable LaserJet printer. Although this high-quality printer is still too large for most mobile professionals, it is a nice machine for those who work out of their car and are able to carry the printer from office to office on consulting or other extended assignments.

If you absolutely must print on the road, and the

other output options explained in this chapter won't meet your needs, go ahead and buy the best quality, lightest printer you can afford. If you need good quality and are traveling by car and staying in hotels, consider taking a small laser printer along. Forget this option if you are spending most of your time in airports, planes, and rental cars—while the smallest laser printer is almost within mobile office standards, its bulk and size may prove your undoing while lugging it from place to place.

✈ Make Overhead Foils on the Road

The obvious way to make overhead transparencies is to print your output and then photocopy it onto transparency film. That's fine if you have access to a photocopier. But if you don't, here's another option: Buy a pack of the special transparency film like the type Hewlett-Packard makes for its color ink jet (PaintJet) printers and use this. This film can take ink jet output and each sheet of film comes with a plastic protector that wraps around the finished transparency to protect it. Let the printed foils dry for five minutes before wrapping them in their plastic protectors. The ink takes about four hours to fully soak into the plastic and darkens desirably as this occurs.

SOME REASONABLE OUTPUT ALTERNATIVES

There are several alternatives that can save you the trouble of lugging a printer along. If you don't use a portable printer, or if you need high-quality output for a special report, here are some options to consider.

- Stay at a major hotel chain that offers computer facilities. Almost all the major chains offer computer output options, including laser printers, fax machines, and copiers.

- Use your fax modem to send your document to the hotel fax machine.

- Go to Kinko's or a similar full-service office services company. Almost every major city in the United States has multiple Kinko's or competitive companies (usually located by colleges and universities) that will provide laser printer output, copying (often in full color), document binding, and other useful services. Most rent time on their desktop computers as well, which is useful if you don't have your own notebook computer along for final changes to the disk file. Look for these companies under Copying and Duplicating Services in the Yellow Pages.

- Join a major airline club (listed in the reference section of the book) and do your printing and other output while waiting for your usually late plane at the airport. The gracious concierges at American Airlines Admiral's Club have helped us on many an occasion to arrange last-minute meeting facilities, make copies, send faxes, and get quality printed output of an important "must have" document. Some of the lounges have computers equipped with modems for use by members, along with standard fax machines and copiers.

- If you need typeset quality output or full-color documents, look in the local Yellow Pages under Desktop Publishing or Typesetting to find companies that can output your documents on their high-quality equipment, most of which can read PC and Macintosh files.

In general, we don't recommend the added weight and hassle of carrying a portable printer, but for some mobile professionals, especially those who work out of their cars or those who must make bids, estimates, and reports on the spot, a printer can be an important device for closing sales or getting information to clients and customers. For the rest of you, use the alternative methods we suggest, and you'll have more room in your suitcase for devices that will serve more diverse functions.

6

ON-THE-GO COMMUNICATIONS

The most important aspect of office-on-the-go tools is the ability to communicate. Communication functions are important for maintaining contact with coworkers, managers, customers, prospective customers, and your friends and family while traveling. This chapter explains the communication options for your office on the go. In later chapters, you'll see how to put these tools to work and learn how to integrate the technologies for superior productivity on the road.

THE PHONE ON THE ROAD

The cellular system concept is simple, but putting it to work requires sophisticated computer technology and investment in transmitters that allow continuous calling while behind hills, in valleys, and in fringe areas of the serviced area. Cellular telephone service really has a lot more in common with two-way radio than standard telephone transmissions. Cellular phone technology has almost nothing in common with desk-based telephone technology.

As you move across a city, town, or rural area with cellular service, your telephone call is routed to the nearest transmitter with a circuit available for your call.

Then as you move away from the cellular station currently handling your call, it is automatically "handed off"
to the next cellular station as you approach the area
(usually) without your knowledge.

Cellular systems are based in each major city (in
the United States) with a maximum of two licensed cellular carriers allowed to service the same city. For this reason and because each city has different carriers, once
you leave the cellular system that you subscribe to in
your home area and enter a new one, you go into roam
mode where the local system lets you use their service
for an additional fee.

Still, once you are connected into a cellular network, you can reach almost anyone in the world who has
a conventional telephone. And where in the past you
could call only cellular telephone users when they were
in their local cellular network, new optional services
(NationLink is one example) allow you to locate a cellular user anywhere in the North American continent (if
the person wants to be located).

One version of this feature allows users to call you
directly on any system that supports this feature while
you pay for the long-distance and cellular charges.
Another version of the option tells callers the codes and
numbers to use to reach you. For this second option,
callers pick up the long-distance and cellular charges.
Cellular networks can be used for standard telephone
and data needs, and cellular fax modems can be put to
work in your car as you drive. Additionally, the cellular
network can be used for a variety of data transmission
needs and this is a rapidly growing area of cellular technology.

CELLULAR PHONE OPTIONS

As with most technologies, there are several kinds
of cellular phone models, with the most compact being
the most expensive. The prices of phones are plummet-

ing, and more and more functionality is being added to models even as they become less expensive. The basic choices include the types of phones described in this section.

Car-Based Phones

The most common kind of cellular telephone is mounted into the car and can be used by speaking into a small microphone positioned near the rear-view antennae. This arrangement is called hands-free because the only contact you need to the phone is to dial numbers or pickup calls.

Some units even avoid this contact by allowing you to give the commands by voice, although this technology is not yet all that accurate. Naturally you can still pick up the receiver on a car phone and talk as you do with an office phone. The very cheapest car-based models don't offer the hands-free option, or it may be offered as an expensive add-on kit. Car telephones have the widest range in transmission capabilities because they have the highest wattage output when combined with the right antennae.

✈ Get the Best Antennae

While few purveyors of cellular systems will bother to talk about antennae systems, just like on a portable radio, the antennae is a key link in limiting the range of a car phone. The most common antennae are ones that mount on the inside and outside of the rear window. These jump the radio signal across the glass which is sandwiched between the antennae and the wire that carries the signal to the transmitter. As a result of this arrangement, these antennae lose some of the signal. A better alternative is an antennae that is directly wired to the transmitter. Your cellular dealer has several kinds of antennae options that can be wired this way. Some dealers may not want to sell you such a unit because they are more work to install than the ones that simply stick on the glass.

Handheld Phones

The most convenient cellular phones are hand-held. These can be carried and used almost anywhere except inside of steel buildings or deep inside other large structures where the level of interference may make such calls impossible. These phones vary in size from units with weight measured in ounces to larger phones that weigh several pounds. Naturally you want the most compact unit possible, but beware of small units with limited battery life. Handheld telephones are much more limited in power output because placing a high-power radio transmitter next to your braincase while using the phone is probably not a good idea.

Transportable Phones

When shopping for phones you may run into an inexpensive-sounding phone deemed a "portable." Not to be confused with handheld phones, these units are much larger and consist of a telephone receiver that is wired to a box that houses the system's electronics. These units usually have more transmission power than a handheld. They may have longer battery life as well because, with their larger size, there's room for a bigger and much heavier battery pack. The largest of these phones fits in a small gym bag-like case to carry them around in.

Dockable (Convertible) Phones

Just like there are dockable computers that allow you to plug a compact notebook unit into a full-sized desktop unit back at the office, there are dockable cellular phones. These consist of a car-mounted unit offering full transmission power and a handheld phone that acts as the hand set while the phone is docked in the car mount. To go fully mobile, you detach just the hand-set portion of the phone which becomes a compact hand-held unit. Naturally the smaller handheld portion of the system has less transmission power than the full system. Quality dockable systems tend to be expensive, and you have to pay for the installation in your car in addition to buying the phone. Even so, if you spend a lot of time traveling in a car, these phones can be an ideal solution for communications on the go.

SHOPPING FOR A CELLULAR PHONE

The first decision to make is to the kind of phone you need for your mobile office based on your specific usage requirements. Handheld or dockable phones are usually the best solution for most travelers, but other systems have their place for special requirements. When shopping for the ideal cellular phone, look for the following:

Proven Transmission Range

Each manufacturer rates its phones by transmission wattage, with a higher output rating meaning longer range. Most car phones are 3 to 5 watts. Most handheld phones are a much smaller (and safer) 0.6 watts. In our experience with cellular phones, the manufacturer's ratings don't always translate into actual transmission capability. When we compared three handheld units with an identical 0.6 watt rating in the field, two of the three had superior transmission abilities, and the third unit was very noisy and dropped calls frequently.

Proven Battery Life

If your phone runs on batteries, you want to make sure that the manufacturer's rating translates into real battery life. Unfortunately, the only way to do this is to test units under consideration to see how they hold up. A typical compact handheld unit offers battery power that provides half an hour of talk time (time on the phone making calls) and/or twelve hours of standby time

(time with the phone turned on ready to send or receive a call). Always buy at least two batteries for handhelds or you spend more time waiting for the battery to charge than calling anyone.

✈ What's in a NAM?

Most handheld phones now support more than one numerical assignment module (NAM)—that means that as you travel, you can have phone numbers in more than one city and on more than one cellular system. This is one way to avoid roaming charges or access fees when entering a second city that you frequent on business trips.

A Deep-Cycle Battery Charger

Handheld phones tend to have problems with batteries failing to take a charge as explained in the battery section in Chapter 16. You pick up your phone and head out on the road, and the freshly charged battery dies before dialing your first call. Avoid this problem by buying the phone manufacturer's deep-cycle charger which fully drains and then charges the NiCad batteries.

An RJ-11 Jack for Your Computer

Even if you don't plan to communicate with your computer via your cellular phone, look for a unit that features the requisite RJ-11 jack because, who knows, you might want to use this capability in the future.

The Right Feature Set

Cellular phones typically offer memory functions where you can store frequently used phone numbers and a variety of other features. If the number memory function will get a lot of use, follow the unit's instruction manual and try storing and recalling a phone number. With some phones this is easy and intuitive, but with other units it's like performing brain surgery. In addition to saving frequently called numbers with alphanumeric look-up capabilities, there are other esoteric features that some expensive phones offer. Many of these will be completely useless to you, but study each unit's manual to determine what is offered and how you may find it helpful.

Our favorite feature is the one that cuts off the car stereo audio anytime a call comes through or when you press the Send button to make a call.

✈ Data Access via Cellular Phone

When shopping for a cellular phone, if you plan to use it with a modem built into your computer, make sure that the two units are compatible. We recommend that before purchase, you test the two to ensure full compatibility and clean transmission quality.

Good Audio Quality

Again it is difficult to test a phone's quality without actually using it. Some phones simply sound better than others. An inexpensive phone may make you sound as if you're talking through a tunnel. Calling on clients with such a phone will not add much credibility to your image, and clients with hearing problems will have trouble understanding you.

Hands-free phones can suffer from awful audio problems. For example, we put a General Electric phone in one of our "on-the-road" cars because the price was right. But after hearing that the system made us sound as if we were talking through a hollow log, we promptly replaced it with another system with superior audio quality.

Digital Cellular

The cellular telephone business is quietly undergoing major change: The present systems that provide largely two-way radio operation are becoming extremely overloaded in busy markets such as New York and Los

Angeles. As a result, to make it possible to accommodate new subscribers, the systems are being switched over to digital equipment that can handle a much larger volume of calls by using one "line" to carry multiple conversations. These systems provide advanced features such as sophisticated paging, much better interference control, and reduced likelihood of losing (dropping) calls. Sounds great, doesn't it? Unfortunately, digital phones are (currently) much more expensive, and existing cellular equipment is not yet compatible with digital systems. As a result, a hybrid phone that can work on both systems is the right choice for now.

A BRIEF CELLULAR GLOSSARY

The terms surrounding cellular technology can be daunting to the uninitiated. For that reason we include this cellular glossary here so you won't get hoodwinked by cellular sales reps.

A/B Switch: Allows you to switch between the two cellular carriers in a local area.

Alphanumeric Memory: Allows you to look up numbers by name. This is especially useful because instead of trying to remember which one of 99 numbers you're looking for, you can search by name instead.

Call-in-Absence Indicator: Lets you know that someone tried to reach you when you were away. The question then is, who?

Call Restriction/Locking: Limits the kinds of numbers that can be dialed on a phone or locks the phone completely when your car goes into the shop or to a valet.

Call Timer: Tells you how long your last call lasted and how many call hours and minutes that you've used. Not really of much use for computing your phone bill because the timer can't tell the difference between a connected call, a long wait for a ring on the other end, or a busy signal. It counts time any time the Send button is pressed until the End button is pressed or a handheld phone's battery croaks.

Dropped Call: Refers to calls that are dropped if you get out of range of a cellular station or if there are defects in the cellular systems. ("Cellular speak" for losing a connection.) Calls are also dropped when a phone's battery gets weak. Usage: "Sorry Phil, I *dropped* you because my phone's battery got low."

Hands-Free Answering: Enables automatic answering of the phone so you can talk hands-free. This feature works best when combined with an option that mutes the car's stereo; otherwise the caller may get a dose of your taste in music instead of you.

Hands-Free: Allows you to talk on a car phone while keeping your hands on the steering wheel. Hands-free is the only way a driver can safely use a car phone.

Home System: Refers to the carrier that provides your service in your home system. When using your phone outside of this system, you are said to be roaming, and additional charges and restrictions will apply to calls.

Mobile-Mounting Kit: Mounts handheld and transportable phones into a car. Usually these kits boost the phone's output to a full three watts.

NAM (Numeric Assignment Module): Refers to your telephone's electronic identification. In the case of phones with the capability to support multiple

NAMs, you can use more than one cellular service as your home system.

Roam Mode: Is activated when you are using your phone on a system other than the one that provides your service, in which case you are said to be roaming on the system you are using to transmit calls. When roaming, extra charges will apply to your calls, and if your home system has no roaming agreement with the carrier you're using, you may get asked for a credit card to charge your calls.

Scratch Pad Function: Allows you to silently enter numbers into your phone if someone gives you a number during a call. Just remember how to turn this feature on or your phone will create touch tones, interrupting your call.

Signal-Strength Indicator: Takes the form of a readout on the phone that shows how strong the signal is at any given time. This gives you a clue when a call may be dropped. On a handheld phone, when the signal strength appears low, moving around in a room (or driving through an intersection when using a car phone) may improve it. Watch the signal-strength indicator to see where the signal is stronger. Sometimes just moving a few feet will substantially improve or diminish a signal.

Standby Time: A measure of the phone's remaining battery life if no calls are made.

System A (System B): The names of each of the two cellular carriers in any city. Typically one carrier is the area's telephone company, where the second carrier may be independent or affiliated with an out-of-the-area telephone company. You can change carriers from A to B by using your phone's A/B switch or code.

Talk Time: A measure of a phone's remaining battery life while the phone is in use making calls. Talk time is usually improved when several short calls are made rather than one long call.

Voice-Activated Dialing: Attempts to operate your phone through spoken commands. Good luck trying to make it work.

✈ Pass on the Porsche-Brand Cellular Phone

Some automakers such as Chrysler have installed cellular phones in their upscale cars in the driver's sunshade. To use the phone, pulling down the sunshade conveniently reveals the controls and it uses a space in the car that really has no other application. But many automakers offer ordinary off-the-shelf cellular phones with their insignia added. Priced outrageously, these phones should be avoided. Do you really need an overpriced phone just because it has a BMW insignia?

TELEPHONE PRICING

When comparing cellular telephone deals, keep in mind that the current low purchase price of many models reflects a hidden commission paid by the cellular service provider (the phone company) to the telephone seller. The logic (or lack there of) is that once you get a deal on the phone, you'll sign a one-year or longer service contract with the cellular carrier. These commissions represent several hundred dollars, so more and more inexpensive phones can be "purchased" with new cellular service for free. In addition to the purchase price of the phone, you will (usually) be charged an account set-up fee, an advance for one month's service, and several other incidental charges. If the telephone will be installed in a car, a hefty installation charge may also be involved, although installation charges have been reduced in most cities as a larger number of experienced phone installers are available.

✈ The Cellular Phone Book

Mobile professionals will want to purchase a copy of The Cellular Telephone Directory. *It's a complete guide to roaming in North America with information on roaming arrangements and a map showing where each system provides coverage. Call (206) 232-3464 from your cellular phone (or any other phone for that matter) to order a copy.*

Cellular calls are priced by the minute. Most savvy users buy a block of time each month at a discounted rate. For example, you might purchase a three-hour block of time for about half the price of paying for calls by the minute. If you exceed your three hours, each additional minute is charged at a flat rate. Of course, long distance charges are added to the airtime charges. Other services are also available for an extra monthly charge, including voice messaging and call forwarding to name just two. Only add these services if you are actually going to use them, as the little extras can turn a reasonable monthly rate into a monster bill in no time.

CELLULAR PHONE CARRIERS

When you purchase a phone the dealer will usually set you up automatically with the cellular service provider the company works with. This isn't normally a problem because in most cities, competing cellular systems are fairly identical in capabilities, available features, cellular service coverage, and signal quality. But before signing up through a service, you may want to get recommendations from other cellular phone users.

Forget asking the dealers for recommendations; they will simply praise the service they work with and badmouth the competition. In some cities, one carrier (the cellular phone company service provider) may offer better coverage of outlying areas or use newer, quieter equipment that drops calls less often.

✈ No "A" Service? Try "B" Instead

While it may seem like the "A" carrier will exist in areas with only one carrier, it is really the "B" system that is likely to be up and working in areas with only one system. If No Service appears in your phone's display when in an area that appears large enough to have service or on an interstate freeway, switch your phone over to the "B" system to see if service is there. To sign up with your selected carrier, purchase your phone through a dealer that works with the service of your choice. Because the phone you buy is usually heavily subsidized by the carrier to keep its purchase price low, you'll be locked into a one- or two-year contract with the carrier when you buy your phone. (Demand a one-year contract.) The only way out of these contracts is to pay a hefty cancellation charge or wait out the contract.

For example, in our base city, one carrier charges slightly more but offers better coverage of the city and calls have less interference problems. The other carrier, strapped for cash until a larger company recently purchased them, offered lower calling rates, but their equipment frequently dropped calls and their coverage of some outlying areas of the city left something to be desired. Smaller cities may only have one carrier, although most areas have second services at least in the planning or construction stage.

PAGERS AND PAGING

Before cellular phones became popular and affordable, the only ways to reach someone on the road were via pager, painfully expensive car telephones ($3 just to pick up the telephone receiver), or mobile radio. Today, cellular phones have supplanted the original car phone systems and two-way radios, except those used by taxis and emergency response teams. But for some mobile professionals, pagers are still a less expensive and viable option. Many mobile professionals carry both a cellular phone and a pager. Some PDAs now incorporate the functions of a pager and there are paging add-in cards for notebook computers that can be used to tie into wireless networks.

Essentially there are two kinds of pagers: basic and "intelligent" models. Basic pagers work something like the units of yesteryear. They beep, buzz, or vibrate silently to tell the wearer of the page. The tiny readout at the top shows the number to call or a disembodied-sounding voice transmits the message, and that's pretty much the extent of their services.

More sophisticated pagers have large readouts that not only provide the phone number but a complete message. You can scroll through the pages received throughout the day, making immediate responses to important calls, and then looking up numbers for less important calls later in the day. To send messages to these units, a keyboard must be purchased in addition to the pager. This combination costs more than a cellular phone, although monthly fees are lower.

What to Look for in a Pager

Choosing a pager is relatively easy compared to choosing a computer. There are a growing number of options available, especially in the higher end models, but they are generally simple to understand. In addition to obviously durable construction, when shopping for a pager look for:

A Unit That Meets Your Needs

Buy only the amount of pager you need. Units with alphanumeric readouts are very convenient for tracking messages, but they are much larger than a simple unit and more expensive to purchase. For "silent" paging, choose a unit that vibrates when you are paged instead of beeping. Other systems are built into very utilitarian looking wristwatches. One system, from BellSouth and Swatch, the Swiss manufacturer of brightly colored watches, is built into a colorful wristwatch for added convenience. Unfortunately, the Swatch pager is targeted at latchkey kids rather than mobile professionals.

✈ Paging Receivers and Pagers on a Card

SkyTel's portable messaging service and Motorola's EMBARC (Electronic Mail Broadcast to a Roaming Computer) are one-way paging services that allow broadcast messages to be sent to anyone with an appropriate modem. Paging modems are available for mobile computers to act as message receivers for these one-way services. There are paging receivers and high-speed modems on the drawing boards for incorporation into PCMCIA cards, targeted for release sometime in 1993. Where a typical pager stores up to 6,000 characters, a pager modem can store around 32,000 characters. A 300-character message over SkyTel runs about $6, whether it goes to one person or a few hundred.

Services That Meet Your Needs

You can choose from a wide range of services— related to additional features and the size of the area that you can be paged in. Typical services include voice messaging when you aren't available. Paging areas can include your local city, the state you live in, or an entire country. Worldwide paging is also possible but, as you can imagine, it's pricey.

Ease of Use

In advanced models, choose a unit with easy to use controls and features. For all pagers, make sure that the display is highly readable and that you understand the functions and buttons of the system without referring to the instruction manual or your paging service's instruction sheets.

One neat function is a pager that looks up incoming numbers in its memory and then displays the caller's name. Of course this only works for phone numbers that you have stored in the pager's limited memory.

✈ Paging Terminals and E-Mail Connections

If you will be using a pager with an alphanumeric readout (recommended), you will also need a special keyboard terminal that allows your assistant back at the office to send you messages, or you will need to use a software gateway product like PageIT! from Infinite Technologies, which transmits electronic mail (E-mail) messages created on standard personal computer networks directly to alphanumeric or full-text pagers. If you choose a dedicated paging terminal system, you may need more than one keyboard terminal if several people who work apart from each other will be picking up your messages. If you use a system like PageIT!, people can send standard E-mail messages (from MHS-compatible E-mail programs) from any personal computer and the messages will be automatically routed to the pager. With these systems, businesspeople in the field need only carry a pager with a small display to receive any message and they no longer have to stop and use the phone to determine the nature of the page.

The Right Service

Pagers work through a paging service provided by

a telephone company or private service. You should choose a service (which often provides the pager) that's right for your budget and range capabilities. When shopping for a service and pager, you may find a variety of price cuts and perks available among several companies. Look for the best deal, but also keep in mind that some companies provide superior service than others. Check it out with people who use the services.

CELLULAR PHONE OR PAGER?

For most mobile professionals, a cellular telephone is the way to go. But, for others, a pager or pager *and* cellular telephone is the right way to keep in touch. Here are some pros and cons so you can choose the communication method that's right for you.

Cellular Phones

Pros:

✔ Equipment carries full voice communication and can transmit computer data and faxes.

✔ These phones can be used anywhere that a receiving cell is available to link the user to the cellular net.

✈ Save Money by Renting

*For mobile professionals who only need a pager or cellular phone for short durations when visiting other cities, rental units are priced reasonably for short-term use. Look in the Yellow Pages under **Paging and Signaling Equipment and Systems**.*

Cons:

✖ Cellular service is expensive, especially in major markets such as New York, Los Angeles, and the San Francisco Bay Area.

✖ Service is not available in many parts of the country, including towns and rural areas not close to a major interstate highway. At this writing, even much of the interstate system lacks cellular access.

Pagers

Pros:

✔ Generally, pagers are less expensive to operate than a cellular phone.

✔ Pagers offer *much* longer battery life than cellular phones.

✔ Paging functions are now integrated in some PDAs and offered on add-on computer cards, eliminating the need for an additional bulky device in the briefcase or on a belt.

✔ Depending on the kind of service you use, you can be reached almost anywhere—even in remote wilderness areas providing you aren't down in a narrow valley or canyon.

Cons:

✖ No two-way voice capabilities—that means a trip to a pay phone to establish communications. Between the telephone charges for long distance calls made from a pay phone and pager charges, a cellular phone may be almost as economical and you can skip the trip to a phone.

✖ If customers or others have you paged, until you call them back, they have no idea whether you received their message or not. A cellular phone is the best choice for direct calling while on the go. While you can't (legally) make calls in flight, these phones can be used almost anywhere else that cellular service is available. Using a quality phone, you can spend unproductive hours driving around town setting up appointments, booking travel arrangements, and keeping in touch with your business or family.

Choose a pager if your travels take you away from the cellular network for long periods and if immediate communication with the party paging you is not essential. Pagers are, as mentioned, cheaper to operate than cellular phones, but they are also proportionately less capable devices—even ones with a complete readout and message forwarding capabilities.

✈ Getting Credit Where Credit Is Due

When arranging cellular or pager service, the carrier will check your credit and make sure that you pay your bills on time. This isn't because they are unusually paranoid, instead it's because some users have run up cellular phone bills in the thousands of dollars and then gone south. By checking your credit, the company ensures that your are likely to pay for the calls you make in a timely manner. If your credit is thin, bad, or if you don't have steady income, a deposit may be required which will be held for six months to two years (some systems pay interest on your deposit, some don't). For users with overtly bad credit, this may range from $500 to several thousand. Deposits tend to be larger in cities with more would-be cellular users than space on the cellular system.

For people who spend their life on the road in cars, a combination of pager and cellular phone may be the best alternative. With a statewide, nationwide, or worldwide paging service you can be reached on any road or in any town as desired; you can then call in if you need more information about the message upon reaching cellular service, with your cellular phone.

MODEMS ON THE GO

We've mentioned modems several times already

without providing much explanation. If you are new to computers, a modem is an electronic device that can send and receive computer files over telephone lines. Modems can work with cellular phones to transmit over the cellular phone system. Modems are useful because they allow you to exchange files and information with your office and access information services where you can perform online research or use the service's electronic mail features.

Today's modems are tiny devices that are contained either in a small outboard box or completely inside the computer or organizer unit. Some modems are available as PCMCIA cards. Most notebook modems for serious mobile professionals are installed inside the computer and offer a faxing option as well as data transmission capabilities. (Fax/modems are discussed next.) The modem is controlled via telecommunications software that runs on your computer. Once set up, you can log on (connect) to the office's computers or to CompuServe or other online services with a single command. This makes it easy to read electronic mail or browse the news, weather, and sports information available through any one of several online services. (Online services are discussed in detail in Chapter 9.)

✈ Modem Software

Many modems and fax modems designed for notebook computers come with software to operate them, although not all these programs are easy to use or intuitive. Usually the faxing software is easier to use than the communications software that you use to access electronic mail. Fortunately, you are not limited to the fax software that comes with the fax/modem. You can choose from a wide variety of off-the-shelf communications packages that can handle the faxing functions as well as general modem communications functions.

Built-in or External Modem?

When choosing a modem for a notebook computer,

you usually don't get much choice because many of these machines only work with modems made by the computer's manufacturer. Some notebook computers such as Apple's PowerBooks, are popular enough that other companies make modems that fit these machines at a price that's lower than that charged for the manufacturer's equipment. If you are using an external modem, your choices broaden considerably, but you then must carry around another piece of equipment.

Obviously, a modem that is integrated and built-in to the notebook computer case is easier to work with (most of the time) than one that has to be attached from the outside. Still, there are reasons to use an external modem—such as the ability to put it where you need it. External modems are typically sturdier and faster than internal modems as well.

Some power users employ both an internal 2400 bps (bits per second, also referred to as the "baud rate," an older and less accurate term) modem for general communications with online services and electronic mail and an external high-speed modem for occasional transmission of large data files from corporate databases.

Fast-Lane Transmission Speeds

Speedy transmission is a key to getting the most from a modem because it saves time, cuts down on long distance phone bills (or cellular time), and reduces connect time charges for online services. Today, the most commonly used modem speed is 2400 bps with 9600 bps rapidly replacing it as modems improve in capability and the price of their components continue to collapse.

If you buy a 2400-bps modem, all you have to look for is Hayes compatibility, and you can talk to any computer that supports the speed. But, if you buy faster modems, you need to be aware that for two modems to communicate, they must use the same transmission standards.

The most important standards for high-speed modem communications are V.32, which controls 9600-

bps communications, and V.32bis, which controls 14,400 bps communications.

Any modem that uses V.32 can talk to any other V.32 modem at 9600 bps. And, a V.32bis modem can talk to other V. 32 modems at 9600 bps or to a V.32bis modem at 14,400 bps. Be careful, however. There are standards called V.42 and V.42bis which are error correction and data compression standards and have nothing to do with the true transmission speed of the modem. People who make 2400 bps modems to V. 42bis standards often claim that their modems have "9600 bps throughput" or "an apparent speed of 9600 bps" because the modems can transfer text data at that speed with compression if talking to another V. 42bis modem that can accept the compressed data. This is not true 9600-bps transmission, but it is a superior feature compared to a 2400-bps modem without it.

Yes, this is all very confusing. To keep it straight, just remember that a modem with V.32bis is actually a much faster modem than the V.42bis modem in most cases, even though most people think the bigger number means the standard is better.

✈ Fax/Modem Speed and Modem Speed

When shopping for fax/modems you will find run-of-the-mill modems that are rated at 9600-bps fax speed. Keep in mind that fax speed is measured differently than modem speed. Such units usually provide only 2400-bps modem speed not 9600 bps.

There are some modems on the market that offer even better performance for data transmission, like the Telebit QBlazer. This compact external modem allows transmission of data at 38,400 bps. The modem runs at 9600 bps but uses compression technology to squeeze data together and thus realizes much faster transmission speeds. The catch is that you need an identical or compatible modem at the other end to get this kind of performance. Thus some people may want to use two modems on the road—the internal, built-in modem that uses 2400 or 9600 bps for sending E-mail, accessing online systems, and performing other basic communications functions where 2400 bps is still adequate. For sending long documents and dumping files to corporate databases, a faster modem with compression capabilities is probably a good addition, if you need to make large file transfers on the road.

Speed must also go hand in hand with accuracy and dependability; however, check the PC and Macintosh magazines for modem recommendations. They run reviews of new modems at least once a year.

Of course, just as 9600 bps is becoming the standard for transmission, the newer 14,400-bps modems and even faster ones are becoming more affordable and compact. The super-fast modems are still quite a bit more expensive, but for someone who does a lot of online work, the expense of the modem can pay for itself in transmission bills in no time. And you can expect the fast modems of today to be replaced by even faster ones in the future.

✈ Hot Work

Some fast external modems get really hot while engaged in their work. This is normal. But if you're transmitting from a really warm location, give the modem a break to cool down every twenty minutes or so.

Capabilities and Features

As mentioned, if you buy a modem for use on the road, you might as well choose one with fax capabilities. Other features may include useful software for communications (a fax/modem must have its own software) that fully automates connecting to commonly used online services and other numbers, and the ability to add an acoustic coupler should you require one (discussed shortly). If you are choosing a modem that will not mount inside your computer, look for one with status lights and a volume control. The lights and ability to control the unit's sound as it operates help you isolate problems. One unit we used without a volume control was so loud that we finally took it apart and disconnected the tiny speaker.

TIPS FOR THE FREQUENT TRAVELER

Some older hotels, and ones outside North America, have telephone systems that are not "plug compatible" with the kind of telephone connectors that are now standard in the United States and Canada. To get around this problem, buy an acoustic coupler (a unit that "listens" to the phone when you place the handset into it) to work around the incompatible phone system. Add extra periods into phone numbers to make the modem pause while dialing. Your modem translates periods into pauses. This gives the telephone system extra time to access an outside line before your modem spews forth the next set of digits. For really troublesome connections, add four or five periods before the phone number, between the number that gets an outside line, and after any country codes or area codes. Dialing slowly this way gives a telephone system that may be an antique time to catch up.

If none of this works, talk to the hotel staff directly (who may know absolutely nothing about computers or the hotel's phone system), or if you speak the language, call the phone company or a local computer store for advice. Or, change hotels if necessary after identifying one that better suits your requirements. The largest and newest hotels are usually your best choice for modem connections since their phone systems weren't installed in the 1930s or purchased from the local equivalent of Radio Shack. There are always solutions—it just takes time and experimentation to find them.

Two other ways around problem telephones: (1) Manually dial the number and then stick the handset into your acoustic couple or (2) purchase a device that goes between the handset and the telephone itself to access the circuits. Hardcore international travelers may need to carry several kinds of connectors to tame the local telephone system in each country. A kit of screwdrivers and wire strippers is a good companion for such desperate tactics. While you might assume that Third World countries have the oddest phone systems, most of Europe is just as bad.

✈ Get the Right Modem Software

From within a hotel, to make long distance calls, you may need to dial a three digit code plus the area code and number. Make sure that your modem software can handle more than just nine or ten numbers in its internal "telephone book." Another fix is to skip the software's phone book and type the number directly as ATDT 011-342-876-1234, for example. The ATDT command tells your modem to dial a number directly using as many digits as you please.

When using obviously bad telephone systems such as those found in much of Mexico and the Third World, you can also make things easier by shifting to a lower gear with your modem. While it may do 9600 bps while operating in the United States, on a noisy phone system, or one with very limited audio capabilities, try slowing the transmission speed down to 1200 bps to allow your modem and the remote modem more time to recognize what they are saying.

FAXING SYSTEMS ON THE GO

A full-sized office fax machine is obviously not a practical item for toting around on trips. Still, the fax machine has become almost indispensable in American business, so it's good to know that mobile alternatives are available. There are two ways to send and receive faxes while on the road—via a fax/modem built into a notebook computer, PDA, or organizer or using a cellular telephone faxing system. The first option is convenient because a fax modem typically weighs only a couple of ounces and is completely contained inside your computer. A cellular faxing system is easier to use, but the machine that handles the faxing is about the size of a battery-powered printer. Some electronic organizers offer optional faxing capabilities which allow users to send fax information to standard office-style fax machines via telephone.

✈ Modems and Cellular Phone?

The answer to this question is increasingly yes. If you are working on a system that is relatively noise free and you are not in a fringe area where a call can be dropped, it can be done. To get your computer talking to your cellular phone (this may not be possible with older models), contact that phone's manufacturer and request a cellular to modem connection kit. This set of cables may be expensive (Motorola's connector runs $300), but just think of the time you can save. This same connector allows you to send and receive mail electronically and also to log onto online services. In the near future, the intelligence contained in the cable may be built into modems. Also, in the near future, the introduction of the much anticipated cellular digital packet data (CDPC) service, developed jointly by IBM and McCaw Cellular Communications, will be available to transmit data over analog cellular lines at 19,200 bps. CDPD is a nonproprietary protocol that may be used by any cellular company. To use CDPD you will need to buy a special modem, which should be available in 1993. The CDPD is an interim step between the unreliable analog cellular connections of today and the digital service that is starting to be available in select areas. Because the switch over from analog to digital networks will take a few years, you can expect the new cellular phones and modems to be switchable between digital and analog mode.

Fax/Modems

Fax/modems are devices that allow you to send and receive computer data and faxes on a computer. To receive a fax with such a system, the tiny modem requires data like a standard fax machine, so it can effectively communicate with standard office models. It saves data as a file on your computer instead of spewing out paper. For small portable computers, that fax/modem for the system is usually made by the computer's manufacturer and may be so small that it measures about the size of four quarters placed end to end. While a fax/modem is a great convenience on the road, some units are easier to use than others. A well-designed fax/modem automatically sends a cover sheet page for you, makes sending and receiving faxes easy, and relatively automatic, and doubles as an effective general-purpose modem as well.

Selecting a Fax/Modem

When shopping for a fax/modem, you are usually locked into one or two units that are made by your notebook computer's manufacturer. For this reason, you may want to evaluate several different notebooks or PDAs along with their respective fax/modems before purchasing the machine. We recommend that you actually send and receive a fax or see how simple the modem's software is to use and get a feel for the speed with which you can send and receive documents. While these devices work quite well now after the first few year's technical problems, some fax/modem software is awkward, slow, cryptic, and intimidating. But, by sending and receiving a few faxes, you'll get a genuine feel for ease-of-use issues. To run your tests, use the conventional fax machine available at most computer dealer's stores to ship a few pages back and forth.

Cellular Faxes

Easier to use, but heavier and more expensive to purchase and operate are cellular telephone-compatible fax machines. These devices hook into your cellular phone to send and receive faxed documents. You can use one anywhere that you have access to the cellular network—be it in your car during rush hour or on a job or customer site. To a large degree, these machines work much like an ordinary office fax, and unlike a fax/modem, they do not require a computer or computer skills to run. Unfortunately, these systems are very slow on the analog cellular systems still in wide use today. Unless your fax requirements are limited to a page or two, or if you don't mind large bills for airtime and the wait, you may want to convert to a hybrid phone that can work on both analog and digital systems, so that you can send faxes in high-speed digital mode.

INTEGRATED BRIEFCASE SYSTEMS

NEC's office in a briefcase

There are now options that combine a notebook computer, cellular telephone, and modem in two connectable units packed in a specially designed briefcase. For example, NEC, NCR, and other companies offer a cellular phone option that allows the unit to connect directly into the computer. Using this connection, the notebook computer's internal fax/modem can communicate using its over-the-cellular network. This allows communications with remote fax machines and other computers and provides online functions for electronic mail updates and other services. Total weight? About ten pounds with everything.

Of course, as PDAs evolve, the integrated notebook systems will seem bulky and clumsy by comparison. For now, they are an elegant solution for putting an entire office on the go with full-function computer power in one convenient package.

At this point, you have been introduced to most of the hardware components of a typical mobile office. In the next chapter, we'll look at software that brings the mobile office to life and keeps you productive on the road.

7

ON-THE-GO SOFTWARE—THE PROGRAMS THAT GET THE WORK DONE

In the last few chapters you have met a number of the basic "hardware" options for empowering the office on the go. In Chapter 1 we discussed the six functions that every office on the go must accommodate: communication, reporting, information gathering and research, analysis and forecasting, planning and scheduling, and organization and record keeping. And, of course, there are also the personal functions of education, entertainment, and relaxation. It is largely the software you choose that allows you to perform these functions. Thus we urge you to explore further the hardware options we have already discussed *after* choosing the software tools you will need.

CRITERIA FOR CHOOSING ON-THE-GO SOFTWARE

The software for use on the road divides into two categories: (1) fully featured applications like the ones you use back at the office and (2) compact programs that save space on your portable's hard disk that you use when you're traveling. When purchasing software or loading your office applications onto a notebook computer you'll want to keep these categories in mind in order to make the most of traveling with a computer.

Programs You Use in the Office and On the Road

Everyone who has a computer employs a word processor and most businesspeople use a spreadsheet program as well. You may also use a personal information manager with a large database of contact and customer information and computerized schedule. Modern word processors like Microsoft Word and popular spreadsheet programs such as Microsoft Excel and Lotus 1-2-3 tend to be quite large. If you want to use a number of these full-featured programs, it may take up too much room on your notebook's hard disk. Before you add too many programs, consider the room you need for other software and data files. Use the full-featured programs that you use at the office only if you really have room for them or choose the program that is most important to you and install that one on your hard drive, and then choose more compact but capable programs for your other applications. For example, if you are a journalist, you may want a full-featured word processor—but you need a spreadsheet program only on rare occasions for simple budgets. In that case, take along the trusted word processor used on your desktop computer and choose a pared down version of a spreadsheet program.

Here is our guideline for program selection: If you spend more than 50 percent of your working time on your computer with a single program, put it on your computer, even if it's quite large. The reasons for this are simple: You already know this program intimately so there's no learning curve. It offers all of the features you are accustomed to having, and there's no data translation necessary when going from your notebook computer to a desktop system because the same program is used both places.

Making These Monsters Fit

Even if you decide to use the same programs on the road that you use at the home office, it doesn't mean that you have to install all 15MB of Microsoft Word for Windows, for example, on your notebook computer. Instead use the program's minimum configuration available though the software's installer program or strip out unnecessary files yourself. If the minimum configuration option is not available when you start the installer program, look for Customize and choose Quick Install or Easy Install. This choice allows you to place only what you want or need on the hard disk.

✈ How to Save Space

Both Windows and the Macintosh operating system can waste many megabytes of precious hard disk space by installing everything but the kitchen sink. With Windows, install only the screensavers, games, wallpapers, and accessories that you really need (if any). On the Mac, choose Custom Install from the Installer's Windows and select only the system for the model you are using and printer and network drivers that you require. Power PC users can delete some of the DOS functions, README files, and help files from its directory as well because many of these never get used.

In a large program there's no need to install the sample files, the tutorial, or extra functions as long as the program can work without them. So, to minimally install a word processor, install the program and the spelling dictionary, but leave out the help files, the massive grammar checker files (unless you can't live without this function), any README files, and the Thesaurus, if you don't use it very often. If the program installs its own installer on your hard disk (common), erase it. PC users: Many DOS and Windows programs also add a host of fonts to your hard disk that can be removed. Extra printer and display drivers can be deleted as well. Only one driver is required that matches your system for each program under DOS, and most Windows users have absolutely no use for these files, so they should be deleted. Of course, if you have a large-capacity hard drive in your notebook computer, all these concerns about program size are less relevant.

Integrated Programs

When traveling you may use software that doesn't get used back at the office. Typical examples include communications and faxing software, games and entertainment packages, and online road maps to guide you on your travels. The exact mix software will depend on your needs and how you travel. After adding one or two full-function programs to your hard drive that you use for the majority of your work, you may still need other software to handle less frequent chores, or you may only use a word processor to dash off a memo or two. To address these needs, a number of companies make multipurpose programs called integrated software.

Because of convenience, compact size, and flexibility, many notebook users choose to use an integrated program that offers multiple applications in one package. These programs include Claris Works, Microsoft Works, CA-Simply Business, and many others. The individual modules may have fewer overall functions than their standalone program counterparts, but the good ones are quite capable for performing all but the most complex computing requirements.

A typical Swiss army knife package is ideal for use on the road because typical ones contain a word processor, spreadsheet program, communications package, database, and even feature simplified drawing tools for doodling while traveling. Some even contain scheduling and client management tools. Almost all mobile travelers will want to purchase some kind of integrated system. Typically the applications are easy to learn because they all work in similar ways and share commands for printing, layout, and set-up. The programs are usually more compact than choosing five or more standalone programs with similar functionality.

The combination of modules and functions in an integrated program varies considerably from product to product—as does the ease of use and ability to share data between the modules. Select the program with the set of functions most important to your work.

If you decide that an integrated program is right for your work on the road (and we recommend these programs to most people who are just starting out with their mobile offices because of the flexibility), then make sure the programs are able to exchange data directly with your full-featured programs at the home office. For example, Microsoft Works can share word processing files with Microsoft Word and spreadsheet files with Excel. The data exchange compatibilities for the programs should be listed in the sales literature or on the packaging. If they aren't, choose another program.

✈ Bugsville

In our experience, one of the downsides of many integrated software packages on both PCs and Macs is that they have errors in their code that make them crash or freeze unexpectedly. Before purchasing one of these programs, find someone who uses it (preferable using all of its functions) and check with them on the software's stability.

Software Selection Criteria

When selecting software for use on the road, you should use mostly the same criteria you would use for selecting any computer software. But, with the exception of one or two large applications that you use at the office and can't live without on your portable computer, there are additional criteria for selecting the programs you'll travel with. You want software that is more compact than a program you might add to an office computer, and it helps if the software opens quickly rather than chugging along for a minute or so with the hourglass or watch on the screen as do larger packages. Since the files you create with this software may need to be imported to office-based software, look for compatibility between office-based software and office-on-the-go software.

Another important criterion is that the package be intuitive to use. Don't use programs with cryptic commands and strange operations sequences that send you scurrying to the manual for help. A well designed program under Windows or on the Macintosh should be easy enough to understand without requiring a trip to the instruction manual. The reason for this is obvious— four or five programs would require you to tote seven to ten pounds of instruction manuals on your travels. Looking things up wastes time and makes work all that more wearisome.

✈ Help!

When choosing software for use on the road, carefully check out the product's online help function. A well-designed help system can eliminate the need to bring along the instruction manual, making your travel "load" much lighter. Forgetting even one command can be a roadblock to working on the road. Pay special attention to the help system's command information because commands are often the easiest to forget, especially in MS-DOS programs.

THE BASIC SOFTWARE OPTIONS

The basic software that most travelers rely on includes old standbys: Word processors, spreadsheets, and databases containing prospect and customer information. This kind of software is well known by almost anyone who works on a computer so we won't go into it here. Instead, we'll discuss the software that is more germane to maintaining productivity on the road. We'll also look at a key piece of software that is a database of sorts—the personal information manager (PIM). This tool can be like traveling with an administrative assistant. The right PIM, configured to your needs, is always there to help you schedule your activities, find customer information, and keep track of to-do lists. In the new PDAs and some notebook computers, the software functions of a PIM are integrated with the hardware system.

Communication Programs

Communication is vital to life on the road. Communication programs work with your modem and are used to keep in touch, for entertainment, and for research on your company's database or through data supplied by online services. Most mobile office professionals use their computers for some kind of communications. They may send and receive electronic mail (E-mail) from their office, read the latest news on online services like CompuServe, Prodigy, and America Online, or send faxes of documents created on their computer.

The choice of telecommunications program is both easy and difficult because the communications module of an integrated software package or one thrown in with the purchase of a modem can do almost everything an expensive communications application can achieve. The difference lies in the program's abilities to log you on automatically to an electronic mail system with a single command (called macros) that handles the four to ten commands normally required for such a feat. An inexpensive program makes you do all the steps every time you log on. That's fine for the occasional user, but for someone who must "pick up" their electronic mail ten times a day while on the road, this can be an irritating inconvenience.

There are other differences between communications programs to consider. Expensive programs include better error checking capabilities and support more of the many communications models (called protocols) of which there are a large number. Popular protocols include ZMODEM, XMODEM, and Kermit. Generally, basic electronic mail and online services use the software's default setting for protocols, but if you plan to dig through files connected to a mainframe, you may need to choose the right protocol first and that means having a communications program that supports the communications model you require. Check with the mainframe operator in your company for more information on this.

Do You Need to Buy an Expensive Communications Program?

Generally, if your needs are limited to occasional access, almost any telecommunications program will do. The software that came with your modem or the communications module included in your integrated software package will suffice. Shareware products such as ProComm are also available from online services and user groups. The better of these products support the ability to automatically log on and they may also feature several modem protocols. Most modern programs support larger phone books than the ones of yesterday. This is useful for travelers who must log onto several systems or access their company's computer via different local access numbers as they travel. The frequently called numbers are simply entered into the phonebook for future use.

If you plan to run at a very fast 14,400 bps or access a mainframe with a quirky communications interface, a dedicated telecommunications program is a must. Choose a professional-level package such as for ProComm (PC) or Microphone (Mac) for such jobs.

Messaging Systems and Electronic Mail

Keeping in touch while on the road is vital for most travelers. While the phone is the easiest and most obvious vehicle for advising your office on your travels, schedule, and progress, electronic mail and messaging systems can play an important role in making your presence known. These systems are especially useful for secondary communications that don't merit a phone call or when you are working internationally in opposing time zones. For the average traveler, the electronic mail system has already been selected by the company, and using the system is simply a matter of learning the logistics of logging on and reading, creating, and replying to mail that appears in the mail box. A communications program as described in the last section and a modem are all that's required, although you may have to wrestle with the hotel's phone system to make this work, especially when traveling across international boundaries. Chapter 15 explains how to do this.

Some of the popular PC E-mail packages (some of these support Macs as well) include Microsoft Mail, QuickMail, cc:Mail, and the oddly monikered Beyond Mail and Da Vinci eMail. Other packages run on larger computers that serve big corporations. Mail packages in most organizations must be cross platform and run on PCs as well as Macs and even Sun SPARCstations. Usually, a dedicated server (a single computer that does nothing but handle the mail) is used. To read your mail in the field, you can dial up into this machine to access the latest and greatest in your in-box, or you can use a linking program to access your desktop computer to read mail, although this will usually be slower. Microsoft Mail has the handy ability to run inside Microsoft Word. This allows you to compose longer documents from within your word processor and ship them to a recipient without leaving the program.

Other Mail Options

You can send and receive E-mail directly via the office's mail network, or use someone else's mail system where you rent time or pay by the message. Examples of such systems include online services like MCI Mail where you can send and receive mail from any other subscriber. Your office (as a subscriber) can then access your mail at their convenience and reply to you. CompuServe, with its huge installed base, also allows you to send mail to all sorts of people by looking up their mailing "address" via the system. You need only know their city and name to find an address. Mail can also be sent to a variety of companies, and this system may provide technical support for software or hardware products you employ on the road. In addition, there are electronic mail products, like PageIt! (discussed in Chapter 6), that allow E-mail messages to be transmitted to pagers.

Companies such as AT&T provide EasyLink, which is another E-mail system used by large companies and SkyTel offers links which allow users to send messages to other computers or to pagers via satellite. Software and hardware add-ons are required for the SkyTel system. And everyone who has called a company or corporation within the last two years is intimately familiar with voice messaging options that most business telephone systems now provide.

Time and Client Management Tools

One of the worst things that can happen when you travel on business is to become so tired that you become disoriented and let time slip through your fingers. Jet lag, long car rides, and sleepless nights on lumpy hotel beds all contribute to baggy eyes and a state of inertia that is neither productive or restful. You can avoid this problem by using a calendar program or personal information manager to schedule your time to help you keep track of tasks and appointments. The choice of one of these programs should be made very carefully because they vary somewhat in what they're best at and one may match your personality better than another.

Calendar Programs

Calendar programs are used to keep track of events and activities, much like a conventional book-based calendar. But, being electronic, these programs can remind you of upcoming appointments, warn you when you've missed a meeting, and even print your schedule on paper so that you can put it in your organizer. Most calendar programs (at least the ones you should be using) track recurring events such as weekly meetings and annual events such as birthdays, presenting you with a timely reminder of important dates and events.

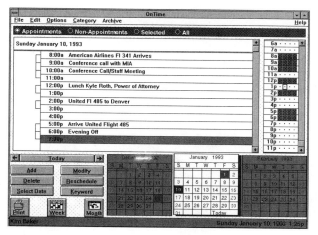

On Time, one of the handy calendar and scheduling programs that runs under Windows and on the Macintosh, is typical of the capable programs for scheduling your time on the road. It, like others, is so easy to use you probably never need to crack open the user manual.

Client Management Tools and PIMs

Electronic Rolodexes and address books have been a part of the personal computer scene almost since Day One. Now they have matured into very powerful packages called personal information managers. These programs have largely replaced standalone databases for keeping track of clients although many people still use database programs such as FoxBase for this purpose. Your company may already use a database for managing clients. If so, you'll be saddled with this instead of a more versatile PIM. PIMs are more sophisticated than calendar programs, with many features and diverse functions. They are also larger programs than calendar packages on your hard disk and when in memory. Since many PIMs are tied to database-type information, when fully loaded with client data and personal information, PIM files can be quite large. A typical PIM contains a calendar system, contact management capabilities, and an electronic repository for personal information. Some PIMs almost resemble simplified project management software; others are strong at maintaining data of all sorts, with the ability to edit and save large blocks of text (like a mini-word processor).

✈ On-the-Go Finances

One of the onerous tasks of traveling on business is keeping track of expenses. Many travelers spend their first day back in the office after a trip hunting down misplaced receipts and filling out expense reports. If this sounds like you, consider choosing a PIM that handles this task for you. With a PIM handling the expenses, while perusing your calendar in the evening or before breakfast, you can quickly log the day's receipts and print detailed reports on your trip when you get back to the office that will satisfy even the most particular boss or finance department manager.

On the PC side, PackRat is a well-rounded PIM that, despite its unpromising name, is a very elegant tool for tracking everything down—from your trip's phone calls to your personal finances. For those wavering between an easy-to-use calendar program and a PIM, PackRat offers a beginner's mode that makes the program work more like a calendar program at first. Then as you get comfortable, you can switch to Normal mode with its much larger feature set.

On the Mac side, After Hours' Datebook when used together with the same company's Touchbase makes a powerful PIM system. These programs track time, calendar events, contact management, and even print calendar pages in either DayTimer and Filofax formats. They allow you to keep track of other information as well by providing a text import and export feature that's handy for keeping track of information relevant for an upcoming meeting or appointment.

PIM or Calendar Program—Which Is Right for You?

If you're new to computers and don't handle that many client accounts, a calendar program is the easiest to learn and use. Start out with one and then later buy a PIM after you feel completely comfortable with electronic scheduling. If you're a more experienced computer user or someone with a hoard of clients to manage and a lot of data on each client account, a PIM is the only way to go. Choose your PIM based on time spent with each program at a dealer if possible or at least an extended session with the program's instruction manual. This will allow you to evaluate the program's functionality and ease of use. You will find that some of the programs meet your needs and lend themselves to your style of working better than others. Since your PIM is so important to working on the road, take the time to choose the one that's right for you. There are many programs listed in the resources section to get you started on your search.

On-the-Go Reporting and Publishing

One of the most persuasive sales techniques for winning over new customers is to assemble a report overnight. For example, let's say you had a long meeting with a prospective client and went back to your hotel room with another meeting scheduled for early the next day. Then to the astonishment of your clients, who know you're billeted at the local Holiday Inn, you pull a multipage proposal or report from your briefcase complete with white binding and a color cover featuring their logo! As they carefully flip the pages, you know you've clinched the deal. But how did you do it?

A mixture of preparedness, tenacity, knowledge, and drive to close the deal without needing to make yet another trip out to this customer site. First, part of the document exists as boilerplate on your hard disk along with a scan of the client's logo. You prepare the report and make the type look nice and print it on a 360-dpi (dots per inch) ink jet printer. The financials were created in your spreadsheet program and pasted into your document.

The color cover is prepared within the word processor in which you import their logo, change its color, and add a title. Then you print the cover on the same printer now equipped with a color ink jet print head. Last, for the binding and clear plastic protective covers, either you cheat by running down to the local 24-hour copy center, or if you're traveling by car, you carry GBC's smallest binding system (about 15 inches long and 5 inches high and deep) and a box of colored binding combs for just this purpose.

✈ How to Keep Technically Supported

One list you should add to your mobile computer in your PIM or organizer is the phone numbers for each software company's support department. That way, should you need help while on the go, you can call in for technical help from your cellular phone or pay phone. In addition to the phone number, note your copy's serial number as well, as this is often the first thing support people ask for after saying "Hello."

The software for such a venture consists of a high-end word processor such as WordPerfect or Microsoft Word (both are available for Windows and for the Mac). A single powerful program can be used to create a sophisticated document without much technical expertise, and a tiny color printer can perform wonders to dress up your report.

OTHER SOFTWARE

There are many specific software applications that you might use on the road depending on your profession. For example, an auditor might use barcode software for checking inventory and equipment on a remote site. Or a group of accountants might do financial analysis with advanced financial software using notebook computers networked together in the boardroom. There is software out there for almost any application— you just have to look for it. Here are some general software products that we recommend to almost everyone on the road.

✈ The Talking Moose

Er ... well, it's not exactly a productivity tool, but it can make your trip more fun and keep you smiling while camping out in a hotel. We're talking about The Talking Moose which is available for Apple's Macintosh and PowerBook computers with their built-in sound capability and speakers. The Talking Moose speaks to you after a given period of inactivity and when you start or shut down your computer. His choice of odd phrases (he sounds something like Bullwinkle Moose) is frequently timely and certainly a way to break the silence of a dreary hotel room. On starting our PowerBook, we have been greeted with, "You're here at last." Shutdown sometimes brings, "Live long and prosper" or "Farewell and thanks for all the fish." Other phrases have the Moose fixing a loose RAM chip in the computer with a hammer. A separate routine, MooseProof, can read text with the animated moose speaking your memos and reports. It is especially entertaining to have the Moose read your electronic mail out loud after a long day on the road. Even the most scathing memo from your boss acquires a new levity.

Roadmapping Software

While traveling by car to unfamiliar cities, even the most experienced travelers find themselves thoroughly lost on occasion. Buying a roadmap helps, but what if you can't find a store? And for the traveler who lives on the road going from city to city, an armload of maps is awkward at best. Now, programs such as Automap make life easier because you can install reasonably detailed maps of the entire country (or another country) on your notebook computer and let the program tell you where you are and how to get to where you want to be. The software shows you what signs to look for and computes distances along while showing you the quickest route from point A to point B. With this product and a little luck, you'll never get lost again.

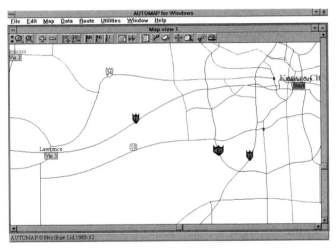

AutoMap for Windows—Maps and info on the go

Maintenance and Utility Software

You must carefully protect your computer's hard disk contents because losing this information could ruin your entire trip. Make regular backups via floppy disks for key files or use backup software for the job for large files. The easiest way to make workable backups that fit comfortably on a few disks is to use a compression program such as PKZip (PC) or StuffIt (Mac) to shrink files and then copy them to your backup media. Vital files should be further protected by sending them to your office PC via linking software on a daily basis. Remember, your machine could get lost or stolen and the data would be lost with it unless you back up the files. To prevent loss of data by theft, store your back up disks away from your computer and carry them with you whenever possible. To protect your data further, use virus detection software and keep it up to date!

This chapter has examined the basic business-oriented software for running your office on the go. In the next chapter we'll look at advanced technologies (both hardware and software) for your mobile office that you may want to consider.

8

ADVANCED MOBILE OFFICE
TECHNOLOGIES FOR THE
FULLY-WIRED TRAVELER

In this chapter we'll profile technologies with advanced functionality that not every mobile professional requires. For example, almost all readers will require communications and workstation technology (cellular phones and notebook computers), but not everyone will require sophisticated market mapping software systems for evaluating national and international market penetration or analyzing delivery routes from airports to clients. The chapter profiles other powerhouse technologies as well. For example, there are new portable digital cameras that allow readers to take photos of products, job sites, and the competition and then input the images into a notebook computer for instant integration into presentations, reports, faxes, and databases.

CD-ROM TECHNOLOGY

A CD-ROM is a computer version of the compact disks used to play music that can store massive amounts of information. These silver platters are becoming a popular medium for storing large amounts of data and picture files which tend to be quite large. CD-ROMs are available containing encyclopedias, dictionaries, the complete 1990 census (yes, they do hold a lot of information...), and a variety of games and software. You may want to add a portable ROM player to your mobile office to take advantage of this convenient new media. Some of the new notebooks and PDAs offer a CD-ROM drive instead of a floppy disk drive. Prices have fallen sharply for ROM drives and a host of new CD titles are entering the market. One downside: not many battery-operated CD-ROM drives are available, although this deficiency, we hope, will be addressed as the units come down in both size and price.

✈ MarketPlace: Market Research on the Go!

Data that would choke an ordinary hard drive fits with room to spare on a CD-ROM. One of the more interesting CD-ROM titles is called MarketPlace—a ROM that contains information on almost every company large enough to have a business credit record with Dun & Bradstreet. (The ROM contains information on approximately seven million businesses.) MarketPlace is a subscription ROM in which the manufacturer sends you a new disk with updated information several times a year. Information on MarketPlace includes the name, address, telephone number, Standard Industrial Classification, principal officer, annual revenue, number of employees, and other information on listed businesses. MarketPlace is the perfect tool for the traveling salesperson looking to make contacts on the go. The data contained in this ROM can also be used to feed market mapping software explained later in the chapter.

ACCESSING YOUR COMPUTER AND NETWORK BACK AT THE OFFICE

One of the most useful functions for the mobile traveler is the ability to access the office computer or network while traveling. Linking software is available from many companies that allow you to run your desktop PC from a telephone anywhere in the world. This is especially handy for E-mail and for retrieving a file that you didn't bring with you because you "knew" you'd have no use for it. Programs such as Norton pcAnywhere or CarbonCopy for Windows allow you to run your desktop PC as though your were sitting at its keyboard. For simple PC to PC file exchange, LapLink Pro is another alternative.

Apple's PowerBooks ship free with a routine that allows you not only access to your office Mac but the entire Macintosh network at the office. The ability to get at your office computer is handy for grabbing data files, adding software that you didn't know you'd need, looking up a memo or letter, or dumping files from your notebook's overpopulated hard disk. You can even run a database on your office computer to look up a customer's name, address, and account credit status that you need. These packages usually ship as a two-pack, one copy of the software for each machine. Some packages also ship with a modem, and obviously both machines will require one to exchange files. Keep in mind that communications of this kind is slow, even with the fastest modems, but it's superior to a trek back to the office to grab a "must have" file.

Getting Turned On

Linking programs are great, but what can you do to turn on your office PC or Mac? There are three ways to do this. The third method is by far the most elegant:

- Leave your office PC on while you travel and connect a timer to its power cord that turns it on once a day when you might need to access it and then turns it off. Make sure that any peripherals turn on as well or your machine may fail to start up.

- Call a co-worker and tell him or her to kick your machine on for an hour or so.

- Buy a remote control computer switch, such as PowerKey Remote that turns the machine on when you phone in. Several companies make these systems and they work well.

Hooking into the LAN at Work or on the Road

In most companies today the desktop computers are linked together in a network called a local area network (LAN). LANs allow you to share programs, data, printers, fax machines, and other devices to hook into the network. To access the LAN a special network interface card is required, along with cables to connect to the network.

Most notebook computers do not have slots for installing a network interface card. (If you use a dockable system, the desk-based unit should have the required slot for the network, but that doesn't do you much good if you are in someone else's office.) Fortunately, if you want to use a LAN in your office or on the road, a number of companies have developed LAN adapters that attach to a PC-compatible parallel port or a proprietary bus port on the back of some notebooks. There are adapters for the most common type of LANs, including Arcnet, Ethernet, and token ring networks. These units are typically the size of a cigarette pack and are an attractive alternative to expensive docking stations for many people.

If you want to get files on and off the LAN at work quickly, or if you want to use the LANs in other offices, one of these devices might be the perfect solution.

USING THE MOBILE OFFICE AS A PRESENTATION TOOL

One of the most interesting ways to make presentations to clients and other branches of your organization is to create a complete computer-based presentation that runs itself. A presentation can incorporate graphics, color, and even sound to make it more engaging to sit through. For single client presentations (one-to-one across a desk or over lunch), the presentation can query the client as it runs as to what he or she wants to see next, or the presenter can choose the topics most germane to the presentation, selecting only the relevant sections from a larger repartee.

Presentation Options

There are a few ways you can make your computer presentation with some options being far easier to transport and assemble than others. Hardware (notebook computer and other devices) for presentations is generally more expensive than is required for the ordinary business traveler. But the right presentation can make the rest of your job easier if it includes closing a deal or convincing others to make a decision in your favor.

The Basic Computer Presentation

The easiest-to-manage presentation runs on a color or black and white notebook and works very much like a presentation that is made in conference rooms across America via an overhead projector and foils. In fact, you can connect a device to your computer which is placed over the overhead projector's bed to project the contents of your computer's screen. Such a presentation can be more interesting than a crude overhead display created with photocopied foils because you can animate the movement of type and add graphs and charts that assemble themselves on screen while your clients watch. Other output options include color output to a projection television, but this is a large device to carry with you and not every stop on your journey will have a compatible projection system set up.

Add Sound and Music

Sound capabilities can be added to some PCs and will most likely become standard before long. Apple's

PowerBook notebooks have this capability built in. You can add music and spoken works to your presentations to jazz them up considerably, although you'll have to travel with some kind of small loudspeakers with built-in amplifiers instead of relying on the tinny-sounding speaker in a notebook computer. To support the addition of sound, you'll need presentation or multimedia software that can handle more than just graphics. (This is discussed later in this section.)

Make It a Real Dog and Pony Show

Visits to a major account may require something just short of spectacular to make an impression. If you don't blow them away, your competition may do it for you. A real spectacle requires a computer-driven projection television (supplied by you if necessary—you can rent them in every city), a full-range sound system that gives the narration and music more impact than can mobile speaker systems, and the use of advanced multimedia software that makes the presentation truly compelling.

Assembling such a presentation will require the services of a professional and that will cost you, but if it closes several $10 million deals or convinces a board of directors to fund a major new product or corporate division, then a hundred thousand spent on the show and equipment is chicken feed in comparison to the results.

Market Mapping Presentations

Desktop mapping is one of the hot new data visualization technologies of the 1990s. Mapping software takes incongruent facts and data and then presents them in a map format that makes the toughest marketing decisions a piece of cake. When it comes to choosing a new location for a business, analyzing complex customer demographics, or choosing advertising venues, there is nothing like market mapping technology.

Mapping software can be a significant presentational tool. As you run the mapping program at a customer site on your computer or through a projection system, your customer can try a variety of "what if" scenarios in which the maps reveal answers to each question right before their very eyes.

There Are Two Kinds of Presentation Software

If you plan to dazzle your clients with a presentation that runs from your computer, you'll need software to make it run. Presentation software comes in two forms—multimedia software and presentation programs for slide shows such as Persuasion and PowerPoint. Multimedia software is large and complicated. Most programs require a professional to design a strong presentation because the learning curve is steep even for the newer easier-to-use programs.

Presentation software, while not capable of the level of stunning presentations possible with multimedia programs, offers a much easier alternative. You can most likely assemble a basic presentation without too much experience with the product. But really professional presentations take at least some aptitude with type and design, and presentations incorporating color and images are the most attractive, but not as easy to assemble.

Most presentation software comes with a number of attractive black and white and color templates that let you type over the sample copy to create a professional presentation.

Assembling an adequate presentation with multimedia software is more like putting together a TV commercial where you play the roles of scriptwriter, production designer, director, art designer, soundman, key grip, best boy, composer, studio orchestra, cutting room editor, sound editor, producer, and special effects animator. These are all special skills that you may lack—although a multimedia specialist can fulfill most of these roles with only one or two outsiders to take care of special needs, such as animation or music production.

MARKETING MAPPING SOFTWARE

We just introduced one of the most powerful tools for working while on the road—market mapping software, also known as desktop mapping software, as potential programs for making presentations. These mapping programs allow you to do more than make pretty maps, however. With them, you can study complex data and statistical information in a visual, geographic format that makes complex data relationships easy to understand. For example, if your job is to visit cities and towns and look for new locations for a chain of hamburger outlets, you can assemble a map that instantly shows you the best locations at the lowest price. You can then drive to the sites and choose the right one with little further research. To assemble the map, you might purchase data that shows the locations of competing burger emporiums, which streets are the busiest, and which lots are available within the part of the city you're most interested in. Then, using the software, you will see a comparison of the available locations and where the competition is already located. You can instantly identify which locations look the most promising based on adequate street traffic.

Packages that can carry out this kind of work consist of Tactician from Tactics International, Atlas GIS and Atlas Pro from Strategic Mapping, MapInfo from MapInfo Corp., and Scan/US from Scan/US, Inc., to name but a few. This software (with the required data) can be expensive and has a learning curve associated with it, but for someone who studies markets, locations, or trends, it's worth every penny. For more information on market mapping applications in business, pick up a copy of our book, *Market Mapping: How to Use Revolutionary New Software to Find, Analyze, and Keep Customers* (McGraw-Hill, 1993).

OTHER ADVANCED TECHNOLOGIES FOR THE OFFICE ON THE GO

The variety of technologies that can make the mobile professional more productive on the road are endless. Some are highly specialized, but as you read this section, you may see something that brings out the response, "Oh, I could use one of those!" Remember, the rule of balance discussed in Chapter 1—evaluate your need before adding new tools and technologies to your load. Otherwise, carrying all your equipment and useful gadgets may force you into traveling in a 32-foot motor home instead via plane or passenger car. (One senior sales representative we met on the road does just that. He dislikes hotel rooms and is paranoid about planes, so he travels with his cats, computer equipment, and large boxes of samples and crisscrosses the continent in a luxurious, top-of-the-line motor home.) Once in a while, some tool will come along that's worth a corner in your briefcase or suitcase. Always study your load carefully. Are you lugging around some "vital" unit that never gets used? If so, don't pack it next time. Use the space for a tool that counts!

Portable Copiers, Cameras, and Video Options

A portable photocopier? Yes, there is one—although it won't handle five hundred copies of the latest marketing proposal. Instead this machine (available from Radio Shack and other sources) copies a 4-inch wide image and outputs continuous photocopies from a roll of narrow paper. While this may sound useless initially, this machine is fully capable of copying a standard column of text in a book, most reports, newspaper and trade press articles, and photographic prints. The machine is very handy for "grabbing" information while on the go. You can also copy articles and competitors' ads from magazines and newspapers, and the "photocopier" is not much bigger than your hand.

✈ Handheld Scanners

*If you have a large capacity hard disk on your notebook comput-
er, Caere's Typist or other handheld scanner can capture
information just as the handheld copier does, except the copy is
stored on disk instead of printed on paper. You can copy photos,
handwritten notes, competitor's ads, checks, and text from any
source while on the go. These can then be printed on your
portable printer or stored until you get back to the office. But
there's another plus: You can use this machine's optical character recognition capabilities to convert scanned text (not
handwriting) directly into word processing text. The converted
text can then be inserted into reports and databases or stored in
your PIM.*

Pictures on the Road

When traveling, you may need to record image
data (photographs) of prospective building sites, competitor's trade show booths, company property, or if you
work in law enforcement, evidence and confiscated property. Several options exist that make this easier and
allow you to transmit your data to your computer for
inclusion in reports and paperwork.

Small electronic cameras have already entered the
market that instead of shooting 35mm film, capture your
image the same way a computer scanner does, as a
scanned image. The resulting computer file can then be
placed in a word processing document or page layout
program, added to a presentation in PowerPoint or
Persuasion, or placed in a database that accepts pictures for later recall. While these cameras are somewhat
limited in their ability to capture quality images (unless
you purchase the multithousand dollar Sony unit),
instant computer compatibility and the ability to bypass
film processing charges and hassles make this a useful
medium when working on the road. Digital cameras are
also compact and easy to carry.

Another option is the use of frame grabber technology. Video camcorders are used to record footage of

everything from used yachts to homes to police evidence. Traveling with a tiny 8mm video camera allows you to capture long sequences of detailed information. (A picture is frequently worth a thousand words.) Once you shoot a video on location, a board can be added to your desktop computer (or to any portable computer with an expansion slot) that can capture frames of video. The captured image can then be used as a digital scan for placement in any program capable of accepting images (many word processors, page layout programs, presentation software, some databases) or printed to a black and white or color printer.

Another new option is Kodak's Photo CD technology, which allows conventional 35mm images to be scanned at a shop offering this service and recorded on a CD-ROM. The resulting images are directly compatible with your computer if you have a late model CD-ROM drive and can be used in the same software that accepts images from electronic cameras, handheld scanners, and frame grabber boards.

Mailing Services

Want to mail to fifty customers important news on a product from a hotel room? In addition to sending E-Mail, services such as MCI Mail allow you to log on to their system, send in the text of your letter, and send in the addresses of the recipients, and the mailing service will print physical copies of your electronic letter, each addressed to a person on your mailing list.

This kind of service is especially useful for traveling salespeople. Each time you get a referral to another potential customer or identify a likely candidate located in city that's later on your travel itinerary, dash off a letter to them explaining your product or service and let them know you'll be coming to town in a few days and would like to meet with them. Then follow up a couple of days later with a phone call. Your prospect will already know who you are and what you're selling, which is a superior alternative to a cold-call when you breeze into town.

Microfiche on the Road

As anyone who has ever perused a piece of microfiche knows, massive amounts of printed information can fit on a small, index card-size piece of durable film. Microfiche is a real boon on the road for the mobile professional who must carry vast amounts of densely packed information. But traditional microfiche readers are large, clumsy devices that take up about as much room as a passenger in a rental car. Fortunately, there is an alternative that makes "feesh" (as it's generally known) compatible with travel. Several companies make small microfiche readers. We've even seen a miniature microscope that fit around a sheet of fiche to read the data. Unfortunately, the diligent worker who was using it didn't know where it came from and the unit had no visible name, model number, or company of origin. Oh well, we'll keep our eyes out for the specifics for the next edition of the book.

Talking in Tongues

As international business has become more important, more pocket-size language translators have begun to appear in business stores, department stores, and even supermarkets. Most of these translation devices resemble pocket calculators. In addition, most of the most popular electronic organizers have plug-in modules for language translation.

These electronic systems vary greatly in their usefulness. Some devices handle only one language and others offer common phrases in five or more languages on one card or device. Unfortunately, these systems while useful are limited. Everyone has heard of the computer translation routine that when demonstrated to a high ranking delegation of visitors took the English input of "See no evil, speak no evil," and translated it into Chinese. Then, because no one in the delegation could read the Chinese, the results were translated back into English, except that the results read something along the lines of, "Unspeakable idiot." Well, some electronic translations by these pocket-sized translators are even less intelligent.

There are a few basic formats available in the electronic translators on the market today:

1. Phrase-only translation systems. These are best if you have no knowledge of the target language and need to use standard phrases for getting from place to place and ordering meals.

2. Word-only translation systems. These are like electronic dictionaries and are most useful if you have some knowledge of the syntax and pronunciation of the language, but only a limited vocabulary.

3. Combination systems. These translate both words and phrases.

If you buy an electronic translator, look for one that not only translates "survival phrases" ("Where is the bathroom?" or "Where can I find a doctor?") but a range of other phrases as well. If you get one with dictionary functions, evaluate the number and range of words contained. Some contain many more words and/or phrases than others. Obviously the more words, the better.

Look for a system that works both ways as well—from English to the target language and in reverse, from the target language back into English. Also, look for one that writes the phrases on-screen using both standard English characters and the local alphabet or writing system. In this way, if people can't understand your pronunciation of the phrase, they can read it on the screen to get the message. And if the system works in reverse, they can use the system to hold an electronic "conversation" with you. Of course, if you're going to be traveling to the same country frequently, we recommend that you get some language training tapes to listen to in your car and on the plane trips or one of the computer-aided language courses available that will run on your notebook computer. In the long run, your business will go better if you pick up some of the native language on your own, and your trips overseas will be more interesting as well, because you'll understand more of the things going on around you.

Scientific and Engineering Calculators for Notebook Computers

Electronic calculators have been around a long time, although the latest and greatest are far more powerful than they once were. A basic model is included with both Windows and the Mac's operating software. Otherwise, buy a sophisticated math or engineering calculation program for your notebook computer. Programs are available that allow you to design your own calculator with whatever scientific or engineering functions you need on your computer. Your finished calculator appears on-screen complete with buttons you operate with the mouse or with the numeric keys on your keyboard. Results are displayed on the pseudo-machine's display and using Window's or the Mac's operating system, you can cut, copy, or paste numbers into spreadsheet or word processing documents as you work. One of these programs received an ecstatic review proclaiming it to be "nerd heaven."

This is but a sample of some of the many tools that may prove to be of special use to you on the road. We left out some of the more esoteric handy on-the-road devices such as one that measures room sizes through ultrasonic waves that anyone working in property management would die for and skipped a discussion on how you can design custom machine parts while on the road with AutoCad and Renderman software! Just keep up with the computer magazines to discover even more specialized tools you can use on the road.

9

ONLINE
SERVICES—GATHERING
INFORMATION AND
KEEPING IN TOUCH

If you travel on business, you absolutely must get turned on to the online world, now commonly referred to as cyberspace. Once a territory embraced by computer nerds, today online services such as CompuServe, America Online, GEnie, and Prodigy have become so easy to use that anyone with a computer and modem can access them through foolproof point and click-type software and successfully navigate through the layers of functions, databases, and information. More important, through competition prices have come into line so that the formally $300+ monthly bill for long sessions online today typically range from $12 to $50—a price that more users can afford to pay. These 24-hour services can be used to send and receive electronic mail, access data when in the field to locate new customers, to keep up to date on the latest news and local weather, and for entertaining oneself. There are two kinds of online services: full-service information systems and single-service databases. We present the capabilities of the major services in each category in this chapter.

ONLINE SERVICES OVERVIEW

There are a variety of online services and they break roughly into two kinds—single-service and full-service products. We explain them because it will help you better understand the differences between the services—more of which are entering the online arena every year.

Single-Service Databases

Single service databases are usually data sources for professionals working in specific fields. For example, the Multiple Listing Service provides a large database to realtors working in specific areas of the country that list houses for sale along with locations, pricing, and feature information.

Other single-service databases include the massive Dialog system which provides access to 450+ databases described in a 122-page catalog. DIALOG offers information on everything from the world's production of coffee (COFFEELINE) to United States copyright filings from 1978 to the present.

✈ Airlines with Modem Connections

USAir recently announced that on some flights, modem communications will be available to passengers. This will let you schedule the rest of your trip through GEnie or read your E-Mail instead of taking yet another peak through the dog-eared airline magazine you read last week.

Complete issues and back issues of many industry publications and major daily newspapers are also available. Searching for an obscure article in a back issue of *The Akron Beacon Journal* or *Consumer Reports* can produce its complete text in a minute or so. Searches of such massive amounts of information and the sheer availability of so much knowledge in one place is a testament to the awesome power of the computer as a tool for research and the management of knowledge and information. The only caveat: Because this information is expensive to collect, with DIALOG and other services paying the data source a licensing or royalty fee, searches can be very expensive. (A brief search might cost about $42.00.) But, since this data helps companies do business better, the high cost is easily justified.

Full-Service Information Systems

Full-service information systems are much different from single-service systems. A typical full-service system is CompuServe, which is one of the largest of its breed, both in the amount of information and functions available as well as in the number of subscribers. CompuServe provides access (gateways) to single-service systems such as DIALOG, has its own large databases, allows you to keep up with the Associated Press' latest news, and as already mentioned, allows you to send and receive E-mail.

It also provides access to systems such as American Airline's EasySABRE for scheduling your trip on the fly. Online discussions on narrow topics such as desktop publishing are available in forums, and there is a chat line via the CB radio simulator. Forum texts are saved and edited for later retrieval from the forum's library.

These services offer all kinds of games, ranging from sophisticated interactive games you play while using the systems to smaller amusements that you can download and play at your leisure. Most full-service systems also contain a host of freeware and shareware software that handle a wide range of application need. Software manufacturers often post bug fixes to their applications on these systems to avoid the cost of mailing out thousands of floppy disks containing the fix.

There's so much on a good full-service system, you could spend your life in there if you had the time and could handle the charges! Some users describe the online experience in such a system as "being lost in Cyberspace."

Local Bulletin Boards

Every city has an array of people and organizations who run bulletin boards that function something like an online system. You access the systems and navigate through whatever services are available. Called BBSs, these systems range in sophistication from a twelve-year old's set up with an old computer and a modem to large companies that disseminate information about their products and services online. Many computer user groups offer BBS services containing information on software and hardware problems, shareware software, and classified ads where you may find used computer equipment for sale. Some merchants have online BBS systems set-up for customers to browse their wares and place orders.

Depending on the bulletin board you log onto, you may find people looking for dates and mates, crude interactive games, oddball chitchat sessions, Sherlock Holmes stories, free software, listings for local entertainment, electronic mail support (free usually), fishing information, or a dead line when Mom and Dad disconnect Junior's telephone. Most BBSs are free, although single's BBSs and ones of an "adult nature" (not uncommon) charge a subscription fee through a credit card. To find out about the BBSs available in a city, pick up the local computer newspaper (such as *Bay Area Computer Currents* in the San Francisco Bay Area). BBSs open and close on a daily basis, and there is no single, comprehensive guidebook to all of them.

ACCESSING ONLINE SYSTEMS

To access the online services you may need to dial only an access number and answer the system's questions, or with services such as America Online and Mead

Data Central's Lexis/Nexis, special software is required. Both CompuServe and Prodigy offer starter packages that allow you to work through a graphic interface to operate the system. (Most companies provide both PC and Mac versions of their software.) Starter packages are available in most computer and software stores, or you can order them directly by calling the system's phone number listed in the back of this book. These systems make navigation through the program's many features much easier for the novice user. A system like CompuServe is huge with many levels and functions to get you lost in. Therefore, the information management software they provide can make the system much friendlier.

MEET THE MAJOR ONLINE SYSTEMS

As you've seen already, there are many online systems and services available. Here we provide a description of some of the largest and most useful of these services.

CompuServe, GEnie, America Online, and Others

These full-featured information services provide a relatively similar range of services as described earlier in the section on full-service information systems. Still, the richness of individual features and functionality varies from system to system. Subscribing to one (or more) full-service systems is a must for the traveler who wants to take advantage of the sheer wealth of useful functions these systems provide, and access to airline and hotel reservation systems online is a must while on the road. Common services on a full-featured online system include electronic banking, online stock trading, educational programs, and access to special interest groups where people discuss topics of interest to you (called SIGs, these forums are available on almost any topic imaginable), electronic mail, bibliographic services, movie and book reviews, and the ever-popular CB simulators.

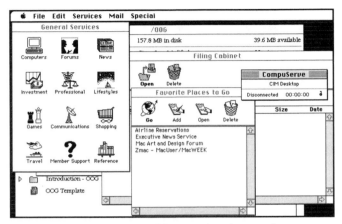

CompuServe's Information Manager is a front-end pro-
gram that makes it easier to use the system. Clicking on
any of the icons takes you into that service. For example,
double-clicking on the Travel icon opens a submenu that
allows you to choose from airline reservation systems,
visa information, state department travel advisories, and
even forums on traveling and aviation.

Many mobile professionals will find forums on these systems that cater directly to their business or skill. Note: There is a disparity of pricing in these systems with some still charging by the hour for access during daytime hours within the working week. On such systems, daytime access can amount to a major bill at the end of the month. Other systems provide a flat rate for access and then charge for certain popular services or ones that cost the service money to provide to users. We prefer the latter arrangement because the new user exploring the system doesn't have to worry about the charges for looking over the various online offerings, unless they choose to use a premium service.

Prodigy

Prodigy is a unique full-service system designed primarily for households and families. While all full-service systems provide shopping capability with mail-order delivery, in many cities Prodigy, like other services, allows you to do your holiday and gift shopping online—this is useful for the mobile professional who wants to send a birthday gift while on the road. Many of the online shopping services will wrap the gift, enclose a hand-signed card, and get the package there the next day. You can also manage your personal finances if you choose a hometown bank that is hooked into Prodigy. The system provides news and entertainment as well as games. One of its annoying features is the barrage of commercial messages that display randomly most of the time you are online. Unlike other systems, Prodigy's interface is colorful and highly graphic. It's almost fun to use, but outside of shopping, playing games, making a reservation, or getting the latest ski report from Vail, the system still lacks the depth of information resources of other full-service systems.

DIALOG and Knowledge Index

Already described as an example of a single-service database, this system is a powerhouse of information for professionals. The system is a cornucopia of all kinds of news and information, and it contains massive databases that can answer queries on topics ranging from labor laws (LABORLAW I and LABORLAW II) to providing biographical information on 3 million persons. Containing more than four hundred databases and 330,000,000 million records, DIALOG is probably the single most powerful information system on Earth.

For the home user, the Knowledge Index is available. Costing far less than DIALOG searches, this system is somewhat less capable than the full DIALOG system, but is still an awesome power source of information for after-hours browsing. DIALOG also offers the DIALOG Business Connection and DIALOG Corporate Connection for business users.

Lexis/Nexis

Mead Data Central's Lexis is a massive legal research database designed for powerhouse searches of laws, cases, and precedences. Nexis is a massive compilation of press information in which a keyword search can be used to locate all of the information in press accounts of the topic. Journalists, writers, and researchers find this system a rich source for instant research into the history of a topic, event, person, company, or trend that they plan to write about. It is also great for competitive analysis. Because the systems are relatively expensive compared to general-purpose information systems, it is important to master the searching techniques fully before going into long queries. The expense makes Nexis inappropriate for just keeping up with the news.

EasySABRE

EasySABRE is American Airline's simplified version of the powerful SABRE system used by travel agents to make reservations for airline flights, hotels, and rental cars. Like most single-service systems, you can access this system from the full-service systems or dial in directly to the single-service database. The service is available through CompuServe, Prodigy, and other information services.

NewsNet

NewsNet is a one-stop resource for keeping tabs on news as it comes off the wire from the major wire services. Services that read the system range from A (Associated Press) to X (Xinhua from the People's

Republic of China). The system also contains business news from business wires as well as six hundred plus newsletters in every type of industry. The system allows access to Dun & Bradstreet business credit reporting as well.

Dow Jones, Dun & Bradstreet, and Standard & Poor's

Business news and stock and commodity quotes are available via several online quoting systems for stock watchers. Services such as Dow Jones News Retrieval can be used to look up the latest in world and business news or to read the *Wall Street Journal* online and Dun Financial database contains financial information on more than 750,000 companies. The Dow Jones system also includes online access to the *Grolier Encyclopedia*, and you can send and receive E-mail. You can access Standard & Poor's database system through Dow Jones.

MCI Mail

Mentioned earlier in the book, MCI Mail is widely used by corporations as a way to send electronic mail from business to business and between office and employee. MCI Mail can be used a standalone E-mail service. MCI Mail addresses can also be accessed through CompuServe and other full-service online information systems. The system is not friendly to use, but if you need to communicate to other businesses on a regular basis, it's a good investment because of the sheer number of subscribers who use the system.

The Internet

The Internet is different from other online systems because it is a not-for-profit system dedicated to serving research and communications needs of educational institutions and government agencies around the world. The diversity of material available on this largely free system is surprising. The Usenet newsgroups on the Internet, a sort of quasi-conferencing system for people with shared interests, offers lively discussions of almost anything you can imagine. There are also E-mail services and diverse subject-specific databases.

A dedicated corporate connection to The Internet, meaning the connection is always open, can cost more than $1,500 a month. These connections also require that your company have a UNIX-based server to access the system. There are also a number of companies that sell affordable, private user Internet account. These allow you to log into their computers with a local telephone number that ties into a national network. InterCon's personal Internet client software for use with PSInet, called WorldLink, provides an easy-to-use interface for accessing the global network services of Internet from most major cities.

Public access systems are also available for Internet, such as Panix in New York, SuperNet Inc. in Colorado, and The Cyberspace Station in San Diego, California. Some of the public systems offer bulletin board services and local E-mail in addition to their Internet access.

The Internet is becoming the place to be—and almost everyone who is anyone on the road is a frequent visitor to Cyberspace on "the net." As a business traveler, your own Internet account is probably the way to go if you want guaranteed access from anywhere you travel.

This chapter has introduced the universe of Cyberspace—the online services that can be used to educate, inform, and delight you on the road. As a businessperson on the go, it's imperative to become a frequent Cyberspace visitor.

10

TAKING THE MOBILE
OFFICE WITH YOU—
MAKING A CASE
FOR A CASE

The basic mobile office includes the components you've read about in the last chapters—a small computer (or computer notebook alternative such as a palmtop or one of the new PDAs), cellular phone, and optional cassette-sized stereo/tape recorder and other assorted gadgets. You'll obviously need to carry these items with you when traveling in a briefcase or other compact storage system. The number and size of your office components governs the kind of case that's best, and we examine the options in this chapter.

CASES IN GENERAL

The choice of case for your office components is essentially one of form versus function—protecting your equipment and making the system easy to carry—with cosmetic concerns thrown in for good measure.

The key criteria for choosing a case for your mobile office are:

- The case should be durable and protect its contents against impact and weather. It must have quality latches (or zippers) that can't pop open.

- Special requirements require special cases. If your work includes geological field work, for example, a fancy leather briefcase is not the case for you.

- The case should be able to hold everything you will take with you on a typical trip and leave room for important incidentals such as prescription drugs that you may want to keep with you and travel documents such as tickets and passports.

- The case should not make up more than 25 percent of the total weight of your complete office (and 15 percent is better). The exception to this rule is cases that will be checked during transport—which we don't recommend unless necessary.

- The case should be compatible with your personal style of dress and grooming. You may be carrying it with you into clients' offices and meetings, so you want it to present the appropriate image.

- The case should be comfortable to hold, even when fully loaded.

- The case should not be too ostentatious, or it may catch the attention of thieves.

 Rule of the Road

Never let the case containing your office equipment out of your sight when traveling. Never check the case or allow someone to carry it to your room for you—it's too easy for it to get lost or stolen. If you have put substantial work into a project contained in your case, you may lose it as well as your possessions. Instead, keep it with you whenever possible and rest its edge on your toe when you put it down while standing in line, waiting for transportation, or in hotel lobbies. With the weight on your toe, if a sneak thief tries his craft on you (common in busy places), you will instantly notice the theft in progress and you can grab your case back or at least yell out.

In addition to these criteria, the case should match your physical stature. A 5' 2" woman weighing in at 112-pounds will look ridiculous carrying a monster 24" by 40" briefcase that weighs half as much as she does. Again, a large briefcase makes an attractive target for thieves who will wonder why such a small person is struggling to carry such a big, heavy case. If this is a problem for you, either carry fewer components or, better still, shop for the most compact tools you can buy—even though these may cost a little more. In the long run (a pun), the expense is worth it.

If you don't want to carry a traditional briefcase, there are attractive, functional mobile office cases made from nylon and other synthetic materials. Many of these are available for a fraction of the cost of a quality leather case. Available at computer stores, sporting good stores (often free with the purchase of Nikes or other sports shoes), and other outlets, many of these look like padded briefcases and can carry your equipment with no problem. Beware, however, if the bag has a handle made from the same nylon material as the bag, it may be scratchy and uncomfortable to carry, especially when heavily loaded.

There are also the trendy plastic or aluminum cases used for portfolios and notes by graphic designers and architects. These can be purchased at art supply stores and large business supply stores such as Bizmart, Office Depot, and Staples.

There are a number of different kinds to choose from. If you want the best in these cases, Zero Corporation makes aluminum cases that can be ordered with custom foam inserts to hold each component of your mobile office snugly in place. These cases can take very heavy physical abuse while protecting their precious contents like so many fragile eggs. They aren't cheap, however, and they are a bit on the heavy side for some people.

✈ Latches and Handles

In addition to the obvious construction of your case, pay special attention to the latches and handle. Many briefcase latches are made in the countries in the Orient that lack substantial quality control. As a result, the latches may pop open usually when the case is fully loaded and you're scurrying to an appointment. Handles are equally important. The handle must be comfortable to hold, especially when the case is full, and it must be securely mounted to a the case. Pay special attention to leather briefcase or combination briefcase/purse handles. Often these are designed for case containing no more than a manila folder of papers, and the weight of a notebook computer and other mobile office paraphernalia may prove too much over the long haul.

CASES FOR THE FREQUENT AND

INTERNATIONAL FLYER

If you watch lots of frequent flyers—especially those who regularly fly overseas—you'll see a lot of soft carry-all bags. The most savvy frequent fliers never check luggage—it's a waste of time. They take only one carry-all bag and a briefcase on even the longest trips. They wear their coats on the plane, so they don't waste valuable storage space in the bag. If you're still spending time waiting for luggage in crowded turnstile areas, think about getting another kind of bag.

When one of the carry-alls is empty it looks like a floppy bag (often black or brown leather) with all kinds of compartments and heavy-duty nylon zippers. Although they don't look too substantial when they're empty, they hold an inordinate amount in a small format and can keep things organized for easy retrieval. The best ones incorporate small wheels and a heavy-duty shoulder strap for carrying (or dragging) the bag in different terrain. Another advantage of these bags over other luggage is that they don't have to be checked through. The best ones are sized to meet airline on-board baggage requirements. You just take the bag with you and stow it on the plane. Because it's flexible, it can be stowed almost anywhere, even when full. The trick to making the bags work is to stuff them so they take on shape and substance. As long as you don't mind a few wrinkled shirts or blouses, you can take just about everything in one bag. As a result, there is no risk of lost or delayed luggage—which is so frequent in international travel.

Quality carry-all bags are priced from $300 to $1000. Beware of less expensive imitation bags that use a patchwork of leather (or vinyl) and cheap zippers. These imitations lack the heavy-duty construction and amenities of the more expensive bags and can't carry as much.

The ingenious design of these carry-all bags allows them to hold everything from clothes to computers and still fit under the most cramped airline seat. The best bags can hold enough clothes and technology for a two-week trip (if you pack conservatively). The bags have numerous sections and compartments, and many contain special clothes hangers that are built right into the bag. One design we reviewed has a soft pull-out briefcase that unzips from the main compartment. This allows you to shed the larger bag at your hotel before heading off to a meeting.

✈ Test Each Case "Under Load" Before Purchase

The best way to shop for a case is to take the components you plan to carry to a luggage store and stuff them into prospective cases while testing each one for comfort when carrying it. If you don't match the components to the case, you may wind up purchasing something that is too small, holds your tools awkwardly, or that comfortable in the store, but once loaded down, cuts into your hand.

These bags are found in quality leather goods shops, luggage stores, high-end department stores like Neiman Marcus, and sometimes through mail order. Avoid purchasing leather compartment bags through the mail unless there is a liberal return policy because each model is different in its construction, and some bags will fit your needs much better than others.

If you plan to shop without testing the actual components, put three or four red bricks into sealed plastic bags and place these in cases to test weight and comfort. While the salesperson may treat you like you have a screw loose, remember it's you not him or her that has to carry this case around the state, country, or world.

A final word about cases—take the same critical, needs-based approach to choosing the case for your office that you used to choose the precious contents. If you do, you're going to get a lot more done using your office on the go because the case will protect your equipment and supplies, while at the same time, keeping them organized, easy to get to, and easy to cart around.

Section Two

PUTTING
MOBILE OFFICE
TECHNOLOGY TO
WORK

11

=============================

DOING
BUSINESS ON THE
ROAD

Now that you have decided on the equipment, it's time to put the technology together with business procedures and time management skills to make the system effective in real-world situations. This chapter explains how to develop the system, process, and consistency necessary to use mobile office technologies for maximum productivity.

The fully wired businessperson travels and does business proactively instead of frittering away the time when waits between planes push most people into the "hurry up and wait mode." This kind time of wasted time is not only unproductive, but it builds stress that saps energy, creates an attitude problem, and ultimately weakens people. You, however, can effectively manage your own time on the road instead of allowing airlines and other people's schedules to do it for you. By taking control of the situation, you can turn travel into a positive experience and make your traveling time even more productive than time in the office.

There are standard places where you will find yourself when you travel: on the road, driving or as a passenger in an automobile; in the airport; in the air during your flights; in the hotel; and in client or company offices. Each of these "offices" has different work and productivity possibilities, which we describe in the next pages.

OFFICE ON THE ROAD

Time spent driving is time to spend on the cellular phone (when in range of a city system), making appointments, checking up on activity back at the office, and following-up on calls from clients. The fully wired businessperson doesn't let the phone messages pile up at the office, instead this professional responds almost as quickly as if sitting at the office desk. And in today's time-sensitive markets, returning a client's phone call may make the difference between making a sale or losing it to someone who does return the call. For important contacts, the fully wired business traveler provides them with NationLink (or other similar system) access that allows important contacts to call from anywhere in the United States where compatible cellular phone service is available. This allows a client with a problem to reach the fully-wired businessperson instead of stewing with frustration when your office tells him they don't know when you can get back in touch.

When the cellular phone readout says No Service because you're on the open road, it's time to pop in a tape or compact disk and relax to music, enjoy a story from a talking book, listen to a motivational tape, bone up on a foreign language, or study with one of The Teaching Company's great college lecture tapes. Not one minute of time needs to be wasted, though always remember that relaxation is a necessary part of life on the road.

What Your Car Should Have

If you travel in your own car or a company car that is yours for a while, install a quality tape player if the car doesn't have one. Have it hooked into a quality sound system, even if that means replacing the manufacturer's tinny- (or boomy-) sounding speakers with more expensive ones. Consider adding a compact disk system as well. (Tape and disk capability is a superior choice over tape or disk because you have two media sources instead of one.) A ten-disk compact disk changer in the trunk can provide enough soothing music and other entertainment for an eight-hour drive.

✈ Before You Leave...

Try to store every phone number you may need for simplifying dialing on your cellular phone. The best solution would be a phone that accepts spoken commands, but as explained earlier, none of the ones we've tried with this capability work adequately. Instead, they make you repeat things until you give up and end up dialing manually. Hopefully, voice recognition technology will improve over time.

You also want a hands-free cellular phone with a quality microphone as explained in Chapter 6. This may mean either purchasing an expensive dockable system or having a handheld phone and a car phone. Hands-free is the only way to use a cellular phone because you can keep your hands on the car's controls except for dialing phone numbers. A handheld phone is awkward to hold while driving, and these phones have a limited transmission range compared to a regular car phone. They lose a city's signal long before a car phone will and may fade in and out as you talk. "Dropping" calls is far more common with handheld phones as well.

Another consideration that may save you from the specter of having your mobile office set-up stolen (and maybe your entire car as well) is to install a sophisticated car alarm system. Female travelers take note: You want one with remote activation that also lets you unlock and lock the doors from a finger-size transmitter that also contains a remote panic alarm. This makes a pitstop at a rural gas station all that much more secure because you can take the transmitter with you and sound the car's horn using the system's panic button if you are accosted. This system will also attract attention if you park your car near your room at a motel or hotel and someone tries to enter your room during the night. (Make sure you park in range by unlocking and locking your car's doors from your room.)

A good car alarm costs between $250 and $600 (including installation), but that's a small expense compared to the prospect of losing your mobile office and all your work. Most alarms that come with cars at the time of purchase are not sophisticated enough, and an after-market alarm is a must.

In a Rented Car

Your options are more limited in a rental car because it's not your car to go cutting holes in the doors or deck lid for speakers or mounting a phone transmitter in the trunk. Instead, to get a decent sound system, rent one of the firm's more expensive models and insist on a car with a cassette stereo system. (More and more rental cars come with these, and some units may have a CD player as well.) If this turns out to be impractical, rely on your tiny cassette player/recorder, but you may need to bring a set of small amplified loudspeakers to provide the audio. Many states have laws against drivers wearing headphones. In California, for example, some local police departments and the highway patrol pull people over and issue tickets for this offense.

Phones are more of a problem in a rental car as well. Since you are renting the car, chances are better that you won't leave the city's cellular net so you can keep in touch with your handheld phone. But a three-watt transportable phone may be a superior option with its greater transmission power if you plan to leave the city or head for the outlying suburbs. Plug your transportable into the car's lighter because the unit's batteries won't last long at three watts transmission power. Of course, many car rental agencies also rent cellular phones for their cars.

In Other Transportation

Sometimes you'll pass on a rental car, instead taking a cab to your meeting or hotel. If you fly into the city's airport and the cab ride will be long consider taking a limousine instead. Often for only 20 percent more than the cost of cab fare you can enjoy the plush backseat of a limousine, some even fitted with a working cellular phone that will let you slip in a couple of calls (negotiate with the driver for charges). A limo is a good place to work, nap, or enjoy the ride. For a long trek from the airport, this is a superior option to the back seat of a worn and dirty taxicab with a driver who chats you up with, "What do you think of them Mets this year, eh." Look for limousines lined up at a stand near the taxi stand. Every city has more limousines than can be used, so drivers with no commitments hope for a fare at the airport. Limousines may be scarce on Friday and Saturday nights, especially during prom season.

✈ Losing Touch

When using a cellular phone in a city's outlying areas, if you begin to lose your signal, try switching to the area's other carrier by changing your phone from system A to system B or the other way around. Typically, one carrier may support an outlying area better than another. In some cities, one carrier may cover the interstate highway all the way to another city, while the second carrier covers only the city and a bay or harbor.

OFFICE IN THE AIRPORT

Airports are uncomfortable places—there's so much tension and emotion in the environment as people say good-bye to friends and colleagues. Everybody rushes, even when there's no need to hurry. While sitting in one of the lounge chairs waiting for a flight, you can almost feel the tension, and that makes it difficult to work productively. You'll probably have six things on your mind and be worrying whether your flight will be on time as well.

To get to work, don't sit in the boarding lounge. Don't even go there until you need to board your flight, because chances are you'll spend the time fidgeting instead of working. Instead, find the closest airline club and settle in. These clubs offer quiet places to think and work and provide flight information right in the club, saving you a trip outside to the monitors. The host or hostess can issue boarding passes, change your tickets, book your flights, and at some clubs, even accept your baggage for check-in. Most clubs also offer complimentary refreshments, soda pop and alcoholic drinks for a charge, and phones you can jack your modem into or use for free local phone calls. Additional services may include access to computers, fax machines, and conference facilities. Why wait in the noisy airport when for a reasonable annual fee you can work in a quiet, softly lit airline club? Join several if you fly frequently, and you'll almost always have a place to go.

What If There's No Airline Club?

While a few airports such as Seattle's Sea-Tac have installed quiet areas for work or a quick nap, most airports have no such facilities unless you can find a bankrupt airline's wing and sit in the abandoned departure lounges. Another choice in airports with no clubs, or where the clubs you are a member of are located in a distant terminal, is a quiet bar (one without a blaring television). Drink a juice or soda water if you aren't in the mood for anything else. Another possibility is one of the large cafeteria-style restaurants common in airports. When they're not busy, there's bound to be a quiet corner where you can hole up for a couple of hours with your notebook computer.

OFFICE IN THE AIR

Most people's picture of traveling while working is sitting in an airline seat in first class with a notebook computer on the tray table. But in our experience, as the prestige of owning notebook computers has worn off because prices have plummeted, most first class passengers are too busy napping or drinking to pull out the computer and tap out a memo or report. That doesn't mean that you shouldn't use yours—we encourage you to take advantage of your quiet time in the air, regardless of whether you're cramped between two Sumo wrestlers in coach or sitting up front in business or first class.

✈ Notebook and Palmtop Computers

When flying with small computers, you need to make sure that you keep track of them. Small palmtops and the shiny surface of many notebooks allow them to slide around when placed under seats. Notebooks placed in overhead bins can slide out of some kinds of bins, especially if they are placed on top of other smooth-surfaced luggage such as a briefcase. When opening a bin, do it slowly or a notebook may land on the head of the passenger underneath.

Working At 35,000 Feet

Flying can be a very productive time for work. Once on the plane, jack into the aircraft's hi-fi or use your cassette player/recorder's headphones to listen to music while you work. Even if you don't turn the music on, wearing headphones will usually discourage seatmates from bending your ear for the entire flight.

Short hauls are a great time for writing a trip report, doing expense reports, and dashing off a memo or two. A morning flight is a good time to schedule your time for the day, and once you are on the plane you will finally know how your arrival time will affect other elements of your schedule. (Until the plane leaves you really don't know how late the flight may be.) Use short flights for tasks that are not too complicated and that don't require intense concentration. Longer flights can be used productively to write reports and complete financial analyses with spreadsheets. Long hauls are better used for work that requires thought because this helps keep you alert and the flight may present a long period of "quiet time" that you rarely enjoy at the office.

Don't work the entire time on a long flight, however, or you may arrive worn out. Instead, mix work with play. Try some computer games (plug your cassette player/recorder's headphones into the headphone jack if your computer is so equipped or make sure that the sound is off otherwise). Or listen to a talking book. An exciting or well-acted book may invigorate you and get you ready for more work. A really dull one may be useful for putting you to sleep.

If you are traveling with a co-worker or boss who will effectively prevent you from working with their ceaseless chatter, make the time useful by scheduling a meeting with them during the flight. A really productive meeting can be held in the air just as well as in an office or conference room. To make this effective, schedule the meeting time formally and bring an agenda of what's to be discussed. This won't work for long flights unless you have an unusually long list of discussion points.

Unloading Undesirable Travelmates

One of the least productive arrangements is sitting next to officemates who may waste your flight with chitchat about office politics or other mundane nonsense. Avoid this problem by doing one of the following:

- Quietly call the airline and request a new seat assignment away from the one you had. If you don't have a seat in mind, choose an unlikely location at the rear of the plane. On international flights, sit in smoking if your travelmates are non-smokers if you can stand the smoke.

- Change your flights from the ones the company's travel agent assigned you. Have a reason for leaving at a different time, "I promised my wife that I would drop the kids off at day care before I left, so I'm taking a later flight."

- Upgrade (or downgrade) your tickets so you sit in another class.

- In a partially empty plane, change seats for a "better view." Look especially busy by spreading papers and equipment all over the seats next to you. This will discourage your travelmates from coming and sitting next to you when they become bored.

- Travel only with people who, like yourself, plan to work on the flight and make the time productive.

Coach, Biz Class, or First Class?

The most comfortable travel arrangement is a roomy seat in first class, but for most of us, this remains only an occasional luxury. Most of us must still sit in coach, squeezed into smaller seats than ever, as airlines scramble to "pack 'em in." The choice of class does have implications that may justify an upgrade if your budget can stand it.

Large people, tall people, and individuals with a full load of carry-on luggage should consider upgrading to business class (or first class) unless the flight is short and you can put up with the discomfort. If you are really big, flying in coach may make not only you uncomfortable, but your seatmates as well.

While upgrading is more expensive on long trips than short trips, moving from coach to business class will allow you to work and maybe catch some sleep more comfortably than back in steerage class.

Remember George Bush fainting at an important function on a visit to Japan? This is what can happen if

you have an important meeting right after a long overseas flight. Upgrade to business class so you have a
better chance of arriving rested.

✈ Beware of Charter Flights
*When traveling to Europe and other destinations, some airlines
offer charter 747 flights that cost even less than regularly scheduled flights. Before taking one of these, check to see what kind of
seating the plane offers. If it turns out to have no business class
or first class, it's an all coach flight and the seats will make a sar-
dine can look roomy in comparison. An eight hour flight on such
a plane will become torture for large people. Don't expect to get
rest or work accomplished on one of these bargain airlifts.*

Generally the cost of upgrading from business
class to first class is not as big a jump from upgrading
from a discount coach fare to business class. But what
do you get for your money? On domestic trips, the seats
are larger and many 747s and 767s have comfortable
sleeper-seats that recline and have foot rests. You also
receive better food, wines, and more selections of everything, although this is more in terms of cost of
ingredients rather than anything substantial. Business
class food is already a major step up from the meals
served in coach that too often taste like cooked cardboard.

Also important are the rest room facilities if you're
taking a long trip. First class (usually) offers large
restrooms and restricts other passengers from using
them. This is in contrast with coach, in which once the
sun rises in the morning after an all night trip, there may
be long lines to get to the tiny facilities. And this may be
hard to take early in the morning after a night of poor
sleep. These lines will wake you up as well if you happen
to be one of the passengers seated near the restrooms.
(And the airlines wonder why fewer people are flying!)

On overseas 747 flights, a carrier may actually

have four classes, with the top category offering beds and truly royal treatment. In business class and above, in most airlines you also receive handy travel kits containing eyeshades, razors, and toothbrushes (and toothpaste) so you can clean up your act before deplaning. Some other amenities, depending on the airline, include colognes, slippers, hot towels before meals, and very expensive champagne.

Frequent Flyers

Almost every airline has a frequent flyer club. You should join all of the clubs (usually free except in Canada) so that as you fly, you will earn mileage credit that will provide you with a free upgrade from coach to business or first class. Earn enough mileage and you will become a special guest of the airline and upgraded for no charge, even without accumulating enough mileage. For example, American Airlines' frequent flyer club, called the AAdvantage Club, provides free upgrades after so many miles are flown, no matter whether you or your company buys the ticket. The miles are awarded to the person whose name is on the ticket if he or she is a member of the club. Make sure that when you check in, your membership number appears on your tickets. Travel agents and ticketing personnel are often remiss in doing this, and the only other way to claim your mileage is to mail in ticket stubs with a letter.

Then, if you fly on American more than about 95 percent of the people in your home area, you receive a Gold AAvantage Club Card (we have one!), which entitles you to special booking privileges, free (or low cost) upgrades to business or first class if seats are available, and a host of other perks. For higher distance fliers there is also a platinum level that provides even more services and amenities. If you aren't a member of these organizations and you fly a lot, all we can say is, "Join the club."

✈ Don't Print in the Air

Most small printers are ink jet based and make less noise than a dot matrix printer, but their ongoing whining and other noises make your fellow passengers want to string you up if you begin printing a twenty-page document. Another reason to use care relates to a leak we once had from the print head at 32,000 feet that made a huge mess inside the printer and on our hands. Fortunately, the print head did not contain enough ink for a really serious stain on our clothes or the aircraft's seats! No one from the printer's manufacturer could explain this, but we assume that even with a pressurized cabin, the pressure inside the cabin was too low to keep the ink in place inside the moving head. Instead of printing in tiny drops, larger drops oozed out.

OFFICE AT THE INN

Almost every business traveler should set up an office on the go in the hotel room. This can be your command center as well as a home away from home. The choice of hotel is important because the right lodgings keep you productive while letting you get a good night's sleep. Never leave the choice of hotel to the company's travel agent looking for the best deal. Otherwise you may learn at 4:00 a.m. that the room backs directly on to the local commuter train line complete with flashing lights and noisy bells, as we once experienced.

The Suite Life

In our opinion, the best kind of hotel for the mobile professional is usually a suite hotel. These provide two rooms in addition to a bathroom, an arrangement that allows you to keep work in one room and relaxation in another. In other words, you can get away from your job by walking into another room. Many suite hotels provide a dining room table or small desk to make working at your computer that much more comfortable. This arrangement also works well for couples traveling. One person can go to bed early without having to listen to the TV until the other person goes to bed. And, if people hold a meeting in your room, you can keep your bedroom private by holding the meeting in the suite's living room. Since most suite hotels cater to the business traveler, they typically provide extensive business services, in addition to a free entertainment hour with complimentary cocktails and breakfast each morning.

What if There's No Suite Hotel?

Always choose a hotel that caters to business travelers instead of families on vacation. Identify hotels that have been extensively remodeled within the past five years, and that are located close to where you plan to do business. Why? Rooms in hotels that cater to families are often less expensive to rent but may be noisy and full of surprises. Older properties that have not been remodeled may not only be run down (hotel room interiors require gutting and remodeling about every four or five years) but force you to tear the phone apart if you want to hook up your computer's modem. And you might as well stay near your business to avoid making long trips back and forth to your room.

Where Not to Stay

If you notice that there are no listings for the cheapest hotel chains in the back of this book that's because we don't recommend that you stay at them. Not only are these places minimally comfortable (to put it nicely) according to a 1992 *Wall Street Journal* report, they aren't all that safe. The story reported that one of the largest chains has an appalling record for murder, rape, and robbery on its properties. You, traveling alone and carrying your mobile office equipment, could be singled out for "special" treatment. Women should be especially careful if forced to stay in one of these places. Be careful after dark, and keep the door locked at all times. If you feel especially vulnerable, nudge the room's bureau (if it's not nailed to the floor) in front of the front door. Position it so that should an emergency arise you can still get the door open quickly.

✈ Bring Your Smoke Detector

When traveling, especially if you will be staying at cheap hotels, bring a smoke detector and possibly a burglar alarm that trips if someone tries to enter your room. Some cheaper hotels, in violation of state laws, have no smoke detectors, or they may be present but equipped with dead batteries.

Be Careful About Airport Hotels

For easy access to the airport there are many hotels that cater to business travelers located at the airport. Before booking one of these make sure it's not directly *under* the glide path as was one we spent a sleepless night in at Dallas/Ft. Worth. The hotel's corporate headquarters later sent an apology when we complained that said everything we objected to had been rectified. We assume they dug up the twelve-story hotel and moved it to a quieter location or made the airport close its runways at night.

Working in a Hotel Room

For the fully wired business traveler, a comfortable hotel is as close to an office as you can get. If your stay will be for more than a night, enjoy the luxury of spreading your computer and papers out on the desk or dining room table in your suite. Hang up your clothes, fresh for the morning. Arrange your toiletries neatly in the bathroom as you do at home. What luxury after a day spent in coach seats or driving around a strange city!

Then after you're set up, use the dayparts methodology (explained next) to plan your time—unless it's late or you're truly beat. You can do almost anything in a hotel room that you can do at your office, other than hold face-to-face meetings or dig through your desk's file drawer. But, to make yourself productive, unpack a little. A workstation (your computer and papers) set up the night before is more inviting for work in the morning than is one still locked away in its carrying case.

✈ No Place to Stay

For a variety of reasons you may find yourself checked out of a hotel by noon, but with a long wait before boarding an evening flight. (Try to schedule so that this rarely happens.) When you do find yourself in this situation, there are three activities that you can engage in to make the time either productive or relaxing. First, head for the airport club and plan on an afternoon of work and relaxation. Second, schedule client meetings or follow-up visits. Many clients will appreciate the extra attention, especially if you take them out to lunch. Third, use your rental car for a nice relaxing drive before turning it in. Depending on the city you're in, you might take a drive by California's oceans, Kansas' prairies, or Arizona's deserts. Stop along the way and enjoy the view wherever possible. Pack a camera if possible and shoot pictures for your family.

For Quick Stops

If your stay will just be for one night with a morning checkout and departure, stay as packed as possible, only jacking your computer in to check mail and type a few memos. Short stops, especially ones where you arrive late at your hotel and are tired either because of a day of meetings or late arrival, are best used for short term activities that don't tax your brain. Do your expense report over room service dinner and sack out. This is a more productive approach because you'll last longer on the road.

✈ Fill'er Up!

Always plug in and recharge all your equipment that has been used on battery power, even if only making a one-night stop.

MANAGING YOUR TIME AWAY FROM THE OFFICE

Should you schedule every minute of your trip two days before you leave or take things as they come when you travel? If you plan a schedule too specifically, delays such as canceled flights and longer than planned meetings will ruin your trip. Plus, such an arrangement can make you stressful as you try to keep the pace and make up lost time. Eventually you'll wear yourself out and get nothing done as a result. Not having a schedule is just as bad because as you travel, you may not be able to get any work done.

A superior solution is to schedule your time in a loose fashion using a technique we call dayparts. A daypart is a defined segment of a day. Examples of dayparts include lunch time, evening, morning, early morning, and so on. These loosely defined time periods allow you to schedule your time effectively but without creating a rigid schedule that will be almost impossible to keep. By scheduling via dayparts instead of minutes and hours, a late flight won't devastate your priorities. Arriving late at a hotel after getting stuck in rush hour means that your afternoon of scheduled work simply starts a little later. But if you had scheduled work from 1:45 p.m. to 3:30 p.m., arriving late would force you to change your schedule and make you feel late—that leads to stress and stress makes you unproductive on the road. The only things you should schedule rigidly are events that require you arrive at a predetermined time. Examples of such events are meetings and air travel.

Here's an example schedule containing a mixture of rigidly scheduled events and daypart events:

7:30 A.M. Leave Dallas on AA flight 345

9:45 A.M. Arrive in Dallas

Morning: Settle into hotel and make client calls

Noon meeting with Ted and Andrea at the hotel

Afternoon: Write Steven's proposal

Dinner: Read proposal over dinner

Evening: Relaxation time

Late Evening: If time, get E-mail and read news updates online

In this example, you can see that events with rigid starting times are scheduled that way, but events that have no defined start times become a daypart. For example, if lunch with Ted and Andrea runs late because the conversation is lively, starting on the Steven's proposal at 2:00 P.M. rather than 1:00 P.M. won't break the schedule, and you won't feel late as a result.

When Should You Create Your Schedule?

Schedules are like rules—they are meant to be broken. If you sell on the road, you may locate new clients and set up meetings that weren't originally in your travel plans, or untoward events may occur that force substantive changes in your schedule. Getting bumped from a flight throws off even the most carefully crafted schedule. For this reason, we recommend that you schedule only one day at a time, instead of trying to create a detailed schedule before hitting the road and then having to erase it and change it as you go.

✈ Schedule After Dinner

The best time to create your schedule for the next day is right after dinner. Otherwise, if you've assigned the evening as time off, doing your schedule before bed will nag you all evening or you may be tempted to put it off until tomorrow. Also, by reviewing your schedule before you're sleepy, there's less risk of forgetting an early morning meeting or flight.

Before you leave, pencil in all activities with set times such as travel time in the air and meetings, and then fill in the other space as you travel. The best time to set up other activities in dayparts is usually the night before, because by then hopefully all unforeseen events will have occurred that may affect tomorrow's schedule.

CREATING A FOOLPROOF SYSTEM FOR WORKING ON THE ROAD

If you aren't already "fully wired" or at least "partially wired" and use some of the equipment we talk about in this book or if until now you rarely traveled on business, on-the-road productivity takes time to master. At first, you will feel strange carrying a briefcase full of technology that you do not fully understand. Initially you may carry too much equipment as well as instruction manuals for everything until you learn how to work it all. (The manuals should go with you at first, but make it a goal to learn the products well enough to leave them behind for all but the most labyrinthine software programs.)

Getting Started

Lighten the load and go easy on yourself at first by bringing on new tools a trip at a time. For example, travel with your cellular phone and maybe your notebook computer on a couple of trips and make a point to learn how to use both of them. Using a cellular phone is easy, but to explore some of its more advanced features, you may need to sit down with it and learn how to access its special functions.

A computer may take you longer to learn simply because this device is capable of so many different functions. For this reason, you want a computer that's easy to learn and use as explained in Chapter 2. An easy-to-use machine substantially cuts the learning curve. After you learn how to get the machine powered up and ready for work, learn how the word processor works (assuming you have one) because most travelers use this tool the most. Once you feel comfortable with this software, begin exploring other software, a program at a time. It's important that you keep working with the software so that you remember how to make things work rather than having to dig out the instruction manual every time you want to do some work. Avoid trying to master more than a couple of software packages at a time because you may get confused about which program has which function, and this can lead to frustration.

Organizers are easy to learn, although some of their more esoteric functions may be counterintuitive because the manufacturers build in so much functionality without enough buttons to make some procedures simple to remember.

Last, if you will be taking a multimedia presentation on the road complete with sound and a projection TV, practice hooking it up and making the presentation run until you can do it in your sleep. Setting up such a presentation at a client's office and finding that it won't run or that you've forgotten a part is embarrassing and makes you appear incompetent to your would-be customer.

MOBILE OFFICE TECHNOLOGY CAN MAKE MONEY

You have already seen that a mobile office can make your time on the road more productive. But did you know you can also make money with the technologies? When other employees would be twiddling their thumbs, working on the road can actually generate new business and new sources of revenue. Time on the road is an excellent opportunity to make contacts and personally meet customers who have had contact with your company only via phone, fax, and mail.

In addition to ordinary customer contact, a mobile office allows you to analyze market demographics while in the field and take action to solicit new accounts. Best of all, as you approach a new town or city, you can set up meetings with these prospective new accounts and make sales that add to the already scheduled business you have in that city with established customers. Were you to make these same contacts from your regular office, the sale would need to be delayed several days to set up travel time and make the call. For smaller accounts, the mobile office allows you to drop right in to make a sale. These same potentially profitable, but small, accounts might simply be ignored if you had to set up the meeting from your distant office.

A mobile office also helps you make more money because the tools allow you to take immediate action in the field. Detailed estimates and proposals can be produced in a prospective customer's office or at the hotel room, ready for the next day's meeting. All minor changes and "what if" information can be added as the client asks for it. If you'd prepared such a document at your office before meeting the client, it might be hopelessly out of date. Without mobile office technologies, you have no way to modify the proposal to include new information and changes requested by the client. Using the mobile office, you can make changes, incorporate new pricing information to counter a competitor's moves, and deliver a crisp, accurate proposal right on the spot. Many times this is the difference between closing the sale or leaving it open for the competition.

As you travel with your mobile office and begin really to understand how to maintain your productivity while on the go, you'll reach a point where you can identify what's working and what's not. You may choose at this point to add additional functionality to your office in terms of new equipment or replace something that weighs more than it is useful.

Your goal is to adopt, adapt, and improve your

mobile office until it becomes a part of your routine. When you sit down with it somewhere where you plan to work, getting set up and ready to work should take less than five minutes.

Watch yourself. Are you feeling more confident with your tools or are you still fumbling for instruction manuals in order to figure out what to do next? If so, analyze the procedure to see what is taking so much time. Consider an alternative solution if something you're using is interfering with your productivity and consistently wastes your time.

After your next trip, carefully make a list of what you accomplished using your mobile office and compare this to what you accomplished traveling without one. Chances are, you'll be more productive on Day One because you can keep in touch better with both the office and clients and there is less unproductive waiting, driving, or flying. You may feel better when you come back from trips, showing up at the office with a bright smile instead of commenting, "Boy that was one long trip." Best of all, you can plunk your work down on everyone's desk and bring a smile to your boss's face when he or she sees your meticulously completed expense report. Clients will like you too. Instead of going on the road and essentially disappearing off the face of the Earth, they will have kept in contact with you whether you where in Bakersfield, California, or in the woods of Maine. That makes for happy customers. Over time you'll hone your system into a finely tuned operation that keeps you in touch and on top.

12

MAINTAINING AN ELECTRONIC PRESENCE WHILE YOU'RE AWAY

When traveling, effective communications with other people can be a chore if you don't know the tricks of the pros. Using mobile office technology, staying in touch is easier and more effective than even before. Properly handled, a traveling businessperson can create an electronic presence whether in the next town or a continent away from home base. This chapter shows not only how to keep in contact, but how to use technologies and procedures to make people think you never left the office at all. The results of professionally implemented mobile communications are impressive in terms of employee productivity, customer response, and personal visibility in the corporation or elsewhere.

COMMUNICATION

Communication is a key component of making your presence felt while you're traveling. This requires more than a daily phone call back to the office to check in for messages. Instead, it requires you to make your co-workers aware of your presence by supporting their efforts as you would if you were at your desk. This may require no more than answering E-mail and a phone call here or there, or you may need to exchange work with them on a daily basis to keep the job flow moving back home.

Keeping in Touch with the Boss

Communication is also important to your boss who may have spent a fortune to buy the equipment you are carrying with you. Impress him or her by showing off all the work you accomplish on a regular basis and reporting on your progress with the purpose of your trip by faxing an elegant (but brief) status report every couple of days directly from your computer or organizer's fax. Your boss also wants to be reassured that you are busy accomplishing what you are out to do while on the road. The old adage out of sight, out of mind should not apply to fully wired mobile professionals traveling on business.

Keeping in Touch with Customers

Customers like to stay in touch whether you are on the road or in the office. Surprise them by returning their calls to your office in just minutes via your cellular phone instead of days later as other people do when on the go. It helps if someone at your office has a way of relaying calls to you no matter where you are. A pager or paging cellular phone may be the best solution for this unless you give people a NationLink code that will let clients, colleagues, or customers find you anywhere in the country. Returning their calls promptly tells them that you consider them to be especially important.

Five Ways to Build Presence When You're Not Around

There are several ways to build a presence that belies the fact that you're traveling to the folks back at work. Here are some of our favorites:

Stay Connected to Company E-Mail

When sitting with your feet up watching TV in a hotel room, you can look like you're in the office by staying connected to your company's E-mail. Then as messages come in, return them immediately. This works best with a system that can be set to beep you each time a message comes into your mailbox. For people who know you're traveling, this puts them on notice that you're on your toes. For people who don't know that you're away, they'll assume that you are sitting at your PC answering E-mail as usual.

For travelers on a budget, long distance charges as marked up by a hotel may make this unfeasible, so try it just for a few minutes at a time during the hours when the most E-mail is sent—first thing in the morning as people arrive for work or late in the afternoon at most companies. Or use a gateway via Tymnet or another commercial network set up by your company. Unless you're in Timbuktu, gateways are available all over the country that allow you to access your office's network via a local phone call. Gateways are also available internationally, but these are a little more expensive.

Send Handwritten Notes

The presence of a handwritten note sent via fax reminds people, especially underlings, that you are alive and well and thinking about them. A handwritten communication is very effective for maintaining presence. If you are not at an office or hotel with a fax available, you can have your handwriting converted by Signature Software, Inc., of Portland, Oregon into a font that you can use to write letters. It looks like your writing when you send a document created with it via fax. Your own font is also handy for faxing a note to your kids who will probably be unable to tell the difference between your handwriting and the Signature Software's authentic-looking recreation.

Have Your Office PC Snap to Life

As explained in Chapter 8, you can make your computer turn on and off by remote control so that you can access your files. Linking products are available that actually move your system's mouse and open and close files and windows by remote control. Set your machine up so that others may see this amazing process, and, like the proverbial ghost in the machine, people will know you're "at work."

Call Everybody

To keep your profile high, call everyone that you need to talk to on a regular basis (via cellular phone if you have one). Make them aware of your progress on your trip if they want to know, but try to keep the focus of the conversation on what's happening at work. Make suggestions, clarify points, and call others who you may need to talk with to get a better handle on what's going on or to ensure that you will be included in a decision process. Call clients to check in on what they're up to and make sure they're happy. Don't waste anyone's time, but maintain your presence as an active participant in the process of doing business and keeping the ship of state afloat.

When Traveling Internationally

When traveling ten time zones away, no one will be expecting you to call or respond to E-mail as though you are around the corner. Surprise them by calling at a time when they're hard at work but expecting you to be in bed long ago.

RULES FOR ELECTRONIC MAIL EFFICIENCY

E-mail is a powerful tool for keeping touch. It crosses the time zones between you and the office, and using E-mail systems on CompuServe (or other full-service information systems) you can send mail to large numbers of people not connected with your company. But to make the best of it, here are several suggestions for those who are not yet E-mail pros.

Keep It Short

Most E-mail messages are read quickly. It's not uncommon for a busy professional to receive more than fifty E-mail messages a day. Senior managers in large corporations may receive as many as five hundred messages a day and, as you can imagine, have administrative assistants sort through the morass of mail and "file" the unimportant material rather than waste time with trivia. While five hundred messages a day may see impossible, keep in mind that the higher you rank in an organization, the more people not only send you mail but copy you on correspondence to others. You also become a lightning rod for problems, special causes, and invitations to a multitude of company events.

Keep It Simple

If you are having trouble writing a message about a particular subject because you're not sure how to phrase the message, it may be something better discussed in person or at least on the phone. If you find it difficult to put into words, it may be because the message is of a nature too delicate for E-mail, which is probably the most depersonalized kind of communication after form letters.

✈ Checking for Messages

Always check your electronic mail at least once a day. Some of the messages will be from co-workers and managers who need your feedback to continue their work. Other messages will be from people trying to keep you in the decision loop on some aspect of your business. Timely response is vital to prevent work from stalling or getting dropped from the approval process because no one heard from you.

Writing to Power E-Mail Users

Power E-mail users employ a variety of codes to convey emotions and generally make communications faster. These codes vary from organization to organization, so it may take you some time to understand and put them to work. For example, when communicating in the online services :-) is a representation for a smile or that what has been said is meant in jest. Take you're time to understand the E-mail shorthand fully before adopting it or you risk using it incorrectly. If you don't understand an odd phrase, acronym, or symbol, ask someone who does.

✦ Avoid Double Meanings

When communicating via E-mail, especially with people who don't know you very well, avoid sarcasm and phrases or words that may turn the meaning of your sentence or entire message around. While E-mail appears to be a very straightforward medium of communication, your remarks can become meaningless or really steam someone who misinterprets them on the other end.

Avoid Too Many Blanket Messages

Many E-mail systems make copying your message to ten or a hundred people as easy as entering a single command. To do this, you define a group of people who should receive the same message with an alias for the entire group. (An alias is the system's way of making it possible to mail to a group of people by simply using a single name.) For example, MARKETING could be an alias for the entire marketing group of twenty managers, administrative assistants, and researchers. "Addressing" a single message to MARKETING sends it to everyone in the department.

Sending too much E-mail to people with only a marginal need to see your messages will make them ignore all your E-mail, memos and letters, including important ones they need to pay attention to. So be careful when using aliases. They save time for the right messages, but they can waste it if you involve too many people in an irrelevant issue.

Delegating Work Electronically and Keeping Track of Progress While You're Away

If you manage or coordinate people, you need to keep track of what they are doing as well as their progress, even when you're on the road. For highly motivated workers, this can consist of a weekly phone call to keep tabs on activities and E-mail to discuss fine points and less important business. For less self-motivated employees, more regular contact is required to give them specific direction and answer their questions.

For less trustworthy people working at jobs where they may not show up when no one is around to check on them, calling at the beginning and end of the day will see who is working and who isn't. For example, calling right at starting time in a business with rigid time and attendance requirements quickly discloses who's on time and who isn't. Be arbitrary in timing your calls if you want to catch people off guard. You may be surprised by the dependable staff you have as a result.

Managing Large Projects

If your staff is engaged in a major new project such as a new product launch or if your travels will be extensive, consider using a product such as Microsoft Project to schedule the events that will go into the process and assign dates and tasks so that everyone knows exactly what he or she should be doing. Microsoft Project and many other project management tools allow you to carefully track progress and get an overview of the sequence of events. Milestones are used to check progress at major turning points in the projects so it's easy to see if the work is on time or not, even for projects as complicated a building as fifty-story skyscraper.

On the downside, these products take practice to learn to use effectively and good project management is an art that many managers know little about. While engineering students study project management as a discipline central to their careers, few business or MBA degrees offer substantive classes in this field. If you would like to learn more on managing projects, both large and small, order our book *On Time/On Budget* from Prentice Hall by calling (800) 288-4745. This is a book on project management techniques written for businesspeople, not engineers or construction managers.

✈ Let Your PIM Do It

PIMs, described in Chapter 7, have the ability to schedule projects using a basic project management chart called a Gantt chart. You can create your project plan using your PIM and then print relevant reports for distribution to your staff. You can track progress against plan by checking in with your staff and updating the project plan on your notebook computer while on the go or back at the office.

In this chapter, you have learned the basics of traveling on business while keeping people aware of your presence back in the office. While an electronic presence is not quite a full substitute for actually sitting at your desk, when handled as this chapter suggests, you can keep in touch, stay in control, and look good no matter how much time you spend away from headquarters.

13

KEEPING UP WITH NEWS, TRENDS, AND BESTSELLERS

The well-equipped office on the go consists of much more than a laptop computer used to manage contacts and a cellular phone for chitchat on the cellular phone. It can be a flexible system for work, entertainment, and communication. To expand on the work-related tools covered in other chapters, this chapter profiles useful on-the-road entertainment tools, including mobile music systems and electronic entertainment options that can soothe and revitalize the weary business traveler. For example, the Voyager Company sells compact books on floppy disks that can be read on screen in one window, while stock market quotes are displayed interactively in another. A third window can be used to look up the weather at your destination.

TOOLS FOR KEEPING UP WITH THE WORLD

When traveling, it's easy to lose track of what is happening around you in the greater world. Someone accustomed to starting the day with *The New York Times* may go through newsprint withdrawal symptoms when forced to see the world through the eye's of a small town newspaper. Plus, the personal details of running one's life still must be addressed even when your away for weeks or more. Fortunately, there are steps you can take to keep up and proactively manage your life and affairs while away.

Keeping Up with the News

The familiar comfort of reading a newspaper over a cup of coffee while still in your bathrobe is possible, albeit a little more costly at most hotels. Do what we do. Order a room service breakfast and ask that the best of the local morning newspapers be included. Arrange an early delivery that allows you the leisure of reading the newspaper cover to cover while sipping your coffee. While it won't quite be like home, it's reasonably close. There's another advantage to this approach. If you will be meeting with your client in the city, coming up to speed on the local news gives you a point of conversation that can be used to make communication more personal.

Electronic News

For casual news and information while traveling, you can use the full-service online systems (listed in Chapter 9) to keep up with national stories. If you are a professional journalist, NewsNet is another powerful although somewhat more expensive tool for the same purpose. Services such as CompuServe and America Online let you read the *Washington Post* or other papers online for an extra charge, but there are no pictures, and the paper appears a few hours later online than it does at the newsstands.

Keeping Up with Traffic

If you must travel by car to get across a city or reach the airport in a timely manner, don't forget the morning and evening traffic reports. These can be found on many AM stations, usually numbered at the lower end of the dial. You'll find out about local traffic, news, and weather although it may take a roadmap to show you what parts of the traffic report are relevant to your route.

A superior option, although one not in use in many cities yet, is to use a traffic reporting device that can be installed in your car. Autotalk, Inc. makes a device that receives the transmission of ongoing traffic reports that are broadcast on an extra side band used for television audio channels. Already set up in Los Angeles, known as "traffic jam central," the system provides reports more frequently than heard on most radio stations and offers the audio portions of local television stations as an alternative to local radio.

✈ Keeping Up via GTE Airfone

The telephones available on modern airliners allow you to access news, weather, and other information quickly. The only downside is that you have to pay for this service.

Electronic Weather

While the news may predict sunny warm temperatures for the day, as everyone knows weather can change quickly for the worst. Newspaper weather is inaccurate because many papers set the weather section in color, which means it was put together hours before reliable forecasts are available.

When traveling through snow country or in areas where prospects of deadly lightning storms, tornadoes, or hurricanes, read the local weather reports available through most online services. Or if you're traveling by car, consider carrying a short-wave radio that tunes in the government's weather frequencies. Can't afford such a radio?

Consider purchasing Radio Shack's weather cube radio. Several models are available and are useful for nearly continuous weather updates as you travel by car. Bring extra batteries for portable radios. There are also telephone services for weather reports listed in the resources section of this book.

CONTROLLING PERSONAL FINANCES ON THE ROAD

While traveling you need to look after your personal affairs just as you would at home. Bills that are late because you're on the road will accrue late charges no matter how you plead, and a difficult credit card or mortgage company will add a black mark to your credit without a second thought. Fortunately several solutions exist that are preferable to carrying all your bills and paperwork with you on trips.

Quicken and Checkfree

One of the least expensive and handiest programs for managing personal finances is Quicken. You can use it to track payments, make expense reports, pay bills, and balance your accounts. It can also print checks, but this is a cumbersome option while traveling.

✈ Making Checkfree Work Better

If you use Checkfree to pay bills to organizations with large numbers of occasional customers, make sure that Checkfree has reference numbers for your account so that when your payment arrives, the payee knows how to credit the payment. For example, a bill we paid to a newspaper for a classified ad accidentally was used to start a newspaper subscription because the newspaper did not know what account to apply it to. Apparently they use phone numbers to track ad payments, not names. If we had told Checkfree to add the phone number, there would have been no problem.

Checkfree is another on-the-road option that works

with Quicken. Capable of sharing financial information with Quicken, Checkfree pays all your bills either electronically via the U.S. central bank or if no electronic links are possible, Checkfree issues a physical check which is mailed to recipients. This product can pay regular monthly payments such as your mortgage completely automatically. You can plug in dollar amounts for payment amounts for bills that change monthly such as credit card bills.

Other Electronic Finance Options

You may be able to use your full-service online service to pay bills, and if your bank is connected to the system, you can make transfers, pay credit card bills, and check account balances online. Prodigy, for example, is hooked into major banks in most cities. Some banks also offer this service directly. Using an access number, you can manipulate your accounts and move money around.

You can also do your taxes on the road using one of several tax programs that run on computers and even submit your return via modem. But, unless your taxes are very simple, carrying around the amount of paperwork required to fill out the forms correctly makes this difficult. This is one job that is best done at home for most people unless you plan a long international trip and have no way of otherwise submitting your taxes on time. We suggest filing for an extension with the IRS instead if you don't owe any taxes—or even better— have your accountant do it.

Money on the Road

Almost anyone with a checking account or credit card knows that ATM machines can be used to access accounts for cash. But you may not be hooked into a bank that subscribes to the larger ATM networks such as Plus or Star. Having a cash card issued from a bank that uses one of the larger networks allows you to get cash across most of North America, and links to Europe are beginning to appear, although you may have to personally visit the bank instead of the ATM to get cash overseas.

With the right credentials, you can also get cash at many hotels and airline clubs, although the daily limit may be small. Another alternative is to buy something at a large grocery store chain. Many stores electronically process credit and debit cards at their cash registers. You can purchase some incidental for your trip such as shampoo and then when checking out with your debit card or credit card, choose the cash back option. Depending on the store, as much as $50 to $100 in cash can be withdrawn this way.

✈ Using ATMs Overseas

If you plan to use an ATM overseas, limit your personal identification number (PIN) to four digits. Many foreign ATM systems use only four-digit PINs and won't be able to access your accounts if you use a PIN of different length.

One sticky point while traveling: How can you deposit checks? While there are plenty of ways to get cash while traveling, your paycheck or customer payments made to you are more difficult to process. ATMs dole out cash, but generally only those run directly by your own bank (in the same state) accept your deposits. So, choose a true interstate bank with branches in more than one state—becoming more common as banking rules are being relaxed. Instead of banking with Cucamonga Savings and Loan, consider opening at least a checking account with an interstate bank that has branches in many states. (Ask about making out of state deposits before you open the account.)

A second option is to use overnight services to ship checks to your company or your bank for processing. Shipping a bunch of checks via next-day air to your home bank costs a mere $9 to $14 depending on the distance involved and the carrier you choose and only

$2.90 for second-day service via the U.S. Postal Service. There are many convenient points in every city for dropping off overnight parcels ranging from Federal Express kiosks in shopping center parking lots to stores like Mailboxes, Etc. that can be found almost everywhere. Shipping the checks is probably statistically safer than carrying them around for the duration of your trip—plus you or your company can get faster access to the cash.

✈ Your Paycheck While You're On the Road...

The easiest arrangement for the mobile professional who spends a lot of time on the road is to have the paycheck automatically deposited in the bank. This allows you to access the funds while on the road, and any automatic payments can be satisfied. If your employer doesn't offer such a program their bank probably does. Open a checking account at the same bank that issues your paycheck and arrange for the bank to deposit your check automatically into the new account. It's easy and usually reliable.

Electronic Investments

You can watch your stock portfolio or your company's stock via an online service. While watching the stocks, you can place orders to your broker as you travel via Dow Jones online service or other services. Make sure that if you play the stock market that you're thoroughly rested before communicating buy/sell decisions that you may regret later. Instead, consider watching market activity as a spectator sport while on the road. Full-service online services also offer business news to help you in your investment decisions.

PERSONAL GROWTH TOOLS

You can do many things to "better yourself" while on the road, ranging from learning ways to improve your business skills to acquiring a degree from an accredited university. Many new educational tools are available that can be used on the road that are both educational as well as entertaining. You can take advantage of these tools to keep your mind awake and to acquire new skills that help you do your job better. This is yet another way of turning normally wasted time on the road into productive and beneficial periods of personal development.

UNIVERSITY DEGREES YOU CAN EARN WHILE ON THE ROAD

University of Phoenix Online is one of the new university programs that lets you attend class from your home or office or while camped out in a hotel room. University of Phoenix (among a handful of other schools), an accredited Phoenix, Arizona-based business college, provides complete bachelor's and master's degree programs that can be completed using online technology. Using your notebook computer and modem, you log onto their computer where instructors leave assignments for you to complete and in which you spend time with other students participating in online discussion of the study topics. Completed assignments are then E-mailed back to the instructor, again via modem, to the university's computers. You can attend class almost anywhere there's a phone line. You may hold online discussions with classmates in Hawaii, New York, and Florida, almost as though you're all sitting together in the same room.

If you want to learn about more distance educational opportunities for working (and traveling) businesspeople, pick up a copy of our book *College After 30* (published by Bob Adams, Inc.) at any major bookstore. It includes a long list of accredited online and other degree programs that can be completed on the road.

Software Teachers

Want to learn statistics, bone up on biology, or learn how to use a complicated program? There are software packages that take you through lessons on any number of subjects, ranging from courses on how to build electronic circuits to foreign language courses. You can also use your time on the road to explore the tutorials packaged with the software you buy. For example, if you want to learn how to assemble a database from scratch with a sophisticated database program, work through the tutorial provided on a disk.

Other Learning-on-the-Go Tools

Mentioned earlier in the book, complete college lectures as spoken by distinguished professors are available from The Teaching Company. Sold as a set of cassette tapes (videos are also available, but these are less suitable for travel), the lectures can be enjoyed during a long drive between cities or on the plane. These are not just dreary college lectures that will put you to sleep. Instead they are articulate, thoughtful dissertations that will get your brain thinking about content and controversies. At this writing, The Teaching Company is working to make the lectures acceptable for college credit.

There are many other learning options available. Many business books are available on cassettes, and CD-ROMs are coming to market on a wide range of topics. Cassette books include titles ranging from *Customers for Life: How to Turn That One-Time Buyer into a Lifetime Customer* (Carl Sewell: Bantam Audio) to Alvin Toffler's *Power Shift* (Bantam Audio). On CD-ROM, explore the structure of Beethoven's Ninth Symphony on The Voyager Company's *Ludwig Van Beethoven Symphony No. 9* and a growing range of other titles.

Look up information in *The New American Encyclopedia* CD-ROM, which contains a 21-volume encyclopedia along with pictures and even sounds on one disk. Sony's Bookman is another CD-ROM educational option. A CD-ROM allows you to search an entire encyclopedia for all references to a word or series of words. For example, if you are traveling to Japan and want to learn about it's history and culture, just typing in the word Japan when using *The New American Encyclopedia* brings up more than 700 relevant articles and a map of Japan.

Minicompact disks are also entering the market for this device on a number of topics and Kodak's Photo-CD technology mentioned earlier in the book is allowing companies to create complete courses on CD-ROM complete with high quality photos and sound that can be used to educate on any topic you choose. There are many options to pick from and the number is growing daily.

ENTERTAINMENT TOOLS

There are many ways to keep entertained while on the road in addition to the old standbys: listening to the radio, watching television, and reading paperback books acquired at a hotel or airport book kiosk. While there's nothing wrong with such entertainment and we encourage you to use your relaxation time as you see fit, you may want to learn about some of the other options available to the "fully wired" mobile professional. And you may find some of these alternatives more interesting than watching reruns of *Fantasy Island* or *M.A.S.H.* to pass the evening.

Electronic Books

Electronic books are becoming commonplace with the Voyager Company producing the first three mass-market books (*Jurassic Park* is one of them) on a series of floppy disks. They come in several formats—stored on floppy disks, on CD-ROM, and the new mini CD-ROM formats. You can read these books on the screen of your notebook computer, even "marking" your page for later reference. The advantage of electronic books over physical books is that you can carry many titles with you because they are loaded onto your hard disk or stored on a CD-ROM and the "book" thus takes up little or no space in your suitcase. For example, the single CD-ROM, *Great Literature—Personal Library Series* contains the complete text of 943 famous books along with color illustrations and spoken passages. With this single disk, it's easy to see how you could feel a little behind in your reading!

Books on Tape

One growth industry is books recorded onto cassette tapes. Once the domain of highly abridged titles complete with poor acting and laughable sound effects, the new generation of talking books has become a medium embraced by a large and growing audience. Most cities now have at least one or two stores that contain a massive number of titles for sale or for rent. Before leaving on a trip, check out several titles and listen to them on your personal cassette player/recorder unit or on the stereo of your car or a rental car. You can choose from titles as diverse as romance novels to classic literature to science fiction. While many titles are still abridged (although not nearly as much as the first generation of such books), the acting and thoughtful attention to recreation of the scenes via sound effects makes these tapes entertaining. And you can listen to and enjoy a book on tape long after your eyes are too tired to read a printed book.

Electronic Games

If you will be traveling with a notebook computer, you can not only enjoy the electronic games available via the online services but also access standalone game packages available from companies such as Broderbund Software. Thinking games such as *Sim City* and *Where in Time Is Carmen Sandiego?* pass the time while keeping your brain alert. *Microsoft Flight Simulator* is fun, and it actually teaches you the basics of instrument flight.

Wage war in China via KOEI's *Romance of the Three Kingdoms*. Fail miserably as a surgeon with Software Toolwork's *Life & Death*. These are all games that will keep you occupied for hours over repeat sessions. While some skill games similar to *PacMan* and *Pong* can still be purchased and played on your notebook computer, many of today's modern games are intriguing with far superior animation, sound, and intellectual stimulation.

✈ Games and Copy Protection

Many games are copy protected in some way or another, and if you choose a copy protected game, you need to make sure that you bring whatever is necessary for the game to run with you or you will be locked out of it. Where many games have key-disk protection requiring you to insert the game's original floppy disk even though you loaded the game to your hard disk, others such as Life & Death *require you to use a cardboard phone number wheel to find people's numbers for dialing into the machine. Clever, but frustrating if you forget it.*

Other Entertainment

An emerging kind of entertainment that's not quite an electronic game, but instead an animated, interactive show is exemplified by *Cosmic Osmo and the Worlds Beyond the Mackerel* (no we don't make this up, we just write about it). Available only for the Mac as of this writing, Cosmic Osmo is a CD-ROM that contains an animated adventure in which you travel the universe to seven worlds, calling the shots as you explore each one. Travel commences in a spaceship (complete with fuzzy dice) in which you can load animated compact disks into a disk player and listen to the music.

Bizarre and strangely wonderful is the only way to describe this piece. The music which accompanies many of the adventures can be played in an ordinary CD player although you may have to jump to the second track to make it work.

Movies-on-the-Go

One of the more expensive on-the-go entertainment tools is Sony's Watchman. This (comparatively) small unit accepts tiny videotapes and displays them with sound on a small color monitor. While this format shows promise, there are not many major screen film releases available for this format and you'll most likely need to order tapes through mail. Still, the ability to watch a video movie any time or any place is about as entertaining and technologically advanced as you can get. On the plane, this system is a nice alternative to watching the heavily edited movie shown by the airline and you do get to choose what you want to see. Now if Sony could just figure out how to keep people from watching over your shoulder...

Music-on-the-Go

As anyone who has ever entered a record store within the past twenty years knows, there is an endless amount of music of all kinds available on compact disks and cassette tapes. When traveling, you can listen to tapes on your car's tape player or your personal cassette player/recorder and some hotel rooms have cassette players built into the clock radio. Compact disks, which sound better than cassettes, can be played on a portable compact disk player, a car stereo equipped with a CD player, or a portable CD-ROM player.

✈ CD Player and CD-ROM Player Longevity

While you'll rarely hear this from a salesperson, the lasers used in CD systems of all kinds have a finite life span, and when the unit begins to skip, it's time for a new player, as replacing the laser costs almost as much as a new player. For this reason, should you buy an expensive top-of-the-line CD-ROM player, consider saving it for CD-ROMs and play music CDs on audio CD players which are less expensive to replace.

RELAXATION TOOLS

While maintaining your productivity on the road may seem difficult, relaxing and getting enough sleep may be even more difficult. Together with the underlying tension of travel and unfamiliar places, you may have the pressure of closing a big deal that the people back at the office are worried about. While you may be sitting quietly at your hotel in a comfortable chair, you mind is worried and your heart beating hard. You need to counter the stress, and this section describes some alternatives to do just that.

Relaxing in the Air

Flying time can be used for relaxation, especially on red-eye flights and long trips between continents. While some people can fall asleep almost anywhere or anytime, light sleepers often can't sleep in the air. If it's not the lady in front who turns on all three over-the-seat reading lamps to peruse a copy of National Enquirer, it's the flight attendant dropping the silverware while cleaning up the galley.

Avoid using alcoholic drinks, sleeping pills, or tranquilizers to bring on sleep. While these may indeed make you sleep, some research of in-air shows that it's the people who knocked themselves out chemically who fail to make it off the plane. Plus, you want to arrive rested, not drugged. Dealing with an unfamiliar or foreign city is hard enough when you're awake, but chemically induced sleepiness will make it that much more difficult and you may forget some of your belongings when exiting the plane.

Instead, deal with this by bringing an eye shade (provided free in business class and first class on long international flights) and purchase a relaxation tape designed to put people to sleep. Listen to it on your cassette recorder/player unit. If you're a really light sleeper, wait until the meal has been served and change seats if possible to a more sparsely populated area of the plane.

Avoid sitting near the galleys and rest rooms because these will remain noisy for most of the flight.

Relaxing in Your Car

This may sound like we're suggesting that you go to sleep at the wheel, but what's to be explained here is how to minimize stress while stuck in traffic. Plan your route via map before leaving and allow yourself extra time to get to appointments. Try to avoid rush hour. Listen to a soothing music tape instead of loud rock-and-roll or a talky newscast. On hot days, keep the windows up and use the air conditioner to cool down your temper. If you get lost, observe street signs to see where you are and pull over and read the map instead of going around in circles. If you are visiting Manhattan or other densely packed city for the first time, take a cab or limo, and let someone else worry about the directions and heavy traffic.

✈ Never Say Die

Never keep driving after you begin to get sleepy, especially on long business trips where you may already be run down before starting the drive. Find a hotel and hole up somewhere because falling asleep at the wheel gets harder and harder to fight off. You won't know you fell asleep until you wake up in a ditch or at the scene of an accident, if you wake up at all.

Relaxing in Your Hotel

One of the best stress reducers is exercise. Depending on your taste and physical health, a session in the hotel's gym or swimming pool may be in order or maybe a jog around the neighborhood if you feel it's safe. Do your heavy exercise no later than before dinner, because strenuous exercise late in the evening may actually keep you awake.

If you're a light sleeper, choose a room that will be quiet. Choose a room with double-pane windows that is located away from elevators, busy streets, and the hotel's disco, if there is one (common in Mexican and many foreign hotels). To damp out other noises, set the room's heating and cooling controls to leave the fan on all night. This runs the fan continuously, but activates the heater or air conditioner only as the room's temperature becomes uncomfortable, as it normally does. The same relaxation tapes suggested for plane trips can be used in your hotel as well. And, obviously, if you plan to sleep late, make sure the Do Not Disturb sign is on the outside of your door or the maid may come knocking early.

A New Relaxation Tool

One new tool, made by several companies including Salt Lake City's AlphaLab, is the brain box. Consisting of electronic sunglasses, earphones, and a small control unit, AlphaLab's system simulates a wide variety of meditation states through the use of colored lights mounted in the eye-side of the glasses. These are accompanied by soothing sounds or music piped in through the headphones. (Some of these units can be plugged into a music source such as a Walkman or compact disk player to allow you to use the music of your choice.) As one ad reportedly proclaims, "Meditate Like a Zen Master in Just 30 Minutes." With practice, you may be able to use one of these units to relax before sleep or to wake yourself up in the morning without caffeine. Priced from around $100 to several hundred dollars, these could be the next big thing with mobile professionals who need to keep their act together under stressful schedules.

This chapter has offered a number of options that allow you to not only improve productivity but also to keep yourself happy and rested as you travel. Don't assume that these options include everything available. New technologies and new ideas are rapidly changing the options for working and playing on the road. If you keep your eyes peeled, you'll start seeing all kinds of useful gadgets for your business travels. But remember our earlier advice—don't buy every neat gadget you see or you'll have to carry them around with you. Buy and bring only what you will use.

14

INTEGRATING TECHNOLOGIES FOR MAXIMUM BENEFIT

The full power of the office on the go is not realized until the singular technological elements are brought into harmony with each other where one tool supports another for maximum benefit. If the technologies integrate properly, they can perform more than one role in the mobile office, and more work will get done on the road.

INTEGRATION STARTS WITH COMPONENT COMPATIBILITY

Throughout your mobile office set-up, you need equipment, software, and tools that work with each other in as many ways as possible. For example, carting equipment that runs on four different sizes of batteries means that you might need to carry backup AAA, AA, C, and 9- volt batteries on your travels. This adds weight and means a trip to a store each time you run out of any type of battery. But if all your equipment runs on AA batteries, you can have just one supply of batteries and even cannibalize another unit's batteries if the supply gets low.

It would also be convenient if one AC adapter could run more than one piece of equipment, but currently this is not possible. "Universal" adapters sold by places such as Radio Shack lack the power to run notebook computers and hooking up another device such as a palmtop computer or a cassette player/recorder with the universal adapter set up incorrectly may fry it. We expect this problem to be addressed by notebook/cellular phone combinations that are now reaching the market, but full power support for a wide range of gizmos has not yet crossed the horizon.

Compatibility is available in other areas, however. The same headphones you use for your cassette unit can fit your computer's sound port if it has one. You can plug the output of your cassette player/recorder into your computer's sound port to digitize speech, music, or sound. With state-of-the-art word processors, a quote captured on your recorder can be imbedded into a memo so that others can not only read the words but hear the person speak them.

Computer cables have also begun to be standardized, although many configurations still exist. Fortunately, the office on the go (usually) requires far fewer cables than does a desktop computer with its monitor and multitude of external boxes. Depending on the external equipment you will carry, look for a CD-ROM player which can use the same cable as your printer or an external modem if you use one. By swapping cables among devices when you use them, you can carry one cable instead of two or three. (Power everything down before swapping cables.)

Computer Compatibility

With all its power, a computer can still be the starting point for compatibility problems. Software may save files in formats unreadable by other software. Printers and modems may fail to work, and a host of minor problems may dog your productivity. For this reason, you should test each new component of your mobile office with your computer before purchase. Your machine's modem should be able to plug into your cellular phone, and the two must work together for clean transmission (most of the time anyway). Your phone should have standard modem input jacks as well, or you may have to contact the manufacturer for an overpriced adapter cable.

If your machine will be used to drive external video displays, this can be another can of worms unless you test compatibility before purchase. A manufacturer's statement that its computer is "fully compatible" with external video systems is not going to make you feel any better if the two fail to work together during an important meeting.

Software Compatibility

As explained in Chapter 7, if your software applications will exchange data files, choose products that work well with each other. For example, if you will run market mapping software using data stored in database you also use, make sure that the data can be transferred directly between the applications. Otherwise extensive reformatting may be required. If you plan to place spreadsheet data into your word processor, make sure the files are directly compatible. While you can translate files for many products via PCLink or other translation software, this extra step wastes time and makes work more tedious.

GET THE MAXIMUM BENEFIT FROM EACH COMPONENT

You can often get more than one function from the same device and putting more than one device to work can create a complete system. A CD-ROM can play audio CDs as well as your ROM disks. A computer is also a source of entertainment, education, and communication as well as functioning as a workstation. A cassette player/recorder can be combined with a computer as an interviewing system as well as used to listen to music and relaxation tapes. For example, the unit can be used to interview expert sources for information germane to a research project. The tapes can be transcribed with word processing software from the same cassette system and the document faxed to the office with the computer's internal fax/modem connected to the office via a regular telephone jack or through a cellular phone.

LOOK AT THE MOBILE OFFICE AS A SYSTEM

Remember that your mobile office system is a complete office environment that just happens to fit in a briefcase or bag. Properly chosen, the sum of the parts should be more powerful than the individual components, although the individual power of a PDA, sophisticated organizer, or computer make these by far the most significant contributors to the productivity of your office on the go.

While you travel, your mobile office replaces a more familiar system —your desk-based office. At work, you probably take information from various sources, make written notes, and add up numbers on a desktop calculator. Then manually on ledger paper or using spreadsheet software, you analyze the information and try to reach conclusions, phoning people to clarify points as you go while writing your report on a word processor. You may then have your administrative assistant assemble the complete report from the bits and pieces and photocopy the pasted-up pages into a format suitable for distribution or you may even do the word processing yourself. Taking the finished report to the fax machine, the pages are sent out to interested sales offices.

But, when on the road, a higher level of integration may be required to get the most from limited resources.

Where at the office you may routinely query the company's mainframe ten or twenty times a day for customer data, when on the road, this many queries would run up either your cellular phone bill or hotel long distance charges, so to minimize contact, query the company's computer just once, storing the information in a personal information manager (PIM), or acquire the data before leaving the office. You also don't want to lug a photocopier, office-size fax machine, desktop calculator, and glue and tape on your travels.

On the road the data available in your machine is used to contact clients for appointments with your cellular phone, while at the same time, you may use it to study market penetration, analyze which customers may be ready to make a new purchase, and follow up with people behind in their payments.

At this level of integration, one set of data is used for many functions. And, as you travel and contact the customers, you update the data to reflect account activity and download the modified data back to the company's mainframe. Your mobile office has become a system for client contact, market research, sales lead management, and financial control. Of course, the system also allows you to do many other functions at the same time.

Reports created on the road rely on the higher level of integration your mobile office demands. You word process the text portions of the report, pasting in the spreadsheet to substantiate your written data and then test a couple of calculations using a Windows or Macintosh-based software calculator to determine that your spreadsheet calculations are correct. Finally, you directly fax your report from the notebook computer via the fax/modem and your cellular phone if no conventional telephone hook-up is available.

This integration of tools eliminated the desktop calculator, an office-size fax machine, the need for your administrative assistant, and sundry office supplies. You faxed it directly using a list of phone numbers culled from your PIM instead of having your administrative assistant look up each recipient's fax number from his or her Rolodex. Your computer then automatically dials each person and sends them the fax before going onto the next number. More important, the entire process probably took a fraction of the time it would have taken back at the office. While you could work the same way at your office, chances are you don't because other resources are available that are easy to rely on instead of doing it yourself. But on the road, without easy access to conventional tools, you handle the entire process seamlessly all by yourself.

This automated integration is important for another reason. While many people gather data in the field, they wait to reach the office to do anything with it. You, on the other hand, can analyze the data as it comes in and make decisions before returning to the office. In-field analysis allows you to take action immediately and proactively.

In this chapter we have explained how to integrate the components of your mobile office to make using the system easier and to make yourself fully self sufficient while on the road. From this information you will develop an eye for choosing technologies that complement each other and see how to combine components that form complete systems to help meet your business goals.

15

MAKING INTERNATIONAL CONNECTIONS

When traveling abroad with the mobile office, the trip and the technology must be planned with work in mind. Beyond the obvious power incompatibilities, there may be problems transporting equipment through the customs bureaucracies. In addition, the video, telephone, and other technology standards may be incompatible with your equipment. Hong Kong, for example, uses unusually strong X-rays to check travelers' luggage for explosives and weapons. One dose is enough to damage information stored on disk and will partially expose photographic film. However, with the information provided in this chapter, you will be prepared to carry sensitive data with you through security checkpoints and will know the ins and outs of customs traps and compatibility pitfalls.

IS INTERNATIONAL TRAVEL SAFE FOR THE MOBILE OFFICE USER?

Traveling internationally on business is generally safe and uneventful, but because business is becoming more global in orientation, people are going to places that were previously considered exotic or remote. This means your business travel could place you in areas of potential terrorism, highjackings, and even war. Let's face it, the political situations around the world are far from stable. This makes it imperative to be alert to international events when you travel. While it's unlikely, any international flight can be the target for terrorists or highjackers. If you travel overseas frequently, the risk is greater. Although travel through most of Europe and the non-communist countries of Asia is probably not any less safe than a trip through downtown Los Angeles unless you engage in illegal activities such as smuggling, money laundering, or drug transactions. Come to think of it, those activities aren't very safe right in here in the United States or Canada.

For information on high-risk airlines or political problems in areas where you will be traveling you can contact:

Citizens Emergency Center
Room 4800 N.S.
U.S. State Department
Washington, D.C. 20520
(202) 647-5225

THE MAJOR HASSLE IS WITH CUSTOMS

Generally, the most arduous problem when traveling to foreign countries is passing through the customs authority. Expensive-looking equipment you may be carrying can be confiscated, or you may need to post a cash bond, (hopefully) redeemable when you leave the country with your equipment.

Check with the country's embassy or the State Department before attempting to import a notebook computer. Ship it home if there's a chance of a problem. If possible, get something in writing giving you permission to carry your equipment across borders. Backup documentation such as a copy of the insurance policy on your equipment and purchase receipts go a long way to proving that you bought the equipment for business and you are not attempting to bring it into the country to sell it or give it away as an gift or bribe.

✈ If You Must Post Bond for Your Equipment

Always be as courteous as possible to customs personnel because they can cause you real trouble. But, if forced to do something irksome like post a large cash bond to bring your equipment into a country, graciously ask to talk to a supervisor before doing so. You may, with all your paper proof of being a legitimate business traveler, be able to negotiate the amount of the bond down substantially or even eliminate it. If you must post a bond, ask how exactly you can retrieve your funds when leaving the country and keep careful track of receipts for your money. Put it on a credit card if you can (possible in only a handful of countries), then you can float the bond charges until you straighten them out back at home.

U.S. and Canadian customs can also be difficult about allowing technology back in the country if they think you bought the equipment overseas (even if it was made by IBM). Get a document at the airport's customs office showing that the equipment was purchased in the United States or Canada before you leave. Alternately, if you will travel through a large number of countries and don't feel like explaining your system to customs authorities in twenty countries and fifteen tongues, leave it at home.

If your stay in a country will be extensive, bring carefully protected floppy disks containing copies of your software (not the masters!) and data and rent a computer for the duration. Bring a copy of the receipt for the software so that it doesn't look like you're importing it and that your copies of the master disks are legitimate. If you anticipate hassles when leaving the country or reentering your homeland, bring the data back but erase the software disks, after removing their labels as completely as possible.

Get an ATA Carnet—If You Know There Will
Be a Problem

Get an ATA Carnet. You give a copy of this document to each customs official as you cross the border into and out of the country. Upon returning to the United States, you surrender the final copy to the customs authority. Provided by the International Bureaus of Chambers of Commerce, and good for one year, this document makes carrying even obviously expensive mobile office systems trouble free, although you may still need to post a bond and do some paperwork. Apply early for this document so that it doesn't delay your trip.

If you must leave in a hurry and don't have the time to wait for an ATA Carnet, use an international shipping expediter or custom house broker to arrange a bond and the paperwork before you leave. While there's a charge for this service, posting bond through these companies is often cheaper than the rate customs may try to charge you if they misvalue your equipment. And, while the bond is for the value of your equipment, the full dollar value of which must be paid if you leave your equipment in the country, like insurance, you pay a fee for the bond instead of posting the full amount. Bring all the paperwork to customs when you import or export your system, and leave photocopies in a safe place at home.

Travel Lighter

Things can get dicey in visits to repressive countries, where the police and/or military run things. While most such countries are becoming increasingly accustomed to seeing computer hardware and they will treat you as an honored guest if they let you in at all, a communications-heavy mobile office set-up may make untrained police or customs officers nervous even though cellular phones work only in their country of origin. In the unlikely event that you will visit such a place on business and you can't do it without a computer, leave everything but a small organizer or subnotebook computer behind or get official permission in writing to bring the goods in.

GET A PASSPORT—EVEN IF YOU DON'T EXPECT TO MAKE AN INTERNATIONAL TRIP

U.S. passports are now valid for ten years. A brand-new passport costs $35.00 plus a processing fee if you use a local agency such as a county government office or a post office to process the application. The U.S. Department of State has thirteen Passport Agency Offices located in Boston, Chicago, Honolulu, Houston, Los Angeles, Miami, New Orleans, New York, Philadelphia, San Francisco, Seattle, Stamford (Connecticut), and Washington, D.C. You may apply in person to these agencies and avoid the extra processing fee or other charges.

Normally, a passport takes four to six weeks to process. You can rush the passport through the system in one or two days if you apply in person and have a valid reason for the emergency application. We suggest that all businesspeople maintain a valid passport to avoid this situation—you never know when your skills may be required out of the country. Be prepared for the opportunity—you wouldn't want to miss a big assignment just because you don't have a valid passport.

Register your passport at the U.S. embassy if you are traveling on business in a foreign country, especially if you are traveling to Eastern European, African, Middle Eastern, or Asian countries. This expedites the process if your passport is lost or stolen.

Keep your passport with you at all times. A U.S. passport is a valuable item in some countries; don't give it to someone else to carry and never pack it in your checked luggage. The best place to carry your passport is in a zippered pocket inside your clothes.

Visas

Your travel agency or the airline should inform you about the need for visas on your itinerary. If they don't mention visas, ask about them. If they don't know, call the consulate for that country. If there is no consulate in your area for that country (look in the White Pages of your telephone directory), then call the consulate in Washington, D.C. Different countries have very different requirements—and sometimes they change without notice. A visa is an endorsement of your entry, and when the country grants one it indicates that your papers and intended purpose in the country (travel, work, etc.) are acceptable to that government. The visas for some countries in Asia, Africa, the Middle East, and the former Eastern Bloc are restricted and may take months to get. Inquire about visas well in advance of your trip if you need to travel to Third World countries or areas of political unrest.

PAYING YOUR WAY

When traveling, many people worry about the safest way to carry their money. Carrying cash is risky, and foreign money exchangers may soak you with a serious "service fee" for handling American or Canadian cash. Buying too much local currency may force you to exchange the money twice, making the fee even more usurious.

Credit cards beckon with safety and ease of use, but they are not accepted widely in many parts of the world. And travelers' checks can be clumsy to deal with small denominations requiring a long session of counter-signing for large bills and large denominations are uncashable except at a bank (when they're open) or your hotel. The best way to handle money is probably a mix of all three forms of payment. Here's a little insight about traveling with each.

Traveling with American (or Canadian) Dollars

You can travel with American money because it's an almost universal exchange medium (although not recommended in some countries in the Middle East), and you can change only the amount you need into local currency. Or many merchants will accept American currency directly for payment although the "exchange" rate charge may be exorbitant. Beware of stores, hotels, and restaurants abroad that advertise their goods using prices posted in American dollars. These usually cater only to tourists who don't mind paying substantially more than the going rate.

On the downside, unless your travels are limited to modern countries in Europe, you may need to carry no bill over $20 because larger denominations may make money changers (even some banks) nervous, especially in less developed nations. Carrying enough $20 bills to make it through a long business trip may require that you purchase a suitcase just to hold the cash. That may make you feel like a robbery target, and customs officials will be at least curious about your stash. Money belts and hidden compartments in clothes and purses may help, but there's still only so much cash you can carry without bulging in odd places.

✈ The Almighty Dollar

Carry American currency discretely if you carry any more than is required to pay for the cab back to the airport when you return home and bring travelers and credit cards instead.

Local Currency

The local money may seem more foreign than the country itself with a variety of different sized bills elaborately decorated with pictures of people you don't recognize. Foreign change can be equally intimidating with large, heavy coins that are worth hardly anything.

(Foreigners visiting the United States probably wonder why a dime is worth more than its larger cousin, the nickel.)

✈ Carrying Local Currency

While many U.S. and Canadian banks can order foreign currencies for you, purchase the local currency (preferably through a bank to get the best rates) after arrival. If you must have pocket change, buy it from one of the airport money exchange booths, but don't purchase much because the exchange rates may be usurious. Buy only enough for cab fare and incidentals unless you plan to shop in the local stores where credit card acceptance is questionable. Buying more than you need may require another trip to the money exchange, or if you're on the hurried schedule of many mobile professionals, you may arrive home weighed down with several pounds of pounds sterling.

Credit Cards

While you certainly have heard the familiar slogan, "American Express: Don't leave home without it," VISA cards are the world's most popular credit card. But, if you plan to rely on credit abroad, carry a VISA or MasterCard card *and* an AMEX card so that wherever you find yourself, chances are good that at least one of your cards will be an acceptable form of payment.

In Third World countries, credit cards may be accepted only at the largest (and most expensive) hotels, stores, and restaurants and they are a new phenomenon in many former communist countries.

In smaller outlets that accept credit cards, expect far more scrutiny of you, your card, and often your passport than would be normal in the United States and Canada. This is because smaller merchants have no way of authorizing your card, and if it proves expired, stolen, or substantially over its limit, they will have no way of collecting from either you or the credit card company and will be out the merchandise your purchased as well.

As mentioned, try to carry at least one credit card,

and a VISA (with room on it to charge) and an American Express card will give you more acceptance options. Other cards such as Diner's are accepted, but in far fewer places. Protect your cards when abroad, because even though the AMEX people can replace your card quickly as they advertise, VISA and MasterCard replacement may take longer.

✈ Worth the Wait
When traveling to countries in which the currency is likely to lose value within the next sixty days against the U.S. dollar (Mexico and much of the Third World, for example), charge everything. By the time the bills arrive, which may take anywhere from days to occasionally months, you may gain from the devaluation because the charges made in the foreign currency will now be worth less when converted to dollars!

Travelers' Checks

Local currency is your best bet for getting fair prices on goods and services overseas. It is best to bring travelers' checks (in dollars) on your international trips and exchange them for local currency when you arrive. You can exchange the travelers' checks at a bank for the best exchange rates. Inquire about the fee charged, it will vary from bank to bank.

✈ Become an International Currency Trader
While it slightly complicates figuring out exchange rates, when traveling overseas, consider buying travelers' checks in a stable currency so that your money doesn't change value as you travel. This is especially important during long trips in which you will have no access to your home accounts without a lot of paperwork and waiting. For example, we sometimes order our travelers checks in Swiss francs or deutsche marks before leaving for an expedition to Europe. If anything, our travelers' checks may become worth slightly more in value against other currencies as we travel.

There are also exchange booths in airports and in major cities, but their exchange rates are not usually as favorable. Some stores and restaurants will also accept travelers' checks for payment, but again, the rates they offer are not usually competitive. Exchange only the money you will use—as you will have to pay another fee to convert the foreign currency back to dollars. Of course, if the rates are fluctuating wildly in your favor, you may want to gamble that you will make some money in the exchange process, but this is usually not a good use of your traveling funds. If you want to invest in the monetary exchange markets, we recommend that you do it with the help of an investment counselor or broker—and not with your travel money.

In summary, we recommend that you carry most of your "cash" as travelers' checks. Carry a number of small denominations but convert the bulk of your money into $100 checks to make checking out of hotels easier. American Express or VISA travelers' checks are the most widely recognized.

✈ The Name on Your Checks

When you make international trips, the name on your travelers' checks should be the same as that on your passport—as your passport will be the only acceptable identification for cashing travelers' checks. Don't use your nickname, even if it is how you normally sign your name. You may have problems when trying to cash the checks.

WHAT COMPONENTS OF YOUR MOBILE OFFICE CAN GO INTERNATIONAL?

Most components of your mobile office can go international if you can keep them in electricity during your trip. The one major exception, as mentioned, is your cellular phone, which will be incompatible with the local system except in Canada. Customs authority concerns aside, computers, organizers, cassette systems, and CD-ROMs all work fine overseas as long as you can master the electricity problems.

Power Overseas

Around the world different voltages, cycles per second standards, and oddball electrical outlets must be dealt with to plug in. Plug socket adapters are sold as sets in travel specialty stores and many luggage stores. Buy a complete set of plugs (usually about six different ones) and that will allow you to hook up in most of the world.

Electricity can be another problem. Hotels that cater to American travelers, or at least those people likely to be using American purchased products, may offer 115-volt, 60-cycle power in the bathroom, but nowhere else. Fortunately, as the world really becomes a global economy, everything from hair dryer units to notebook computers can run on more than one voltage and on 50 or 60 cycles. A manual switchover may be required for your computer, but other devices can look at the power thrown at them and change over automatically. Read the owner's manual carefully before plugging a 115-V AC appliance into 220-V outlet or smoke may be the reward for your effort.

✈ Buy Power Plug Adapters *Before* You Go

Surprisingly, the most difficult commodities to find in many countries are the power plug adapters you should have purchased before leaving. Save yourself the trouble by purchasing them in the United States—even if you have to pay the ludicrous price charged for a set at a store in the airport.

Keeping in mind that many office-on-the-go tools use external power supplies containing transformers, check carefully the cycles per second. In North America 60 cycles is standard, but 50 cycles is standard in much of the rest of the world. Plugging a device such as a CD-

ROM player that uses a transformer designed for 60 cycles in an outlet that provides 50 cycles will eventually cook it, maybe taking only seconds for the process to melt the internal components.

Power Adapters and Surge Protectors

There are power adapters that convert 220 volts to 110 volts and you can use these for an electric shaver or maybe even a small radio, but these systems provide "dirty" power for use with a computer unless you are prepared to buy an expensive adapter, which may weigh you down with its big transformer. It is better to have a computer power supply that is directly compatible with the local power.

In addition to the power and plug adapters, you may also want to carry a portable surge protector to protect your equipment from unpredictable foreign power levels. Panamax, Inc. and other companies offer a variety of computer surge protection products for domestic and international travelers.

Checking for Bad Power

"Dirty power" can ruin your equipment. This may stem from accidentally plugging a 60 cycle appliance into a mislabeled 50 cycle outlet, the use of a power adapter that uses cheap electronics to partially convert electricity (most of them), or problems with low voltage because of overdemand or faulty generating equipment. Here's how to at least partly check for dirty power:

- Plug in, and if things appear to be functioning normally, touch the top of your equipment's power supply two minutes after turning it on. If it becomes rapidly warm (or worse, hot) or makes a buzzing sound, unplug immediately. Otherwise, if everything appears in order, recheck the power supply every two minutes for the first ten minutes.

If it gets only normally warm, things are probably fine. For transformers located inside the unit (locate it by balancing the unit in your hand to determine the heaviest corner or edge—that's the transformer), keep your hand on that area to check the transformer for overheating.

- Study the incandescent lights and lamps in the room. If they appear dim, flicker, or increase and decrease in brightness at regular intervals, the local power system may be producing inadequate voltage or dirty power, and you should not plug in.

✈ Run on Batteries

Palmtops and other devices that use batteries can be run that way to avoid having to deal with power conversions or electricity problems. Bring a large supply of alkaline or lithium batteries. Or bring NiCad batteries and purchase a charger compatible with the local power from a hardware store, department store, or whatever passes for the local Radio Shack. Carry this on future trips and let it cope with local power problems instead of your expensive equipment.

USING THE PHONE AND YOUR MODEM

Power plugs aren't the only thing that are different overseas. Phone connectors offer even bigger challenges. Phone plug configurations change between country and country, and also between major cities within a country.

It is possible to buy an American-to-PTT telephone adapter when you arrive in the country or city, if you can find a telephone store. A better solution is to contact TELEADAPT, a company in the United Kingdom, that supplies a range of tool kits and adapter products for international "road warriors." They offer a comprehensive line of "intelligent" adapters, clips, plugs, and testers for making modem, fax, or cellular connections almost anywhere in the world. Their products work with PC-compatible and Macintosh computers. They also offer a newsletter full of hints and techniques for making connections easier and faster.

In addition to placing orders direct to the United Kingdom at the address provided in the reference section of this book, you can also order their products through CompuServe.

✈ Notch Filters

While we have never run into this problem, some countries use a system of tones to track your phone bill. These can interrupt communications and add gibberish to incoming and outgoing faxes as sent or received by a modem. TELEADAPT sells notch filters to zap these tones from the line while leaving the rest of the audio spectrum alone. Because these filters only take out a notch of the audio signal, they are called notch filters. You may need two because different countries apparently use different tone frequencies.

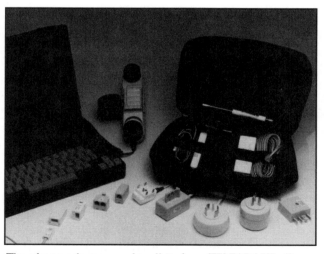

The phone adapters and toolkits from TELEADAPT offer road warriors reliable ways to connect portable modems and fax/modems to phone systems around the world.

INTERNATIONAL ACCESS TO ONLINE SYSTEMS

Though international modem connections to online services were once unreliable, with new satellite linkups, the connections are now clear in most places. Once you get your modem connected with your adapter kit from TELEADAPT, many of the major online information systems can be accessed anywhere in the world.

Before you go on an international trip, contact the services you use and get local access numbers and sign-on instructions. The log on procedures and protocols vary considerably from country to country. In some countries they vary by city. You may need to set up different protocols and use special codes to gain international access to the network. If there are no local access numbers for the service you use (America Online, for example, has no presence outside the United States), the only choice is to dial a U.S. number from overseas.

The main issue in using U.S. numbers is to make access to your online accounts affordable. You obviously don't want to incur long-distance charges to the United States in order to access your online accounts. Charging such a call by credit card can be a nightmare and paying the hotel service charges for such a call could bankrupt you. Instead, ask your long distance provider (AT&T, MCI, or Sprint) if they have a local access number for the cities on your foreign itinerary. These numbers provide an affordable gateway to your stateside telephone network. All you need to use them is a valid credit card.

THE MOBILE OFFICE AND INTERNATIONAL
AIRLINE TRAVEL

At one time, you could not use a computer on a airliner, but today most of these restrictions are a thing of the past. However, small carriers in foreign skies may not have received the good word and still restrict computers because of the unfounded belief that they interfere with aircraft radios and navigation. Ask before turning yours on when in doubt, or if there's a language barrier, open your unit in front of a crew member, pointing to the keyboard with a questioning look on your face.

Language and Culture

We described the translation machine options in Chapter 8. If you don't have time to learn the basics of the local language before your trip, by all means get one of these devices or a software module for your computer. We strongly recommend that you also take along an audio course in the basics of the language. Just a few phrases will make a world of difference in your business interactions overseas. Also, get one of the many good books on international business customs for reading on the flight over. What you consider a nod of approval may mean something entirely different to the CEO of an Asian conglomerate. It's worth some effort to learn about the culture before you try to do business in another country.

In this chapter, you looked at some of the issues of traveling abroad with an office-on-the-go set-up. As you can see, aside from customs concerns and the possibility of power problems in some countries, the equipment can keep you just as productive when traveling abroad as it does in your homeland.

16

TRAVELING WITH THE
MOBILE OFFICE—
PROBLEMS, SOLUTIONS,
TIPS, AND TECHNIQUES

While a mobile office provides a complete work, communications, time management, and entertainment system for traveling businesspeople, frustrating problems with the technology and services may crop up. This chapter provides a number of techniques, workarounds, and tips for managing the office on the go and getting the best from it. The chapter also includes a section of troubleshooting tips for modem-based communications problems and ways to get expert help in a hurry.

WHEN THERE'S TECHNICAL TROUBLE
WITH A CAPITAL T

When traveling with the mobile office, something may break or fail to work, or you may find yourself in the embarrassing situation of not remembering how to use it—especially a problem with some software and when accessing cellular phone numbers. After taking a deep breath here are several solutions for trouble on the go:

- **Can't remember how to make it work?** Call the

manufacturer's technical support line, the dealer who sold it to you, or an officemate who uses the same product be it a software product or an errant beeper. Call a local dealer for the same product, if no one else is available.

- **It's broken or won't respond:** Check that the unit is plugged in and/or that its batteries are fresh. If plugged in, try another wall outlet in case the one you are using is dead or connected to a light switch that's turned off. If its a computer, make sure that the machine's liquid crystal display (LCD) readout controls are correctly set after the jostle of travel or try booting from a floppy disk with system software installed on it to see if your hard disk has problems. Travel with a copy of Norton Utilities to recover crashed hard disks if your trip will be long. Always back up your work, keeping the backups disks safe.

- **If it's really broken:** Many notebook computer makers offer onsite service, and they will come to you with one day's notice to fix or replace your machine on site. Alternately, ship your busted equipment back to your office via Mailboxes, Etc. For other equipment, have your office ship you a replacement unit at the same time you ship yours back. Deal with warranty claims and repairs when you return from the road.

- **It's smashed with plastic parts scattered on the airport floor:** Carefully scoop up all the parts for a surgery later at your hotel room. Find everything that may have flown under chairs for later reassembly. If the main unit is really broken, use tape from your tool kit to hold the pieces together. (Tool kits are discussed later in this chapter.)

- **It's really smashed:** Buy a new one and place a

claim with your business insurance. Or, if you sit on your pager and crush it, instead of bothering your insurance company, just buy a new one and remember not to put it there again. These devices aren't very expensive any more, so it isn't worth the effort of making a claim on the policy.

- **It's stolen:** In the airport, call the police immediately. In a hotel, call the front desk and check one more time that the maid didn't put the missing components in a drawer or somewhere else. When on the road, keep equipment out of site in the trunk and hope no one steals the car or pries open the trunk as is a popular pastime in Italian and Brazilian cities. To make the system less attractive, use one of the software locking or hardware locking systems available from vendors listed in the resources section of this book.

- **The airlines lost it:** First, don't check anything you care about seeing again, especially your office system. But, if you broke this rule (shame on you), file a claim with the airline's lost baggage representative and ask for compensation. You may get a few bucks for clothes and toiletries, and with any luck, your bag will show up on the next flight. If you must check your office equipment, declare excess value for it and cross your fingers, especially when traveling internationally or when connections between planes at stop over points is tight. NEVER check electronic equipment stowed in a soft suitcase. Some airlines, familiar with the problems created by such a bag, will make you sign a release absolving them of responsibility if anything in a soft case gets broken.

- **You don't know what you did with it:** Fight down the panic and start by looking around you. It may be right beside you hidden by a coat you dropped on top of it. If you can't find it nearby, retrace your steps or make phone calls to restaurants or other likely venues where you may have left it.

✈ Tip: Insure It

Since you may have a substantial investment in your mobile office, make sure that your business insurance covers it, even if the deductible is larger than for office-based equipment. A policy that covers data loss is the best kind, in case your computer is stolen and you lose all your work. This compensation will pay you to recreate it if possible or the insurance company may pay an expert to try to recover data from a hard drive damaged in a fire or other mishap, no matter how bizarre.

TOOLING UP FOR BECOMING FULLY WIRED

Wires are an unfortunate reality of the electronic age, and the computer has done little except to make this prescription for working better than before. When traveling with the office on the go, you must make connections, and we're not talking about the kind you make at Dallas/Fort Worth. In addition to the cables required to link your cellular phone to your computer or your computer to the printer, you need several sets of wires to set up in a hotel room. The right set of wires will make your endeavors easy and allow you to set up a working office that works as it should. The wrong set of wires will force you to use your computer while laying on the bed or on the carpet near the room's door.

Bring a Long Extension Cord and a Power Bar

If you plan to work in your hotel room, travel with a long two-prong extension cord so that you can plug in. (Three-prong extension cords are too bulky and heavy, unfortunately.) Many hotel rooms have outlets only near the bed or the TV. Without the cord, you may be forced to work on the bed, or as we did in the People's Republic of China, in the bathroom, which was the only room with an outlet. (Lamps in the room were hard-wired to the walls!) Bring a multioutlet power bar if your mobile office requires AC power for several devices at the same time, and rather than disable the grounding pin from any equipment, buy a three-prong to two-prong adapter for each piece of equipment with such a plug.

Modem Wires

If you plan to jack into a hotel's telephone system (more on this later in the chapter), you'll need a phone cable that can reach from your desk to the room's telephone jack. Bring a longer cord with male-to-male endpoints on both ends (the kind of plug that plugs into your computer's modem).

If your computer's modem has a modem input and output jack for the room's telephone, bring a telephone cord extension to connect the phone so that it will ring even when your computer is connected but inactive. This cord will have a female receptacle that the phone's plug plugs into as well as a make plug at the other end as previously described. If you leave your computer on while not communicating, make sure that any communications or fax software you are using is set not to answer the phone, unless you are waiting for a fax or file to be sent to your machine.

Presentation System Wires

If you plan to make presentations on the road as explained in Chapter 8, you should carry not only the cables to connect your PC to the LCD screen for overhead projects or the video cable to drive an external monitor or big-screen TV, but also cables for your sound system. If jacking sound from a notebook computer such as a PowerBook, buy a long cable that will do the job. If you don't know what kind of system you'll be passing the audio signal (voice and music) to, bring adapters that will convert the output from the machine output to the public address system.

Tell Radio Shack personnel, "I need a stereo phone jack male plug to male stereo phone jack plug with twelve feet of cable." To buy an adapter say: "I need two six-foot extension cables compatible with this cable in case the distance to the sound system is longer" and "I need adapters to convert the male stereo phone jack to male RCA plugs and an additional male mini phone jack." If this leaves the staff dumbfounded (common, unfortunately), ask another salesperson or try another store. If this loses you, the people who sold you the computer or presentation system will know what kinds of cables and adapters you will need.

Repair Tools on the Go

While the prospect of repairing a broken computer case or taking the phone apart is less than appealing to most people, a simple tool kit can be a lifesaver, even if you use only the tiny screwdriver to repair your sunglasses or the flashlight to find the passport you dropped behind the bed. Here's what you need:

- Small flashlight with fresh alkaline or lithium batteries

- A very small straighthead and Phillip's head screwdriver

- One each: standard size straighthead and Phillip's head screwdriver

- Krazy Glue or similar bonding agent that works with plastic

- Electrical tape

- Pair of needlenosed pliers

In addition, you will want to make sure that your bag of tricks includes the following:

- An extension cord

- A telephone extension cord

- A "Y" adapter for standard telephone wall jacks

- An adapter for linking two telephone cords together to make one long cord

While you may not like the prospect of traveling with tools, they ones we suggest are highly useful. A flashlight can do everything from help you escape from a blazing hotel to finding the plug hidden behind the bed in a hotel. These tools can be used to get you wired into uncompromising telephone systems to use your modem, to repair broken plastic parts on electronic equipment, to reach phone jacks in remote locations, or to keep wires in place. (Use the electrical tape to keep wires under control by wrapping an inch or so of tape around bunches of wires running to power or phone jacks so you don't trip over them in the night.)

Keep these tools in a small case or, if nothing else is available, put them in a plastic bag with a "zip-lock" top ready for stuffing into your baggage.

WHAT CAN STOP THE OFFICE ON THE GO?

When traveling you have to be wary of obvious detriments to your work. While a mugger may steal your briefcase, a hard disk crash may effectively "steal" your work unless you take precautions to reduce the possibility of this happening. Here are suggestions to reduce the possibility that you will lose your equipment, saved work, or other functions of your office on the go:

- **Keep it out of sight:** When traveling, keep the bulk

of your equipment and possessions in the trunk of your car or stored under a seat if you're traveling by minivan or bus. Avoid walking through the back alleys common to all cities whether by day or night with a big bag in your hand or under your arm. Never leave your equipment in your car overnight. In Italy, we've seen pried-open trunks after thieves cleaned out the trunks of a row of rental cars parked outside a hotel.

- **Back up your work:** You have certainly heard about backing up your computer work a million times already. We are going to tell you just one more time—back up your work at the office and on the road. If you don't, all your work may be lost. Copy your computer files, photocopy your notes and physical information, and regularly send these via a trusty carrier such as UPS to your office so that you have protection against losing all the work, research, and customer or client data gleaned from your trip(s). You don't need to copy your programs—just the files you use. There are three reasonable ways to do this on the road: (1) Copy the files onto a floppy disk, if you have one, or (2) Send the files over an online system to your own mailbox or to your system at the office via electronic mail or other network connection, or (3) Probably one of the best ways we've tried is a program like CarbonCopy or a linking program that connects your notebook to your desktop computer, as explained in the chapter on advanced technologies, and simply dump the files to your desktop PC in the office.

- **Protect your power:** When traveling, make sure you have batteries, power supplies, and any plug or voltage adapters required. Make sure you bring all the AC power adapters as well.

✈ Dead Computers

If your computer appears to die on the road, carry it through the rest of your trip before giving up on it. Many times, the work you have saved on your hard disk is entirely recoverable even when the miracle software you brought fails to bring your machine fully back to life.

MAKING MODEM CONNECTIONS

One of the most frustrating events that can happen while traveling is to learn about modem communications the hard way—the unit fails to dial or fails to connect. Modems are part of a communication system that can turn into a complex beast. When you're dealing with a computer attempting to connect to another computer or service via telephone lines that may be a part of a hotel's ancient switchboard or connect through Poland's pre-World War II phone system with a satellite thrown in for good measure, here's what to do to make life with your modem easier on the road:

- **Buy a quality modem:** There are a number of really cheap modems equipped with software available for a song. These (or their software) may lack the ability to suppress noise and spurious responses from phone lines. Pass, and buy a decent name brand unit. If your travels will take you overseas or if you must talk to a balky mainframe as part of your duties, purchase professional communications software instead of a $19.95 mail order special.

- **Stay in modern hotels:** While even the newest hotels in other continents may have a bizarre phone system, new hotels in the United States and Canada have modern communication networks that give you a better chance of making effective modem communication links. To make this work, simply plug your modem into the hotel phone's ordinary jack and plug their phone into the other modem port on your computer if it has one.

- **Use an acoustic coupler (if you must):** While you can take apart the phone and even its wall connections, an acoustic coupler (a box into which you place the headset that can listen to the remote computer's signals) may be an easy alternative for overseas travels although limit your modem's speed to slow ones, that is 1200 or 2400 bps, because acoustic couplers add noise to the transmission process and the speed of light (electricity) gets briefly replaced with the speed of sound through the acoustic link-up. Keep in mind also that the antique or ultramodern phones used in many countries will fit in your acoustic coupler like a hand into a shoe, ensuring a poor connection. Use very slow (300 bps) communication rates for such an arrangement.

HARD-WIRED CONNECTIONS

While we don't recommend this to any but the desperate (a surprisingly large group when it comes to trying to make connections), you can take the two wires of a phone wire and connect these to rubber-coated alligator clips and hook in electrically to the phone, the wall socket, or in a hotel with a cooperative staff, the switch board.

Phone Systems 101

If you can find the right two wires, you can tap into almost any vaguely modern phone system, but finding the right two wires isn't always easy. Most modern telephone systems require only two wires to make a phone work, although four wires may be present (or many more on a multiline system). To tap into a system, you can buy a male phone plug and add alligator clips to make it possible to bypass bizarre connectors. Buy a male phone plug connector like the ones that your (modern) home phone uses from Radio Shack and connect two rubber encapsulated alligator clips (also available from Radio Shack) to the two center wires to make a patch into most phone systems. (Have a technician do this if you're a soldering pencil illiterate.) The key wires, at least in North America, are the red and green leads so you or your technician should solder in wires that match the normal telephone system leads, although if they get reversed, it's usually no problem.

When trying to hook into a phone with the modem, unscrew the jack or plug from the wall and clip your connectors directly to the wires. Then hook the other end to your modem as usual and dial.

✈ And That's It, Period!

Most modems (at least the ones you want to use), employ Hayes protocol developed by the Hayes modem people. One of the commands that makes a modem pause is a period. If you can't get an outside line or are having problems making the system work at all, add extra periods before the number asks the hotel's phone system for an outside line and after country prefixes (when dialing internationally), and give the phone system more time to complete your call. For example, "..8......714...555....1234..." gives the hotel and local phone system more time to respond than does an electronic "87145551234" issued in less than a second by your computer's modem. Keep adding periods until it works. This is a useful way to deal with old systems as well as modern digital phone networks that call the shots their way.

Hooking into the Red and the Green

The key wires are red and green (in many countries). Clipping to these two will usually get you a line. You can get to these wires by unscrewing the phone jack wall plate, a box at the floorboard, or sometimes the mouthpiece of the phone and clipping to the wires or connectors after removing the microphone piece. Alternately, you may be able to connect your modem directly through the antique telephone switchboard of an old Paris (or Eastern Bloc) hotel with the right kind of modem-to-phone-plug cable.

A tip to the switchboard operator and the desk clerk may get you access to this rickety affair but don't expect any help with the wiring because they probably don't understand it any better than you do. If the idea of doing any of these procedures makes you uncomfortable, don't even consider them. Phone or send a telex instead.

High Voltage

Do not mess with phone system wiring without insulated rubber covering on alligator clips (and then only as an act of desperation if you know something about electricity). Varying from country to country (worst in banana republics and some Third World places), the voltage used to make the telephone ring may knock you off your feet. Beware!

A Live Wire

You can test a line to see if it will work by using more Hayes modem commands. If, after several tries, your modem fails to dial, try dialing manually using the Hayes command sequence. Type "ATDT" and your number and press Enter or Return.

If nothing happens or you get a dial tone but no dialog, try another line. If you hear the tones of the modem dialing but no response is audible from the phone system, try our suggestion of adding extra periods to allow the hotel and the local phone system's electronics to "hear" your computer's commands or try it with the acoustic coupler.

MAKING CELLULAR CONNECTIONS WITH YOUR MODEM

As you no doubt surmised, connections via modem on a cellular system are more difficult than on ordinary phone lines. As do radio stations, cellular systems suffer from noise because they're really radio systems that link into the conventional phone system. As you travel, your link to a nearby cellular tower is passed on to the next tower as you travel. Between the radio noise and the hand-offs to other cellular transmitters, your modem has a poor chance of perfect transmission, but you can take simple steps to give yourself a better chance of success.

First, if you are communicating with your modem via cellular phone, do it from a location with adequate signal strength. Translated: Communicate from a fixed location and try to do it where the signal strength is good. Watch your phone's signal strength meter if it has one to get a better idea of the available signal from your present location. If this still provides a spotty modem communication, jack into a hard-wired phone line in a hotel and remind yourself that newer digital cellular technology will eventually make all this easier. (We hope.)

Things you can do to reduce the risk of problems include:

- **Stay put:** When sending from a moving vehicle, your chances of getting handed off to another "cell" are much greater. Stay put because hand-offs create transmission glitches that may force you to start over when sending your file. Park instead in a strong signal area until you or your passenger are done transmitting.

- **Send short files:** The longer you stay hooked up to another computer via the cellular system the greater your risk of errors or losing the connection completely. Send short files and complete E-mail transmissions as quickly as possible.

- **Avoid fast speeds:** While you can send information faster at 9,600 bps than at 2,400 bps, the risk of errors increases with speed. On noisy systems, or when you're transmitting with a low-wattage hand-held, keep the speed down. Use higher speeds to get the transmission over sooner when using a higher-wattage phone in strong signal areas.

- **Buy a modem designed for this purpose:** Some modems from companies such as NEC and Mitsubishi are designed to cope with cellular network inadequacies. These suppress (some) errors and do a better job of staying connected even when there are problems with the cellular net. It helps if you have one of these modems on both ends of the transmission.

BATTERIES AND BATTERY PROBLEMS

One of the most irritating aspects of carrying a mobile office is when a $2,000 device can't be used because its batteries are stone dead. Most portable electronic devices run on off-the-shelf alkaline or lithium batteries or rechargeable NiCads which are designed especially for the machine. Lead acid batteries, vaguely like the one used in your car, have also been used by a few companies. And there are many emerging battery technologies poised to enter the market. Here's the low-down on batteries.

Alkaline Batteries

Alkaline batteries are the standard bearer for running electronic devices. They are available in many sizes and shapes, and you can buy 48 Fuji AA alkaline batteries from Price Club for less than $10. Alkalines have the advantage of long life (compared to obsolete zinc batteries), and they have a long shelf life before discharging. Alkalines provide more current for longer periods than NiCad batteries of the same size, but can't be recharged.

Lithium Batteries

Offering even longer life than alkaline batteries, this kind is available now in several standard sizes. Lithium batteries cost more than do alkaline batteries. Lithium batteries also cannot be recharged.

Lead Acid Batteries

After a brief romance with laptop and notebook computer makers, lead acid batteries have largely disappeared as a power source for portable electronics. They have the advantage over NiCad battery packs of costing less to replace but must be replaced more frequently than NiCads because they accept fewer recharges before their lifespan is over.

✈ Unplug the Charger

Many recharging systems can discharge connected battery packs when you unplug the charger from the wall plug. This is because the charger's circuits are still hooked up to the now charged battery and will slowly consume its power. Remove the batteries from the charger or unhook it so this can't happen.

NiCad Batteries

Available in conventional sizes and often molded to fit the case of a specific computer or cellular phone, NiCad (for nickel-cadmium) batteries provide less current and don't have the life of an equivalent alkaline battery, but they can be recharged many times. Note: Unlike other batteries NiCads lose their charge when stored. Recharge them immediately before trips.

Keeping Your NiCad Batteries in Top Shape

NiCad batteries require proper care to maintain their potentially long life span. Otherwise, you may end up with a battery that won't take its full charge effectively shortening the time your equipment can run its battery.

When working with rechargeable batteries, always read the manufacturer's charging instructions and attempt to follow them to the letter. This will not only provide the longest charge periods between recharges but also make the batteries last longer before you need to buy new ones. (NiCads do wear out eventually.)

Before You Use Your New NiCad-Powered Device

NiCads like to be fully charged before use, and anytime you buy a device with new NiCads, follow the manufacturer's instructions to the letter on how long to charge the batteries before using the device. Once fully charged, the first use of the device should allow the batteries to discharge fully before another complete recharge. This will allow the batteries to provide the maximum period of power between charges.

Don't Overcharge NiCads!

While expensive computer equipment uses "intelligent" power monitoring to ensure the batteries don't get cooked if you forget to unplug the charger after a set recharge period, almost nothing else does other than expensive electric razors and some cellular phones. It is possible to overcharge a NiCad. If left charging long enough this will fry the battery, which in turn may burn out the charger. To avoid this, always leave charging NiCads somewhere where you will see them several times a day and remember to take them out of the charger.

Consider a Deep-Cycle Charger

For your office on the go, consider the purchase of an optional deep-cycle charger. This is a device that fully drains your NiCad batteries before fully recharging them. Without this full discharge, you may power up your "charged" battery only to have your equipment shut down in minutes instead of hours because the NiCad can't charge correctly. With computer-powered equipment in which the power monitoring system inside the device shuts it down before the batteries are truly dead, this can become an annoying problem.

A Last Ditch Effort

We've never tried it, but reportedly if you don't care about possibly ruining your batteries, slapping a NiCad against a hard surface a couple of times will break down the crystals inside them, giving you a brief period of power. The only time to even consider this trick (if it works at all) is when your dead cellular phone is making it impossible to dial 911 and a life and death emergency exists. Naturally, slap the batteries after removing them from the phone.

✈ Charge Up from Your Car

While you probably don't need yet another cable around your neck, you can charge your dead notebook computer or cellular phone from your car's battery with the correct cable. Plugging into your cigarette lighter, you can run your phone or notebook computer or recharge it. Buy and use only the cable sold by the equipment's maker, otherwise you may unwittingly run 12 volts of power through a device that can handle only 6 or 9 volts and cook it. Keep in mind that at 12 volts, it will take much longer to recharge a large battery. While you can simultaneously use and recharge a notebook computer when plugged into the wall outlet, at 12 volts either use or recharging is possible, but not both.

Batteries and the Environment

Batteries of almost every kind are environmentally unfriendly. They contain nasty chemicals such as lithium or cadmium, neither of which is safe for people or other living things. The best battery arrangement for the environment is probably the environmentally inhospitable NiCad, which at least can be recharged many times before disposal. An even better arrangement is to buy equipment from a company that recycles its products batteries for you. Apple Computer, for example, asks that you return its deceased power packs to its dealers who ship them back to Apple for safe decommissioning before disposal and/or recycling.

WHEN THERE'S TROUBLE BACK AT THE OFFICE

When traveling, sometimes it's easy to forget what's happening back at headquarters. While you're enjoying the open road and fancy meals on the old expense account, the office may go through significant changes. More than one salesperson or manager has taken an extensive road trip only to arrive back at the office to find out that they have been reassigned duties in the unemployment line or given the "hot" new account territory in the company's equivalent of Siberia. Here are some ways you can spot problems at the office and step in if necessary to fix them.

Communication

While it may sound like shopworn advice, no single activity is more important to keeping your job and status while on the road than simple communication. You must let people at home and the office know your status and your progress. A constant stream of even small success stories fed back to the office is a real public relations tool for maintaining your image as a company man or woman.

If you manage a staff, one of the worst things that can happen is that your boss sees your employees goofing off in your absence. That's why keeping careful track of what people are up to is vital to looking good while away. If you can't trust your people, ask another person to keep an eye on them and be available to answer questions when your staff needs direction. Never assume for a minute that everything is just fine back at HQ when you're away. That's akin to leaving the harbor in a boat low on fuel—you may make it back, but then again, you may not.

Avoid Back-to-Back Trips

Sometimes the pressure to close deals or make contacts means one trip after another with only a day or two back in the office to catch up. This kind of travel wears people out and may run you into an early grave if there's too much of it. It also means that during the brief periods at HQ, you're so tired that you can hardly think, let alone work. Everyone will comment, "Did you see old so-and-so, she looks like she's given up on her job," after seeing your less than energetic performance during meetings. This kind of situation is a gateway to losing control of staff who may begin to doubt your authority because other managers step in and make decisions in your absence on an increasingly frequent basis. If you're asked to go on too many back-to-back trips, start analyzing the priorities for each venture. If the trips are necessary, fine. But you may find that you are on the road more often than necessary. Say no to trips that are only marginally necessary. You'll save your own sanity and some of the company's money in the process.

Pay Attention to the Rumor Mill

Almost every person who works in the field talks to co-workers, and many travel together frequently. Talk to these comrades to learn what's happening back at the ranch. Discount everything you hear by 90 percent. If the remaining 10 percent still appears ominous, like a thunderstorm building on the horizon, delicately check with your boss to see what's really up.

If All Else Fails

There may come a time when a company goes off the rails because its senior managers spend too much time traveling and employees lose touch of what they are supposed to be doing. The overall mission of the business may weaken and customers may begin to look elsewhere for satisfaction. This kind of problem often happens when a senior person goes off on back-to-back trips for months at a time to meet new customers or talk to the press on a press tour. If you feel that you're losing touch or control, take the next plane home and grab hold of the reins. While your sudden cancellation of a meeting may frost a client or make an editor grumble, this is a small risk in comparison to what else you could lose.

When you travel on business, you have to make your equipment work around dicey communications situations and navigate the dangerous waters around problems back at your office. In this chapter, we have presented the basics of keeping your equipment working, solving the standard technological office-on-the-go problems, and making sure that people "back at the ranch" are happy with you while you're gone. If this seems like a tough bill to fill, remember that your office-on-the-go technology makes almost anything possible—even productive business trips!

Section Three

═══════════════

RESOURCES ON THE GO—A REFERENCE GUIDE FOR BUSINESS TRAVELERS

COMPUTER HARDWARE

NOTEBOOK COMPUTER COMPANIES

The following is a listing of mobile computer manufacturers. The list is not comprehensive, but it does include computer manufacturers with whom we are familiar. Because model numbers change frequently, we have not supplied them here. Most of the companies listed offer a range of portable and notebook computers, with different chip, memory, and display options. Please note that a listing for any product or service in this book does not constitute an endorsement of that product or service as being suitable for any specific purpose. We have provided the listings for convenience only to help in your search of products that meet your needs on the road.

MACINTOSH (POWERBOOK) NOTEBOOK COMPUTERS

Macintosh computers use the Apple OS, but can also read most IBM-compatible files produced under Windows or MS-DOS.

Apple Computer, Inc.
20525 Mariani Avenue
Cupertino, CA 95014
(800) 776-2333
(408) 996-1010

Outbound Systems, Inc.
4840 Pearl East Circle
Boulder, CO 80301
(800) 444-4607
(303) 786-9200

PC-COMPATIBLE NOTEBOOK COMPUTERS

The companies listed in this section manufacture notebook and subnotebook computers that employ the MS-DOS operating environment. Most of them (with 386 microprocessors and above) can also run the Windows graphical interface.

Altima Systems, Inc.
1390 Willow Pass Road, Suite 1050
Concord, CA 94520
(800) 356-9990
(510) 356-5600

AMAX Engineering Corporation
47315 Mission Falls Court
Fremont, CA 94539
(800) 888-2629
(510) 651-8886

AMREL Technology, Inc.
9952 East Baldwin Place
El Monte, CA 91731
(800) 88-AMREL
(818) 575-5110

Aquiline Inc.
449 Main Street
Bennington, VT 05201
(802) 442-1526

AST Research, Inc.
16215 Alton Parkway
Irvine, CA 92713-9658
(800) 876-4AST
(714) 727-4141

Austin Computer Systems
10300 Metric Boulevard
Austin, TX 78758
(800) 752-1577
(512) 339-3500

Beaver Computer Corporation (BCC)
174 Component Drive
San Jose, CA 95131-1119
(800) 827-4222
(408) 944-9000

Bondwell Industrial Company
47485 Seabridge Drive
Fremont, CA 94538
(510) 490-4300

Compaq Computer Corporation
P.O. Box 692000
Houston, TX 77269-2000
(713) 370-0670

CompuAdd Computer Corporation
12303 Technology Boulevard
Austin, TX 78727
(800) 627-1967
(512) 250-1489

Compudyne
15151-A Surveyor Road
Addison, TX 75244
(800) 932-COMP
(214) 702-0055

Dataworld
3733 San Gabriel River Parkway
Pico Rivera, CA 90660-1404
(800) 274-2983
(310) 695-3777

Dell Computer Corporation
9505 Arboretum Boulevard
Austin, TX 78759-7260
(800) 426-5150
(512) 338-4400

DTK Computer Inc.
17700 Castleton Street, Suite 300
City of Industry, CA 91748
(800) GRAFIKA
(818) 810-8880

Epson America
20770 Madrona Avenue
Torrance, CA 90509-2842
(800) 922-8911
(310) 782-0700

Gateway 2000
610 Gateway Drive
North Sioux City, SD 57049
(800) 523-2000
(605) 232-2000

Grid Systems Corporation
47211 Lakeview Boulevard
Fremont, CA 94537
(800) 654-GRID
(510) 656-4700

International Business Machines Corporation
1133 Westchester Avenue
White Plains, NY 10604
(800) 426-2468
(800) 465-7999 in Canada
(404) 238-2200

Leading Edge Products, Inc.
117 Flanders Road
P.O. Box 5020
Westborough, MA 01581-5020
(508) 836-4800

Micro Express NB925
1801 Carnegie Avenue
Santa Ana, CA 92705
(800) 989-9900
(714) 852-1400

NCR Corporation (Also offers a networked system with cellular fax and phone.)
1700 S. Patterson Boulevard
Dayton, OH 45479
(800) 262-7782
(513) 445-5000

NEC Technologies Inc. (Also sells a briefcase system)
1414 Massachusetts Avenue
Boxborough, MA 01719
(800) 632-4636
(800) 343-4418
(508) 635-4000

Northgate Computer Systems
7075 Flying Cloud Drive
Eden Prairie, MN 55344
(800) 548-1993
(612) 943-8181

PC Brand, Inc.
405 Science Drive
Moorpark, CA 93021
(800) PC-BRAND
(805) 376-6174

PC Ease, Inc.
5813 Main Street, #10
Buffalo, NY 14221
(800) 4PC-EASE
(716) 626-0315

Samsung Electronics America
Information Systems Division
105 Challenger Road
Richfield Park, NJ 07660
(800) 524-1302
(201) 229-4000

Tandy Corporation—Radio Shack
700 One Tandy Center
Fort Worth, TX 76102
(817) 390-3000

Texas Instruments, Inc.
Information Technology Group
P.O. Box 202230, ITG-9130
Austin, TX 78720-230
(800) 527-3500
(512) 250-7111

Toshiba America Information Systems, Inc.
Computer Systems Division
9740 Irvine Boulevard
Irvine CA 92713-9724
(800) 334-3445
(714) 583-3000

Twinhead Corporation
1537 Center Pointe Drive
Milpitas, CA 95035
(800) 545-8946
(408) 945-0808

Zenith Data Systems, A Bull Company
2105 E. Lake Cook Road
Buffalo Grove, IL 60089
(800) 553-0331
(708) 808-4300

Zeos International
530 5th Avenue N.W.
St. Paul, MN 55112
(800) 423-5891
(612) 633-4591

PALMTOP COMPUTERS, PERSONAL DIGITAL ASSISTANTS, AND ELECTRONIC ORGANIZERS

Newton
Apple Computer Inc.
20525 Mariani Avenue
Cupertino, CA 95014
(800) 766-2333
(408) 966-1010

Hewlett Packard
1000 NE Circle Boulevard
Corvalis, OR 97330
(800) 443-1254
(503) 757-2000

Laser PC4
The Order Center
(800) 336-2777

Psion, Inc.
118 Echo Lake Road
P.0. Box 790
Watertown, CT 06795
(203) 274-7521

Sharp Wizard Division
Sharp Electronics Corporation
Sharp Plaza
Mahway, NJ 07430-2135
(201) 529-8200

Zeos Pocket PC
Zeos International
530 5th Avenue N.W.
St. Paul, MN 55112
(800) 423-5891
(612) 633-4591

PEN-BASED COMPUTERS AND ELECTRONIC NOTEPADS

Apple Computers, Inc.
20525 Mariani Avenue
Cupertino, CA 95014
(800) 766-2333
(408) 966-1010

Dauphin 5000 Series Pentop
Dauphin Technology, Inc.
450 Eisenhower Lane N.
Lombard, IL 60148
(800) 782-7922
(708) 627-4004

GriDPAD (for both PenPoint and Pen
Windows) **and PalmPAD**
Grid Systems Corporation
47211 Lakeview Boulevard
Fremont, CA 94537
(800) 654-GRID
(510) 656-4700

IBM ThinkPad (under PenPoint)
*International Business Machines
Corporation*
1133 Westchester Avenue
White Plains, NY 10604
(800) 426-2468
(800) 465-7999
(404) 238-2200 for Pen-Assist
Developer's Program

Momenta Pentop Computer
Momenta Corporation
295 N. Bernard Avenue
Mountain View, CA 94043
(800) MOMENTA
(415) 969-3876

NCR 3125 (for PenPoint, Pen
Windows)
NCR Corporation
1700 S. Patterson Boulevard
Dayton, OH 45479
(800) 225-5627
(513) 445-5000

NEC UltraLite
NEC Technologies Inc.
1414 Massachusetts Avenue
Boxborough, MA 01719
(800) 388-8888
(508) 264-8000

**WriteAway for the Zeos Notebook
386+**
Arthur Dent Associates Inc.
500 Clark Road
Tewksbury, MA 01876
(508) 858-3745

Z-Notepad
Zenith Data Systems
2150 E. Lake Cook Road
Buffalo Grove, IL 60089
(800) 553-0331
(708) 808-5000

PORTABLE PRINTERS

Canon BubbleJet
Canon USA, Inc.
1 Canon Plaza
Lake Success, NY 11042-9979
(800) 848-4123
(800) 387-1241 (Canada)
(516) 488-6700

Citizen Printers (thermal fusion)
Citizen America Corporation
2450 Broadway, Suite 600
Santa Monica, CA 90411-4003
(800) 477-4683
(310) 453-0614

Itron (dot matrix)
E. 15616 Euclid
Spokane, WA 99216
(800) 635-5461

Kodak Diconix Printers
Eastman Kodak Co.
P.O. Box 22740
M.C. 36200
Rochester, NY 14692
(800) 344-0006
(716) 724-5393

Mannesmann Printers (thermal transfer)
Mannesman Tally
P.O. Box 97018
8301 S. 180th Street
Kent, WA 98064
(800) 843-1347
(206) 251-5524

Seikosha America (dot matrix)
10 Industrial Avenue
Mahwah, NJ 07430
(201) 327-7227

Toshiba ExpressWriter
Toshiba America
9740 Irvine Boulevard
Irvine, CA 92713-9724
(800) 468-7544
(714) 587-6245

MISCELLANEOUS HARDWARE AND PRODUCTIVITY EQUIPMENT

Travel Kit for Notebook Users

This travel kit is only $29.95 and contains useful mobile office items that would take some effort to assemble from individual sources. The items are packaged neatly in a traveling pouch. The kit includes a modular duplex "Y" jack that adapts a telephone jack to accept the telephone and your modem at the same time (useful for hooking up your modem in a hotel room), a 12-foot extension phone cord (to use when your modem cord is too short to reach the jack in a busy airport), a 3-foot flat-ribbon parallel printer cable for connecting to a borrowed printer, a plug that allows two phone cords to be attached together to make one long cord (also useful when you need a longer phone cord in a hotel room or at the airport), and a two-size screw driver: a 3/16ths inch Phillips on one end and a 1/8th inch flat blade on the other end (useful for making connections and minor adjustments to your mobile equipment). To order a kit, call:

MicroComputer Accessories, Inc.
(310) 645-9400

AUDIO ADAPTERS AND RECORDERS

AudioPort
Video Associates Labs
4926 Spicewood Springs Road
Austin, TX 78759
(800) 331-0547
(512) 346-5781

BATTERY PRODUCTS FOR COMPUTERS

Lind Electronic Design, Inc.
6414 Cambridge Street
Minneapolis, MN 55426
(612) 927-6303
(800) 659-5956

Newer Technology, Inc. (Also sells color screens and RAM upgrades)
78030 E. Osie, Suite 105
Wichita, KS 67207
(316) 685-4904
(800) 678-3726

CELLULAR ANTENNAS

ORA Electronics
9410 Owensmouth Avenue
P.O. Box 4029
Chatsworth, CA 91311
(818) 772-2700

CELLULAR DATA LINK

Mitsubishi International Corporation
(708) 860-4200
(416) 677-8000 (Canada)

ELECTRONIC BOOK AND REFERENCE TOOL

Sony Data Discman
Sony Corporation of America
1 Sony Drive
Park Ridge, NJ 07656
(800) 526-2287
(201) 930-1000

HARD DISK SYSTEMS, REMOVABLE OR PORTABLE

Bondwell Industrial Company
47485 Seabridge Drive
Fremont, CA 94538
(510) 490-4300

Epson America
20770 Madrona Avenue
Torrance, CA 90509-2842
(800) 922-8911
(310) 782-0700

Laptop Solutions, Inc.
10700 Richmond Avenue, #114
Houston, TX 77042
(800) 683-6839
(713) 789-0878

Samsung Information Systems America
401 Mayhill Street
Saddlebrook, NJ 07662
(800) 624-8999
(201) 587-9600

Simplicity Computing
126 W. 23rd Street
New York, NY 10011
(800) 275-6525
(212) 229-1625

Vision Logic
283 E. Brokaw Road
San Jose, CA 95112

(800) 437-1719
(408) 437-1000

LAN ADAPTERS

Accton Technology Corp.
46750 Fremont Boulevard, #104
Fremont, CA 94538
(800) 926-9288
(510) 226-9800

CompuLAN Technology, Inc.
180 Charcot Avenue
San Jose, CA 95131
(800) 486-8810

D-Link Systems, Inc.
5 Musick
Irvine, CA 92718
(714) 455-1688

IQ Systems Corp.
20232 23rd Drive S.E.
Bothell, WA 98021
(800) 227-2817
(206) 483-3555

Solectek Corp.
6470 Nancy Ridge Drive, #109
San Diego, CA 92121
(800) 437-1518

Xircom, Inc.
26025 Mureau Road
Calabasas, CA 91302
(818) 878-7600

MEMORY UPGRADES FOR NOTEBOOK COMPUTERS

Logical Connection, Inc.
4660 Portland Road N.E., #108
Salem, OR 97305
(800) 238-9415
Tech Support (503) 390-9375

MOBILE SYSTEM INTEGRATORS

Data One
P.O. Box 870
4530 River Drive
Moline, IL 61265
(800) DATA ONE
(309) 797-3873

NETWORK CONNECTORS AND NETWORKING PRODUCTS

DOS Mounter, NetMounter, SCSI-to-Ethernet Adapters
Dayna Communications, Inc.
50 S. Main Street, 5th Floor
Salt Lake City, UT 84144
(801) 531-0600

PhoneNET Connectors, Timbuktu Remote Control Software, and More
Farallon Computing, Inc.
2470 Mariner Square Loop
Alameda, CA 94501
(510) 814-5000

NETWORKS FOR PORTABLE TO DESKTOP COMMUNICATIONS

Logical Connection, Inc.
4660 Portland Road NE, #108
Salem, OR 97305
(800) 238-9415
Tech Support (503) 390-9375

Xircom and Novell's Network Simplicity
Xircom
26025 Mureau Road
Calabasas, CA 91302
(818) 878-7600

NUMERIC KEYPAD (PORTABLE)

Genovation, Inc.
17741 Mitchell, North
Irvine, CA 92714
(714) 833-3355

POINTING DEVICES, MOUSES (PORTABLE)

The Little Mouse
Mouse Systems Corporation
47505 Seabridge Drive
Fremont, CA 94538
(510) 656-1117

Microsoft BallPoint, Microsoft Mouse
Microsoft Corporation

One Microsoft Way
Redmond, WA 98052
(206) 882-8080

MicroTrac
MicroSpeed Inc.
44000 Old Warm Springs Boulevard
Fremond, CA 94538
(800) 232-7888
(510) 490-1403

Thumbelina, MousePen
Appoint
7026 Koll Center Parkway, #230
Pleasanton, CA 94566
(800) 448-1184

Trackpoint
IBM Corporation
1133 Westchester Avenue
White Plains, NY 10604
(800) 426-9292

TrackMan Portable
Logitech, Inc.
6505 Kaiser Drive
Fremont, CA 94555
(800) 231-7717
(510) 795-8500

SCANNER, HANDHELD

ScanMan Color
LogiTech
(800) 231-7717

SURGE PROTECTORS

Panamax, Inc.
150 Mitchell Boulevard
San Rafael, CA 94903
(415) 499-3900
(800) 472-5555

TRAFFIC REPORTING SYSTEM

Autotalk, Inc.
3350 Scott Boulevard, Bldg. #4102
Santa Clara, CA 95054
(408) 727-8800

VGA TO VIDEO CONVERTER FOR PRESENTATIONS (PORTABLE)

KDI Precision Products, Inc.
2975 McMann Road
Cincinnati, OH 45245
(800) 377-3334

Willow Peripherals
190 Willow Avenue
Bronx, NY 10454-3596
(212) 402-9500

CASES AND MOBILE OFFICE LUGGAGE

Calisé Computer Luggage
23228 Hawthorne Boulevard
Torrance, CA 90505
(310) 375-8406

Compushield Cases
Solidex, Inc.
(714) 599-2666

Targus
P.O. Box 5039
Cerritos, CA 90703
(714) 523-5429

COMMUNICATIONS HARDWARE

CELLULAR TELEPHONES

Antel Corporation
400 Oser Avenue
Hauppauge, NY 11788
(516) 273-6800

AT&T Cellular Hotline
5 Woodhollow Road
Parsippany, NJ 07054
(800) 232-5179
(201) 581-5149

Audiovox Corporation
150 Marcus Boulevard
Hauppage, NY 11788
(516) 231-7750

Blaupunkt
Robert Bosch Corporation
2800 S. 25th Avenue
Broadview, IL 60153
(708) 865-5200

Clarion Corporation of America
661 W. Redondo Beach Boulevard
Gardena, CA 90247
(310) 327-9100

DiamondTel
Mitsubishi Electronics
800 Biermann Court
Mt. Prospect, IL 60056
(708) 298-9223

Ericsson (GE) Mobile Communications
P.O. Box 4248
Lynchburg, VA 24502
(800) CARFONE
(804) 528-7643

Ford Cellular System
Ford Motor Company
Regent Court
16800 Executive Plaza Drive
Dearborn, MI 48126
(800) 367-3333

Fujitsu America, Inc.
2801 Telecom Parkway
Richardson, TX 75082
(214) 690-9660

GE Mobile Communications
P.O. Box 4248
Lynchburg, VA 24502
(800) CARFONE

Hyundai America Corporation
(408) 473-9200

Identity Systems Technology, Inc.
1347 Exchange Drive
Richardson, TX 75081
(214) 235-3330

Kenwood USA Corporation
2201 E. Dominguez Street
Long Beach, CA 90810
(310) 639-9000

Mitsubishi International Corporation
1500 Michael Drive, Suite B
Wood Dale, IL 60191
(708) 860-4200
(416) 677-8000 in Canada

Motorola, Inc.
1475 W. Shure Drive
Arlington Heights, IL 60004
(800) 331-6456
(708) 632-5000

Muratec
5560 Tennyson Parkway
Plano, TX 75024
(214) 403-3300

NEC America, Inc.
Mobile Radio Division
383 Omni Drive
Richardson, TX 75080
(800) 421-2141
1-800-363-2847 (Canada)
(214) 907-4000

Nokia Mobile Phones, Inc.
2300 Tall Pines Drive, Suite 120
Largo, FL 34641
(813) 536-5553

NovAtel
P.O. Box 1233
Fort Worth, TX 76101
(817) 847-2100

OKI Telecom
437 Old Peachtree Road
Suwanee, GA 30174
(404) 995-9800

Panasonic Company
One Panasonic Way
Secaucus, NJ 07094
(201) 348-7000

Pioneer Electronics
2265 E. 220th Street
Long Beach, CA 90810
(310) 835-6177

Sanyo
21350 Lassen Street
Chatsworth, CA 91311
(800) 421-5013
(818) 998-7322

Shintom West
20435 South Western Avenue
Torrance, CA 90501
(310) 328-7200

Sony Corporation of America
Sony Drive
Park Ridge, NJ 07656
(201) 930-1000

Tandy Corporation—Radio Shack
700 One Tandy Center
Fort Worth, TX 76102
(817) 390-3000

Technophone
1801 Penn Street
Melbourne, FL 32901
(407) 952-2100

Uniden America Corporation
4700 Amon Carter Boulevard
Fort Worth, TX 76155
(817) 858-3300

CELLULAR PACKET RADIO

Axsys
Spectrum Information Technologies
2611 Cedar Springs
Dallas, TX 75201
(214) 999-6000

RAM Mobile Data
1 Rockefeller Plaza, Suite 1600
New York, NY 10020
(212) 373-1930

MODEMS AND FAX/MODEMS

AT&T Paradyne
8545 126th Avenue N.
Largo, FL 34649
(416) 494-0453
(800) 482-3333

Cardinal Technologies
1827 Freedom Road
Lancaster, PA 17601
(800) 233-0187

Digicom Systems, Inc.
188 Topaz Street
Milpitas, CA 95035
(800) 833-8900

Hayes
5835 Peachtree Corners E.
P.O. Box 105203
Atlanta, GA 30348
(404) 441-1617
(800) 635-1225

Intel Corp.
PC Enhancements Group
Mail Stop EO3-07
5200 N.E. Elam Young Parkway
Hillsboro, OR 97124
(800) 538-3373
(503) 629-7354

LogiCode Technology Inc. *(QuickTel Modems)*
1817 DeHavilland Drive
Newbury Park, CA 91320
(805) 499-4443

Microcom Inc.
500 River Ridge Drive
Norwood, MA 02062
(617) 551-1000

PSI Integration
851 E. Hamilton Avenue, Suite 200
Campbell, CA 95008
(408) 559-8544
(800) 622-1722

Supra Corporation
7701 Supra Drive S.W.
Albany, OR 97321
(503) 967-2410
(800) 944-8772

SUBNOTEBOOK MODEMS

AT&T Paradyne
8545 126th Avenue N.
Largo, FL 34649
(416) 494-0453
(800) 482-3333

Microcom, Inc.
500 River Ridge Drive
Norwood, MA 02062
(617) 551-1000

PORTABLE FAX SYSTEMS

The Complete PC FAX/Portable+
The Complete PC
1983 Concourse Drive
San Jose, CA 94131
(408) 434-0145

Infinidisc Corporation
7 Littleton Road
Westford, MA 01886
(800) 428-3071
(508) 692-0898

PAGERS AND MESSAGING SERVICES

Ericsson GE Communications
15 E Midland Avenue
Paramus, NJ 09652
(201) 265-6600

Motorola EMBARC Advanced Messaging
1301 N Congress Avenue
Boynton Beach, FL 33426
(800) 362-2724

Motorola NewsStream
1500 N.W. 22nd Avenue
Boynton Beach, FL 33426
(407) 364-2000

SkyTel
200 S. Lamar Street
Security Center South
Jackson, MS 39201
(601) 354-7813
(800) 456-3333 ext. 0124

INTERNATIONAL PHONE ADAPTERS

TELEADAPT
29A Bridge Street
Pinner, Middlesex HA5 3HR
England
44 (0) 81 429 0479
CompuServe: 10011,2713
Applelink: TELEADAPT
FAX: 44 (0) 81 868 1697

SECURITY AND INSURANCE

AUTO SECURITY SYSTEMS

Vocalarm
Electronic Security Products of California, Inc.
21200 Vanowen Street
Canoga Park, CA 91303
(808) 999-0990

Hornet Auto Security Systems
DEI
(800) 274-0200 (USA)
(800) 361-7271 (Canada)
5-531-61-31 (Mexico)

Seco-Larm
17811 Sky Park Drive, Suites D, E
Irvine, CA 92714
(714) 261-2999

Viper Auto Security Systems
Directed Electronics, Incorporated
2560 Progress Street
Vista, CA 92083
(899) 274-0200 (USA)
(800) 361-7271 (Canada)
Computer Locks

Kensington Microware Limited
2855 Campus Drive
San Mateo, CA 94403
(800) 535-4242
(415) 572-2700

PC Guardian Security Products
118 Alto Street
San Rafael, CA 94901
(800) 288-8126
(415) 459-0190

Z-Lock Monufacturing Company
P.O. Box 949
Redondo Beach, CA 90277
(310) 372-4842

COMPUTER IDENTIFICATION AND TRACKING PROGRAMS

Computer Owner Protection Program
IDX Technologies, Inc.
14 Research Way
Setauket, NY 11733
(800) 645-5404
(516) 689-9866

STOP Program
American Connection Information Systems
56 Ocean Drive East
Stamford, CT 06902
(800) 488-7867
(203) 359-9361
Computer Insurance

Safeware (Insurance)
2929 N. High Street
Columbus, OH 43202
(800) 848-3469
(614) 262-0559

ENCRYPTION ROUTINES AND SECURITY SOFTWARE

AllSafe
This product incorporates access control, virus protection, and other security functions.
XTree Corporation
4330 Santa Fe Road
San Luis Obispo, CA 93410
(805) 541-0604

FinderBolt and MacSafte II
Kent Marsh, Ltd.
3260 Sul Ross
Houston, TX 77098
(713) 522-5625

LapGuard
Personal Computer Card Corporation
5151 S. Lakeland Drive, Suite 16
Lakeland, FL 33813

LapSecure
Secura Technologies
P.O. Box 7089
Laguna Niguel, CA 92607
(714) 248-1544

DiskLock
This program is a password protection, data encryption, and hard disk locking utility.
Fifth Generation Systems Inc.
10049 N. Reiger Road
Baton Rouge, LA 70809
(504) 291-7221

FastLock Plus
This is a program that provides password and hard disk access protection.
Rupp Corporation
7285 Franklin Avenue
Los Angeles, CA 90046
(213) 850-5394

MenuWorks Total Security
This product locks the computer's keyboard and disables the computer's ability to boot from a floppy disk.
PC Dynamics, Inc.
31332 Via Colinas #102
Westlake Village, CA 91362
(800) 888-1741
(818) 889-1741

RENTALS OF MOBILE OFFICE EQUIPMENT

Most major car rental firms will rent cellular phones with the rental of a car. Other firms will rent phones, notebook computers, and even portable fax machines and voice mail services—often drop shipping equipment to you overnight so you have it when you need it on the road. Renting a phone on the road provides distinct advantages for some business travelers—it reduces roaming charges and the complex access codes required to reach you on your home-based phone. Rental phones give you a seven-digit local number to reach you on the road. The following lists some well-known mobile office equipment rental agencies. For rental phones and pagers also look in the Yellow Pages under *Telephone Systems* or *Pagers*. For mobile computer rentals, look in the Yellow Pages under *Computers—Rental and Leasing*. If you need to rent computer-based and other presentation equipment on the road look in the Yellow Pages under *Audio-Visual Equipment—Renting and Leasing*.

Action Cellular Rent a Phone, Inc.
1996 Union Street, Suite 200
San Francisco, CA 94123
(415) 929-0400

Authorized Cellular
16280 13 Mile Road
Roseville, MD
(313) 775-8610

InTouch USA
2200 Cedar Cove Court
Reston, VA 22091
(800) 872-7626
(703) 264-1872

Lap Stop Corporation
153 Andover Street
Danvers, MA 01923
(800) 828-8580
(617) 777-5308

Metro Cellular Rentals
2031 Acacia Street, Suite 220
Santa Ana, CA 92707
(714) 757-0400

Road & Show Cellular
13470 Washington Boulevard
Marina Del Rey, CA 90292
(800) 451-6066
(310) 301-2121

SIMS Communications
2875 S. Congress Avenue, Suite A
Delray Beach, FL 33445
(800) 999-1333
(407) 265-3601

SOFTWARE SOURCES

CONFERENCING SOFTWARE

InForum
MacVONK USA
313 Iona Avenue
Narbeth, PA 19072
(215) 660-0606

Pacer Forum
Pacer Software, Inc.
7911 Herschel Avenue, Suite 402
La Jolla, CA 92037
(619) 454-0565

ELECTRONIC CARD FILES

Address Book Plus (PC, Macintosh)
PowerUp Software
(800) 851-2917

Dynodex (PC, Macintosh)
Portfolio System
(408) 252-0420

MacPhonebook (Macintosh)
Synex
(800) 447-9639
(718) 499-6293

**My Advanced MailList and
MyDataBase** (PC, Macintosh)
MySoftware Corporation
(800) 325-3508
(415) 325-9372

PC Tools (PC)
Central Point Software
(503) 690-8090

Rolodex Live! (PC)
DacEasy
(800) 322-3279
(214) 248-0205

Sidekick (PC)
Borland International
(408) 438-8400

TakeNote (PC)
ButtonWare
(800) 528-8866
(206) 454-6a479

TouchBase (Macintosh)
After Hours Software
(818) 780-2220
Fax Software

Hotfax (MS-DOS based)
Smith Micro Software, Inc.
P.O. Box 7137
Huntington Beach, CA 92615
(714) 964-0412

Imara Lite (for Windows**)**
Imara Research Corporation
111 Peter Street, Suite 804
Toronto, Ontario
Canada M5V 2H1
(416) 581-1740

Winfax (Windows based)
Delrina Technology
6830 Via del Oro, Suite 240
San Jose, CA 95119-1353
(800) 268-6082
(408) 363-2345

FILE MANAGEMENT

File Runner
This useful product allows you to keep the versions of files in sync on every personal computer you use—great if you need records up to date on both your mobile and office computers. Includes virus protection and overwrite safeguard.
MBS Technologies, Inc.
4017 Washington Road #4000
McMurray, PA 15317
(800) 860-8700 Answer line
(800) 538-3939 Orders

Imara Lite (for Windows)
Imara Research Corporation
111 Peter Street, Suite 804
Toronto, Ontario
Canada M5V 2H1
(416) 581-1740
Integrated Software

CA-Simply Business
A Windows-based system that handles accounting, word processing, spreadsheets, scheduling, graphics, and even includes the CompuServe Information Manager.
Computer Associates International, Inc.
One Computer Associates Plaza
Islandia, NY 11788-7000
(800) CALL CAI

Geoworks Pro
This product runs under MS-DOS and incorporates a graphical interface, word processing, spreadsheet (version of Quattro Pro SE from Borland), telecommunications, drawing capabilities, and more. A fast, relatively compact program that is almost a complete mobile office.
GeoWorks, Inc.
2150 Shattuck Avenue
Berkeley, CA 94704
(510) 644-0883

Microsoft Works
Microsoft Works, available for Macintosh, MS-DOS and Windows, integrates a word processor, spreadsheet, database manager, and charting functions. No communications programs are included in the Windows version.
Microsoft Corporation
One Microsoft Way
Redmond, WA 98052
(800) 426-9400
(206) 882-8080

Symantec Corporation
10201 Torre Avenue
Cupertino, CA 95014-2132
(408) 253-9600

LINKING SOFTWARE

The following programs can transfer data and programs between your desktop computer and your notebook computer. If you choose a notebook computer without a floppy drive, these programs are for you. They usually include the cables required to transfer the data between the two computers as part of the package.

Carbon Copy
Microcom Inc.
500 River Ridge Drive
Norwood, MA 02062
(617) 551-1000

FastLynx File Transfer Utility
Rupp Corporation
(213) 850-5394

Hotwire
Data Storm Technology
(341) 443-3282

IntelliLink
This program copies information between your favorite applications and your palmtop computer or organizer.
IntelliLink, Inc.
98 Spit Brook Road, Suite 12
Nashua, NH 03062
(603) 888-0666

LapLink and LapLink Pro
Traveling Software, Inc.
18702 N. Creek Parkway
Bothell, WA 98011
(206) 483-8088

MasterSoft, Inc.
This company sells a variety of translation software to transform files from one format into another.
6991 E. Camelback Road, Suite A-320
Scottsdale, AZ 85251
(602) 277-0900
(800) 624-6107

NETWORK AND FILE-SHARING SOFTWARE

Sitka Corporation
950 Marina Village Parkway
Alameda, CA 94501
(510) 769-9669
Presentation Software

Aldus Persuasion
Aldus Corporation
411 1st Avenue, South
Seattle, WA 98104
(800) 333-2538
(206) 628-2320

Curtain Call
ZumaGroup
160 Knowles Drive
Los Gatos, CA 95030
(800) 451-0900 (outside CA)
(408) 378-3838

Claris Hollywood
Claris Corporation
5201 Patrick Henry Drive
Santa Clara, CA 95052
(800) 325-2747
(408) 727-8227

DeltaGraph Professional
DeltaPoint, Inc.
2 Harris Court, Suite B-1
Monterey, CA 93940
(800) 367-4334
(408) 648-4000

Freelance Graphics for Windows
Lotus Development Corp.
55 Cambridge Parkway
Cambridge, MA 02142
(800) 343-5414
(617) 577-8500

Microsoft PowerPoint
Microsoft Corporation
One Microsoft Way
Redmond, WA 98052
(800) 426-9400
(206) 882-8080

SoftCraft Presenter
SoftCraft, Inc.
15 N. Carroll Street, #500
Madison, WI 53703
(800) 351-0500
(608) 257-3300

PERSONAL FINANCE

Quicken (PC, Macintosh)
Quicken is a popular personal finance program that will write checks and produce a wide variety of expense and income reports. The latest versions of Quicken include a special offer to use CheckFree, the electronic bill-paying service, and IntelliCharge, a no-fee credit card with electronic spending reports linked to your Quicken files.
Intuit
155 Linfield Drive
Menlo Park, CA
(800) 624-8742
(415) 322-0573

PERSONAL INFORMATION MANAGEMENT AND CONTACT MANAGEMENT SOFTWARE

ACT! and 1st Act! (PC, Macintosh)
Contact Software International
(214) 919-9500

Active Memory (Macintosh)
ASD Software
(714) 624-2594

AllFinder (PC)
Infinity Technologies
(800) 627-1330
(416) 890-9797

Biz*Base Gold (PC)
Creagh Computer systems
(800) 833-8892
(619) 792-1367

**Business Contacts Information
Manager** (PC)
Disk-Count Software
(612) 633-2300

C.A.T. III—Contacts, Activities, Time
Management (Mactintosh)
Chang Laboratories
(408) 727-8096

Contact Ease (Macintosh)
WestWare, Inc.
(800) 869-0871
(619) 660-0356

Connections (Macintosh)
Concentrix Technologies
(415) 358-8600

Current (PC)
IBM Desktop Software
(800) 426-9402

Data Dex Power Plus (PC)
Optionware
(800) 548-8335
(402) 697-0055

DayFlo Tracker (PC)
DayFlo Tracker Corp.
(714) 474-2901

DayMaker (Macintosh)
Pastel Development Corp.
(212) 941-7500

DeskTop (PC)
Okna Corp.
(201) 460-0677

Diamond Prospector (PC)
Diamond Data Management
(800) 955-3330
(414) 786-9000

Eighty/20 (PC)
Eighty/20 Software
(612) 633-0730

E Power (PC)
SourceMate
(800) 877-8896
(415) 381-1011

Full Contact (PC)
Practical Software
(813) 845-1847

GOLD (Macintosh)
DataSel Software
(800) 322-6160
(619) 793-2950

InfoTrac (PC)
Profile Technologies
(800) 659-9649
(603) 434-4817

Instant Recall (PC)
Chronologic Corp.
(800) 848-4970
(602) 293-3100

Laptrack and Timeslips (PC,
Macintosh)
Timeslips Corporation
(508) 768-6100

Leads! Manager (Macintosh)
Endpoint Software
(800) 433-5322
(408) 737-3831

Market Master
Breakthrough Publications
(916) 265-0911

Maximizer and Maximizer Lite (PC)
Richmond Software
(800) 663-2030
(604) 299-2121

OnTime (PC, Macintosh)
Campbell Services
(313) 559-5955

PackRat (PC)
Polaris
(619) 743-7800

Performer (PC)
Performer Systems, Inc.
(818) 575-3188

PowerLeads! (PC)
Pyramid Data
(800) 972-7972

**ProSell Personal and ProSell
Professional**
Sales Management Systems
(800) 444-9945

Primetime Personal (PC)
Primetime Software
(800) 777-8860
(714) 556-6523

Rendezvous Plus (Macintosh)
PMC Telesystems
(800) 667-0456
(604) 255-9949

Smart Office (PC)
E-Z Data
(800) 777-9188

Sales Ally
Scherrer Resources, Inc.
(800) 950-0190

SalesPro (PC)
SoftPro Group
(314) 576-7656

Sales Pro Plus (PC)
9-2-5 Software
(800) 992-5925

SimpliFiler (Macintosh)
Zicon Software
(503) 635-9622

Super Office
SuperOffice Corporation
One Cranberry Hill
Lexington, MA 02173
(800) 328-6868
(617) 674-1101

TeleMagic (PC, Macintosh)
Remote Control International
(619) 431-4000

TimeBase (PC)
Time/Design
(800) 637-9942

Who-What-When (PC)
Chronos Software
(415) 206-0580

ROAD ATLAS SOFTWARE

**AutoMap and AutoMap Europe: The
Intelligent Road Atlases** (PC,
Macintosh)
This easy-to-use mapping software
will display the best routes for your
trip on your notebook screen, and
you can print them out on your
portable printer if desired.
AutoMap Incorporated
9831 S. 51st Street, Bldg. C-113
Phoenix, AZ 85044
(602) 893-2400

MapExpert (CD-ROM based for use
with Windows)

Street Atlas USA
Offers a map of every street in the
USA. MapExpert has more features
than Street Atlas USA, including the
ability to annotate maps.
DeLorme Mapping
Main Street
P.O. Box 298
Freeport, ME 04032
(800) 452-5931
(207) 865-1234

SPREADSHEET SOFTWARE

Lotus 1-2-3 (PC, Macintosh)
Lotus Development Corp.
55 Cambridge Parkway
Cambridge, MA 02142
(800) 343-5414
(617) 577-8500

Microsoft Excel (PC, Macintosh)
Microsoft Corporation
One Microsoft Way
Redmond, WA 98052
(800) 426-9400
(206) 882-8080

QuattroPro for Windows
Borland International, Inc.
1800 Green Hills
P.O. Box 660001
Scotts Valley, CA 95067
(800) 331-0877
(408) 461-9122

TELECOMMUNICATIONS SOFTWARE

Crosstalk
DCA, Inc.
1000 Alderman Drive
Alpharetta, GA
(404) 442-4000
(800) 348-DCA-1

LogiCode Technology Inc.
1817 DeHavilland Drive
Newbury Park, CA 91320
(805) 499-4443

MicroPhone II and MicroPhone Pro
Software Ventures Corporation
2907 Claremont Avenue
Berkeley, CA 94705
(510) 644-3232

ProComm Plus/ProComm
DataStorm Technologies
P.O. Box 1471
Columbia, MO 65205
(314) 443-3282
(800) 333-4559

Relay Gold
Microcom, Inc.
Still River Corporate Center
55 Federal Road
Danbury, CT 06810
(203) 798-3800

Quick Link II
Smith Micro Software, Inc.
P.O. Box 7137
Huntington Beach, CA 92615
(714) 362-5800

TERMINAL EMULATION SOFTWARE

PacerTerm
Pacer Software, Inc.
7911 Herschel Avenue, Suite 402
La Jolla, CA 92037
(619) 454-0565

MicroPhone Pro
Software Ventures Corporation
2907 Claremont Avenue
Berkeley, CA 94705
(510) 644-3232

VersaTerm Pro
Synergy Software, Inc.
2457 Perkiomen Avenue
Reading, PA 19606
(215) 779-0522

WORD PROCESSING SOFTWARE

Microsoft Word for MS-DOS, Macintosh, and Windows
Microsoft Corporation
One Microsoft Way
Redmond, WA 98052
(800) 426-9400
(206) 882-8080

Signature for MS-DOS
XYQUEST, Inc.
44 Manning Road
Billerica, MA 01821
(508) 671-0888

**WordPerfect for MS-DOS,
Macintosh, and Windows**
WordPerfect Corporation
1555 North Technology Way
Orem, UT 84057
(800) 451-5151

WordStar for Windows and MS-DOS
WordStar International
201 Alameda del Prado
Novato, CA 94949
(800) 227-5609
(415) 382-8000

UTILITIES AND ANTI-VIRUS SOFTWARE

Norton Utilities and Other Programs
Symantec Corporation
10201 Torre Avenue
Cupertino, CA 95014-2132
(408) 253-9600

StuffIt Compression Utilities
Aladdin Systems, Inc.
165 Westridge Drive
Watsonville, CA 95076
(408) 761-6206

SuperStore
This product reduces file sizes signifi-
cantly and thus frees up space on the
hard drive—very useful if you use
large database and word processing
files on the road and are running out
of hard disk space.
AddStor, Inc.
(415) 688-0470

MISCELLANEOUS SOFTWARE TOOLS

**Personal Font for Notes and Faxes
on the Road**
If you want your faxes on the road to
really look personal, and if you use
an Apple Macintosh PowerBook computer, Signature Software, Inc. will
develop a font for you that looks
almost exactly like your own handwriting. Call the company and they
will send you a form to complete that
provides an example of your handwriting. For $179, in about four
weeks, the company will deliver the
font to you.
Signature Software, Inc.
10075 SW Barbur Boulevard
Suite 5-401
Portland, OR 97219-9918
(503) 386-3221

WIZARD SOFTWARE CARDS AND THIRD-PARTY WIZARD APPLICATIONS

Nictrix Corporation
2 Christie Heights Street
Leonia, NJ 07605
(201) 947-2220

NEWS, RESEARCH, AND ENTERTAINMENT

AUDIO BOOK AND MAGAZINE SOURCES

Call these audio book publishers for their catalogs or to place an order.

Audio Renaissance
(213) 939-1840

Bantam Audio
(212) 765-6500

Newsweek On Air (tapes of the radio program)
Mark 56 Records
P.O. Box One
Anaheim, CA 92815
(800) 227-7388

GOVERNMENT INFORMATION

A wide range of government information is available through the commercial online services listed under Online Services in this directory. In addition to your online links, the following government information services may be of use to you on the road.

The GAIN Program
A single phone call will give anyone with a fax machine instant access and a printout of daily information from six government databanks on federal contracts up for bid, sales leads, import/export opportunities, federal grant and loan programs, and home and land foreclosures. The calls provide these leads for about $3 to $6 a phone call per zip code area. Call: (900) 990-GAIN

Congressional Listings
DataSel Software includes a disk of all members of Congress with its Gold contact management software.
DataSel Software
(619) 793-2950

Department of Commerce NTDB Database on CD-ROM
The NTDB database on CD-ROM contains more than 90,000 documents from fifteen federal agencies including basic export information and country-specific information. The information is released monthly, and is especially valuable for companies that have international marketing and exporting interests.
Economics and Statistics Administration
Office of Business Analysis
Room H4878, HCH Building
Washington, DC 20230
(202) 377-1986

COMPUTER GAMES

There are too many games to list. Here are some we play on the road on our notebooks. You'll probably have your own favorites. Just go to any software store, like Egghead, to peruse the options.

Microsoft Flight Simulator
Microsoft Corporation
One Microsoft Way
Redmond, WA 98052
(800) 426-9400

Franklin Big League Baseball (hand-held game)
Franklin Electronic Publishers, Inc.
122 Burrs Road
Mount Holly, NJ 08060
(609) 261-4800

Where in Time Is Carmen Sandiego?
Where in the World Is Carmen Sandiego?
Broderbund Software
(Available from software stores like Egghead Software and mail order companies listed in PC and Macintosh magazines.)

EDUCATIONAL PROGRAMS

There are more sources of recorded educational materials than possible to list here. The following are ones you may not be aware of or cannot find in bookstores or record stores.

The University of Phoenix Online Degree Program
The University of Phoenix offers a wide range of business, nursing, and education degree programs in formats suitable for working adults. The online program allows students to obtain an accredited bachelor's or master's degree in business or management, entirely by using online interaction with the faculty via a computer and modem. Many of the students are professionals who spend a great deal of time on the road. They simply log on from their hotel rooms or from the airport. The online program is based out of San Francisco, California. The University of Phoenix corporate headquarters are in Phoenix, Arizona. For more information contact:
University of Phoenix Online
101 California Street, Suite 505

San Francisco, CA 94111
(415) 956-2121
SuperStar Teachers
SuperStar Teachers is a series of college lectures on audiotape (and videotape) as delivered by outstanding professors from the best universities. Lectures are available in history, humanities, and many other fields.
The Teaching Company
P.O. Box 4000
Kearneysville, WV 25430-4000
(800) 832-2412

Orbits—Voyage through the Solar System (on CD-ROM)
Chemistry Works—Computerized Periodic Table (on CD-ROM)
Bodyworks—An Adventure in Anatomy (on CD-ROM)
Software Marketing Corporation
9830 South 51st Street, Suite A-131
Phoenix, AZ 85044
(800) 545-6626
(602) 893-2400
Electronic Books

Sony Data Discman
Sony Corporation of America
1 Sony Drive
Park Ridge, NJ 07656
(800) 526-2287
(201) 930-1000

Literature on CD-ROM and as HyperCard Stacks
The Voyager Company
1351 Pacific Coast Highway
Santa Monica, CA 90401
(213) 451-1383

BUSINESS DATA ON CD-ROM

Business Lists-On-Disc
American Business Information
5711 86th Circl,
P. O. Box 27347
Omaha, NE 68127
(402) 593-4565
FAX: (402) 331-1505

Competitive Intelligence Tracking Service
Strategic Intelligence Systems
172 Madison Avenue Suite 301
New York, NY 10016
(212) 725-4550

Computer Select
For $995.00 per year, you receive complete information on a monthly CD-ROM on the computing and the computer industry. The CD-ROMs include full-length articles and abstracts, product reviews, buyers' guides, industry news, analyses, and expert opinions published in the last 12 months for over 160 leading computer magazines, trade journals, and industry newsletters, combined with 72,000 hardware, software and communications product specs in hundreds of product categories, more than 13,000 vendor profiles including phone numbers, key names plus 11,000 definitions from two glossaries.
Computer Library
One Park Avenue
New York, NY 10016
(212) 50304400

DIALOG CD-ROMs
In addition to its online database services, DIALOG sells a variety of CD-ROM disks containing domestic and international business and market information. Request a catalog for more information.
DIALOG Information Services, Inc.
3460 Hillview Ave.
Palo Alto, CA 94306
(415) 858-3792

Disclosure Worldscope and Other CD-ROMs
Disclosure Worldscope provides in-depth financial information on 8,000 companies in 32 countries. A wide variety of other CD-ROMs available. Call for more information.
Disclosure, Inc.
51611 River Road
Bethesda, MD 20816
(301) 951-1300

Lotus Development CD-ROMS
Lotus ROM titles include information on banking, private and public companies, and investments. Call for a catalog and more information.
Lotus Development Corporation
55 Cambridge Parkway
Cambridge, MA 02142
(800) 554-5501

MarketPlace Business
For an annual fee , this CD-ROM provides desktop access to data on more than 7 million U.S. businesses drawn from Dun & Bradstreet's files. Comprehensive information includes name, address, telephone number, SIC code, principal officer, annual revenue, number of employees, year started, type of site, ownership, and D-U-N-S number.
MarketPlace Information Corporation
Three University Office Park
Waltham, MA 02154
(617) 225-7855

Market Potential, American Profile, Graphic Profile, Targetscan, and other CD-ROMS
Donnelley Marketing Information Services markets a variety of CD-ROM disks containing domestic and international business and market information. Request a catalog for more information.
Donnelly Marketing Information Services
70 Seaview Avenue
P.O. Box 10250
Stamford, CT 06904
(203) 353-7474

Million Dollar Disc
Dun & Bradstreet
Three Sylvan Way
Parsippany, NJ 05054
(201) 455-0900

Moody's International and Other CD-ROMs
Moody's Investor Services
99 Church Street
New York, NY 10007
(800) 955-8080

Standard & Poor's Corporations CD-ROM
Standard & Poor's Corporation
25 Broadway
New York, NY 1004

CELLULAR TELEPHONE CARRIERS

CELLULAR DIRECTORY AND PUBLICATIONS

For detailed listings of city-by-city cellular telephone information on the rates, access numbers, roaming agreements, and restrictions of the cellular telephone companies across the nation get a copy of *The Cellular Telephone Directory*. The guide includes maps of the cellular zones in the United States for easy reference. To order the directory or the other cellular telephone publications provided by the publisher contact:

Communications Publishing Service
P.O. Box 500
Mercer Island, WA 98040-0500
(206) 232-3464
(800) 366-6731

MAJOR CELLULAR OPERATING COMPANIES

The corporate offices of national cellular carriers are listed on the next several pages. Note that Ameritech Mobile Communications, Bell Atlantic Mobile Systems, Contel Cellular, Inc., GTE Mobilnet, and NYNEX Mobile Communications recently agreed to develop and implement jointly a plan to form a nationwide brand identity for cellular service. If approval is granted, the agreement calls for the carriers to coalesce billing, advertising, promotion, and intercarrier technical compatibility. Cellular One is the result of a similar joint venture sponsored by McCaw Cellular and Southwestern Bell. The following is a list of the largest cellular operating companies which manage systems in multiple cities.

Allcell
3575 Cahuenga Boulevard, Suite 495
Los Angeles, CA 90068
(213) 850-3337

Alltel Mobile Communications
P.O. Box 2177
Little Rock, AR 72203
(501) 661-8500

American Cellular
5600 Glenridge Drive, Suite 400
Atlanta, GA 30342
(404) 847-0400

Ameritech Mobile Communications
1515 Woodfield Road
Schaumburg, IL 60173
(708) 706-7600

Associated Communications
200 Gateway Towers
Pittsburgh, PA 15222
(412) 281-1907

Atlantic Cellular
1770 Hospital Trust Tower
Providence, RI 02903
(401) 421-7090

Bell Atlantic Mobile Systems
180 Washington Valley Road
Bedminster, NJ 07921
(908) 306-7000

Bell Cellular
20 Carlson Court Etobicoke
Ontario M9W 6V4 Canada
(416) 674-2220

BellSouth Enterprises
1155 Peachtree Street NE
Atlanta, GA 30367
(404) 249-4000

BellSouth Mobility
5600 Glenridge Drive, Suite 600
Atlanta, GA 30342
(404) 847-3600

Cantel
10 York Mills Road E.
North York, Ontario M2P 2C9,
Canada
(416) 440-1400

Cellular, Inc.
5990 Greenwood Plaza Boulevard,
Suite 300
Englewood, CO 80111
(303) 694-3234

Cellular Communications
150 East 58th Street , 24th Floor
New York, NY 10155
(212) 319-7014

Cellular Information Systems
8101 E. Prentice Avenue, Suite 800
Englewood, CO 80111
(303) 770-1001

Cellular Plus Mobile
1400 Spruce Street
Avoca, PA 18641
(717) 654-7587

Cellular Systems International
2227 Capricorn Way, Suite 109
Santa Rosa, CA 95407
(707) 573-3500

Celutel
400 Market Street , 10th Floor
Philadelphia, PA 19106
(215) 922-7000

Centel Cellular
O'Hare Plaza
8725 Higgins Rd, Suite 650
Chicago, IL 60631
(312) 399-2644

Century Cellular
421 Fernhill Avenue
Fort Wayne, IN 46805
(219) 484-2500

Century Cellunet
520 Riverside Drive
PO Box 4065
Monroe, LA 71201
(318) 388-9000

Century Communications
50 Locust Avenue
New Canaan, CT 06840
(203) 966-8746

Comcast
1414 S. Penn Square
Philadelphia, PA 19102
(215) 665-1700

CommNet 2000
5990 Greenwood Plaza Boulevard,
Suite 300
Englewood, CO 80111
(303) 694-3234

Contel Cellular
223 Perimeter Center Parkway
Atlanta, GA 30346
(404) 804-3400

**Crowley Cellular
Telecommunications**
18-3 E. Dundee Road, Suite 201
Barrington, IL 60010
(708) 304-4425

GTE Mobilnet (Headquarters)
616 F.M. 1960 W., Suite 400
Houston, TX 77090
(713) 583-7210

GTE Mobilnet (Regional Office)
1100 Perimeter Park Drive, Suite 101
Morrisville, NC 27560
(919) 481-6400

GenCell Management
1891 Woolner Avenue
Fairfield, CA 94533
(707) 425-8000

Independent Cellular Network
2100 Electronics Lane
Fort Myers, FL 33912
(813) 489-1600

McCaw Communications
5400 Carillon Pt.
Kirkland, WA 98033
(206) 827-4500

Miscellco Communications
PO Box 13748
Jackson, MS 39236-3748
(601) 957-8544

Northwest Cellular
901 Kilbourne Avenue
Tomah, WI 54660
(608) 372-4151

NYNEX Mobile Communications
1 Blue Hill Plaza
Pearl River, NY 10965
(914) 577-5200

Pacific Telecom
805 Broadway
Vancouver, WA 98660
(206) 696-0983

PacTel Cellular
3 Park Plaza, Suite 1100
Irvine, CA 92714
(714) 222-7000

Palmer Communications
12800 University Drive, Suite 500
Fort Myers, FL 33907-5333
(813) 433-4350

Radiofone
PO Box 8760
Metairie, LA 70011-8760
(504) 837-9540

Southwestern Bell Mobile Systems
17330 Preston Road, Suite 100-A
Dallas, TX 75252
(214) 733-2000

**Springwich Cellular Limited
Partnership**
555 Long Wharf Drive, Room 750
New Haven, CT 06511
(203) 553-7600

U S West Cellular
PO Box 7329
Bellevue, WA 98008-1329
(206) 747-4900

United States Cellular
8410 W. Bryn Mawr, Suite 700
Chicago, IL 60631
(312) 399-8900

Vanguard Cellular Systems
2002 Pisgah Church Road, Suite 300
Greensboro, NC 27408
(919) 282-3690

ONLINE INFORMATION SYSTEMS

The following is a listing of the most commonly used online information systems. If you want more information about going online, pick up a copy of the very readable *The Complete Handbook of Personal Computer Communications: The Bible of the Online World* by Alfred Glosbrenner (3rd edition, St Martin's Press). Although this edition is a bit dated as of this writing, it is the best book we have found in its genre. The technical information on connecting to the services still works, although many of the services have more modern interfaces today. Contact the companies for more information on interface options and accounts.

AppleLink
(Described in Chapter 10)
APDA, Apple Computer, Inc.
20525 Mariani Avenue
Cupertino, CA 95014-6299
(408) 996-1010
(800) 282-2732

America Online (AOL)
(Described in Chapter 10)
8619 Westwood Center Drive
Vienna, VA 22182
(703) 893-6288

BIX
BIX is a single-service online system where readers of *Byte Magazine* can exchange information relevant to computer topics and conference on the magazine's editorial topics. Contact the service at:

Byte Information Exchange
1 Phoenix Mill Lane
Petersborough, NH 03458
(603) 924-9281

CompuServe Information Service, Inc. (CSI)
(Described in Chapter 10)
5000 Arlington Centre Boulevard
Columbus, OH 43220
(617) 457-8600

Delphi
Delphi is a multi-service online system that provides news, weather, a gateway to the Dialog system, electronic mail, and special interest forums.
General Videotex Corp.
1030 Massachusetts Street
Cambridge, MA 02138
(617) 491-3393

DIALOG
(Described in Chapter 10)
DIALOG Information Services, Inc.
3460 Hillview Avenue
Palo Alto, CA 94306
(415) 858-3792

Dow Jones News/Retrieval
(Described in Chapter 10)
PO Box 300
Princeton, NJ 08543
(609) 520-4000

GEnie
(Described in Chapter 10)
GE Information Services
401 North Washington Street
Rockville, MD 20850

Internet
(Described in Chapter 10)
Commercial (non-academic) access
to Internet is handled through a variety of service carriers. Here are two
of the commercial carriers to call for
more information on Internet service
connections for dedicated corporate
accounts:

SprintLink
Sprint Communications Company
Government Systems Division
13221 Woodland Park Road
Herndon, VA 22071
(703) 904-2167

Netcom
*Netcom Online Communication
Services Inc.*
400 Moorpark Avenue, Suite 209
San Jose, CA 95117
(408) 554-8649

The following companies sell private
access accounts for Internet:

PSI Net
Performance Systems International
1180 Sunrise Valley Drive, Suite 1100
Reston, VA 22091
(703) 620-6651

The WELL
Whole Earth 'Lectronic Linke
27 Gate Five Road
Sausalito, CA 94965
(415) 332-4335

The World
Software Tool and Die
1330 Beacon Street
Brookline, MA 02146
(617) 739-0202

**WorldLink and TCP/Connect II
Communications Software**
InterCon Systems Corporation
950 Herndon Parkway
Herndon, VA 22070
(703) 709-9890
(617) 739-0202

LEXIS/NEXIS
(Described in Chapter 10)
Mead Data Central
PO Box 933
Dayton, OH 45401
(513) 865-6800

MCI Mail
(Described in Chapter 10)
MCI International, Inc.
2 International Drive
Rye Brook, NY 10573
(914) 937-3444

Online Business Link
This online service provides instant
access to the most comprehensive
business database available. Over 9.3
million businesses are described,
including company name, address,
phone number, SIC codes, name of
owner, number of employees, and
annual sales volume. Information has
been compiled from over 5,000
Yellow Page directories. Service
works with PC or Macintosh, and can
be accessed at 300 to 9600 baud rates
using virtually any communications
software. Contact:
American Business Directories
5711 South 86th Circle
P. O. Box 27347
Omaha, NE 68127
(402) 593-4565
(402) 331-1505 (fax)

NewsNet
(Described in Chapter 10)
945 Bryn Mawr, PA 19010
(215) 527-8030

Prodigy Services Company
(Described in Chapter 10)
445 Hamilton Avenue
White Plains, NY 10601
(914) 993-8848

AIRLINE
RESERVATIONS

Aerlingus
(800) 223-6537 except New York

Aero California
(800) 253-3311

Aero Peru
(800) 255-7378

Aerolineas Argentinas
(800) 333-0276

Aeromexico
(800) 237-6639

Air Canada
(800) 776-3000

Air France
(800) 237-2747

Air India
(800) 223-7776

Air Jamaica
(800) 523-5585

Air Midwest
(800) 835-2953

Air New Zealand
(800) 262-1234

Air Nieugini
(714) 452-5440

Air Paraguay
(800) 327-3551

Al NipponAirways
(800) 235-9262

Alaska Airlines
(800) 426-0333

Alitalia
(800) 233-5730

Aloha Airlines
(800) 367-5250

Alpha Air
(800) 421-9353

America West
(800) 247-5692

American Airlines
(800) 433-7300

Antillean Airlines
(800) 327-7230

Australian Airlines
(800) 922-5122

Austrian Airlines
(800) 843-0002

Avianca Airlines
(800) 284-2622

Aviateca Airlines
(800) 327-9832

British Airways
(800) 247-9297

BWIA International
(800) 327-7401

Canadian Air
(800) 426-7000

Cathay Pacific Airways
(800) 233-2742

Cayman Airways
(800) 422-9626

Continental Airlines
(800) 525-0280

Delta Airlines
(800) 221-1212

East/West Airlines of Australia
(800) 354-7471

Egypt Air
(800) 334-6787

Equatoriana Airlines
(800) 328-2367

Ethiopian Airlines
(800) 433-9677

Faucett The First Airline of Peru
(800) 334-3356

Finnair
(800) 950-5000

Garuda Indonesian Airways
(800) 342-7832

Gulf Air
(800) 631-8924

Hawaiian Airlines
(800) 367-5320

Horizon Air
(800) 547-9308

Iberia Airlines
(800) 772-4642

IcelandAir
(800) 223-5500

Japan Air Lines (JAL)
(800) 525-3663

KLM
(800) 777-5553

Korean Airlines
(800) 421-8200

Kuwait Airways
(800) 458-9248

LACSA Airlines
(800) 225-2272

Lan-Chile Airlines
(800) 735-5526

Lloyd Aereo Boliviano Airlines
(800) 327-7407

Lot Polish Airlines
(800) 223-0593

LTU International
(800) 888-0200

Lufthansa Airlines
(800) 645-3880

Malaysian Airlines System
(800) 421-8641

Martinair-Holland
(714) 992-2243

Mexicana Airlines
(800) 531-7921

MGM Grand Air
(800) 933-2646

Midway Airlines
(800) 621-5700

Midwest Express
(800) 452-2022

Mount Cook Airline of New Zealand
(800) 468-2665

Northwest Airlines
(800) 225-2525 domestic
(800) 447-4747 international

Olympic Airways
(800) 223-1226

Pacific Coast Airlines
(800) 426-5400

Philippine Airlines
(800) 435-9725

Quantas Airways
(800) 227-4500

Sabena Belgian Airlines
(800) 955-2000

Saudi Arabian Airlines
(800) 472-8342

Scandinavian Airlines
(800) 221-2350

Singapore Airlines
(800) 742-3333

Sky West Airlines
(800) 453-9417

South African Airways
(800) 722-9675

Southwest Airlines
(800) 531-5601 except Texas
(800) 442-1616 from Texas

States West Airlines
(800) 759-3866

Swissair
(800) 221-4750

TACA International Airlines
(800) 535-8780

Tan-sahsa Honduras Airlines
(800) 327-1225

TAP Air Portugal
(800) 221-7370

Thai Airways International
(800) 426-5204

Tower Air
(800) 221-2500

Trans World Airlines
(800) 221-2000

United Airlines
(800) 241-6522

US Air Airlines
(800) 759-3866

USAir
(800) 428-4322

UTA French Airlines
(800) 282-4484

Varig Brazilian
(800) 468-2744

Viasa Venezuela International Airways
(800) 327-5454

Virgin Atlantic Airways
(800) 862-8621

Wardair
(800) 237-0314

Westair Airlines
(800) 241-6522

AIRLINE CLUBS
AND LOUNGES

Most major airline carriers have membership clubs that offer a wide range of facilities to enhance business travel, including concierge services, fax machines, conference rooms, and even computer facilities. The annual fee is typically in the $125 to $250 range. If you fly first class or business class access to club facilities is provided for free by some airlines. The clubs offer comfortable lounges and some even provide complimentary bar and beverage services. The following list provides information numbers for some of the most popular airline clubs.

Airline	Club Name	Locations	Phone
Alaska Airlines	Board Room	4	(800) 426-0333
American Airlines	Admirals Club	33	(800) 433-7300
America West	Phoenix Club	9	(800) 247-5692
Continental	Presidents Club	12	(800) 322-2640
Delta	Crown Room	32	(800) 221-1212
Northwest	World Club	28	(800) 225-2525
TWA	Ambassador Club	28	(800) 221-2000
USAir	USAir Club	25	(800) 428-4322
United Airlines	Red Carpet Club	27	(800) 241-6522

HOTEL
RESERVATIONS

Admiral Benbow Inns
(800) 451-1986

Americana
Look in local phone book

Aristocrat Inns of America
Look in local phone book

Amberley Suite Hotels
(800) 227-7229

Bally's Las Vegas
(800) 634-3434

Bally's Park Place
(800) 225-5977

Bally's Reno
(800) 648-5080

Best Western
(800) 528-1234

Canadian Pacific Hotels
(800) 828-7447 outside Canada
(800) 268-9411 in Canada

Circus Circus in Las Vegas
(800) 634-3450

Clarion Hotels
(800) 252-7466

Club Med
(800) 528-3100

Comfort Inns
(800) 228-5150

Comprí Hotels
(800) 426-6774

Marriott Courtyard
(800) 321-2211

Days Inn
(800) 325-2525

Dillon Inns
(800) 253-7503

Doubletree Hotels
(800) 528-0444

Downtowner/Passport
(800) 328-6161

Drury Inns
(800) 325-8300

Econo Lodge
(800) 446-6900

Embassy Suites
(800) 362-2779

Marriott Fairfield Inns
(800) 228-2800

Mayflower Hotel in New York City
(800) 223-4164

Fairmont Hotels
(800) 527-4727

Guest Quarters Hotels
(800) 424-2900

Hampton Inns
(800) 426-7866

Harley Hotels
(800) 321-2323

Harrah's Hotels
(800) 648-3773 except Nevada

Helmsley Hotels
(800) 321-2323

Hilton Hotels
(800) 445-8667

Holiday Inn
(800) 465-4329

Howard Johnson
(800) 654-2000

Hyatt Hotels
(800) 233-1234 except Alaska
(800) 228-9005 Alaska (AK)

Intercontinental Hotels
(800) 327-0200

La Quinta Hotels
(800) 531-5900

Marriott Hotels
(800) 228-9290

Meridien Hotels
(800) 543-4300 except New York
(212) 265-4494 from New York

Nendel's Inns
(800) 547-0106

Omni International Hotels
(800) 843-6664

Preferred Hotels
(800) 323-7500

Princess Hotels International
(800) 223-1818

Quality Inns
(800) 228-5151

Radisson Hotels
(800) 333-3333

Ramada Canada
(800) 268-8998 in Canada

Ramada Renaissance
(800) 228-9898

Red Carpet Inns
(800) 251-1962

Red Lion Inns
(800) 547-8010

Red Roof Inns
(800) 843-7663

Regent International Hotels
(800) 545-4000

Residence Inns
(800) 331-3131

Roadway Inn
(800) 228-2000

Sheraton Hotels
(800) 325-3535

Shoney's Inns
(800) 222-2222

Stouffer Hotels
(800) 468-3571

Suisse Chalet
(800) 258-1980 except New
Hampshire
(800) 572-1880 in New Hamshire

Travelodge
(800) 255-3050

Treadway Inns
(800) 631-0182 except New Jersey
(800) 368-2624 in New Jersey

Vagabond Inns
(800) 522-1555

Westin Hotels
(800) 228-3000

CAR RENTAL AGENCIES

Advance Car Rentals
(612) 591-0076 main office
(800) 328-6262 reservations

Agency Rent-a-Car
(216) 349-1000 main office
(800) 221-8666 reservations

Alamo Rent-a-Car
(800) 327-0400 except Florida
(800) 327-9633 Florida only

American International Rent-a-Car
(800) 225-2529

Auto-Europe
Main office in Camden, Maine
(800) 223-5555
(800) 458-9503 Canada only

Avis Rent-a-Car System
(516) 222-3175 main office in Garden
City, New York
(800) 331-1212

Budget Rent-a-Car Corporation
(312) 580-5000 main office in Chicago,
Illinois
(800) 527-0700 world reservations

Budget Rent-a-Car Canada
(416) 486-2919 main office in Toronto,
Ontario
(800) 268-8900 general reservations
(800) 268-8970 Quebec

Budget Rent-a-Car Hawaii
(800) 922-7221
(800) 527-0700

**Connex Int'l European Car Rentals,
Ltd.**
Office in Peeksill, New York
(800) 333-3949 United States
(800) 843-5416 Canada

Dollar Rent-a-Car
(213) 776-8100 main office in Los
Angeles, California
(800) 421-6878 reservations except
Hawaii
(800) 367-7006 Hawaii only

Enterprise Rent a Car
(314) 863-7000 main office in St.
Louis, Missouri
(800) 325-8007 except Missouri
(800) 392-0248 Missouri

Europe by Car
(212) 581-3040 main office in New
York
(800) 252-9401 California only
(800) 233-1516 except California

General Rent a Car
(305) 926-1700 main office in
Hollywood, Florida
(800) 327-7607 reservations

Hertz Corporation
(212) 980-2121 main office in New
York
(800) 654-3131 except Oklahoma
(800) 522-3711 Okalahoma only
(800) 268-1311 Canada
(800) 654-8200 Arkansas and Hawaii
(800) 654-3001 International

Kenning Car Rental
Main office in Chesterfield, England
(800) 227-8990 United States and
Canada
0-246-20-8888 United Kingdom

Marsans International
(212) 239-3880 main office in New
York
(800) 223-6114

National Car Rental
(612) 830-2121 main office in
Minneapolis, Minnesota
(800) 328-4300 reservations

Payless Car Rental System
(813) 381-2758 main office in St.
Peterburg, Florida
(800) 237-2804 reservations except
Canada
(800) 231-6713 Canada

Sears Rent-a-Car
(312) 580-5000 main office in Chicago,
Illinois
(800) 527-0770 except Canada
(800) 268-8900 Canada

Thrifty Car Rental
(918) 665-3930 main office in Tulsa,
Oklahoma
(800) 367-2277 reservations

CREDIT CARD INFORMATION

Call the following numbers if you lose your credit card or need more information about credit services from the card company. A space has been provided for you to list your card number in case of loss.

Air Travel Card
Phone: (800) 854-9600

Card Number: _____

American Express
Phone: (800) 528-4800

Card Number: _____

Carte Blanche
Phone: (800) 525-9135

Card Number: _____

Diner's Club
Phone: (800) 234-6377

Card Number: _____

For VISA and MasterCard, note your account number and the toll-free number from your bank statement or the back of your card here:

VISA
Phone: _____

Card Number: _____

MasterCard
Phone: _____

Card Number: _____

TRAVELER'S CHECKS

If your travelers' checks are lost or stolen you should contact the issuing companies as soon as possible. Make sure you keep an accurate record of cashed checks. Make two copies of the check numbers and keep the lists in two separate places, for example, your wallet and your suitcase or your briefcase and a suitcase.

**American Express
Travelers Checks**
Continental United States
800-221-7282
Alaska and Hawaii
800-221-4950
Canada
800-221-7282
Other countries
Contact the nearest American Express Service Company or a local bank that handles American Express travelers' checks if no service company is available. Otherwise, call the bank where you purchased the checks. Make sure to record this number in a safe place.

Bank of America Travelers Checks
United States except Alaska
(800) 227-3460
Outside United States
Call collect 415-624-5400

**Barclays and VISA
Travelers Checks**
United States
(800) 227-6811
Europe
London Office 937-8091
Other Locations: Call the

bank where you purchased the checks.

Citicorp Travelers Checks
United States and Canada
(800) 645-6556
Mexico
813-626-4444
Europe
London Office 438-1414

**Thomas Cook and
MasterCard Travelers
Checks**
In the United States, except New York,
Alaska, and Hawaii
(800) 223-9920
Other Locations: Call collect (212) 974–5696

VARIOUS USEFUL INFORMATION

TELEPHONE COMPANIES

AT & T Operator (from inside the United States)
10288-0

US Sprint Operator (from the United States)
10333-0

MCI Operator
10222-0

Directory Assistance for Toll-Free Numbers
(800) 555-1212

Hotelcopy FaxMail
(800) 322-4448

SHIPPING SERVICES

Federal Express
(800) 238-5355

DHL Worldwide Express
(800) 225-5345

United Parcel Service (UPS)
Ground to ground, air to ground, etc.
(800) 742-5877
International shipping
(800) 325-0365

INTERNATIONAL INCIDENTS OR TERRORIST EVENTS

Citizens Emergency Center
Contact the center to find out about any specific safety problems in an area to which you are flying. Also ask if there is any reason, relating to terrorism, that you should not fly on certain airlines. Contact:
U.S. State Department
Room 4800 N.S.
Washington, DC 20520
(202) 647-5225

THE WEATHER

Cities in the United States
Airdata, Inc., at the number below, will give you weather conditions in more than 250 cities in the United States, listed by local area code. A nominal fee is charged after entering the proper codes, as instructed during the phone call. Call (800) 247-3282 or (214) 869-3035.

International Weather for American Express Card Holders
You can obtain a three-day forecast for weather around the world.
(800) 554-2639 or
(202) 783-7272 collect.

Domestic and International Weather via *The Wall Street Journal*
You can obtain weather for 650 U.S. cities and 300 international cities by calling a 900 number (95 cents per minute).
(900) 407-8228 and press 1 for domestic weather or 2 for international weather.

INDEX